I0729629

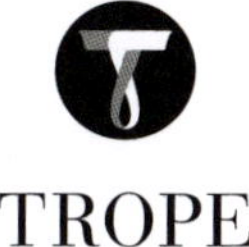

TROPE

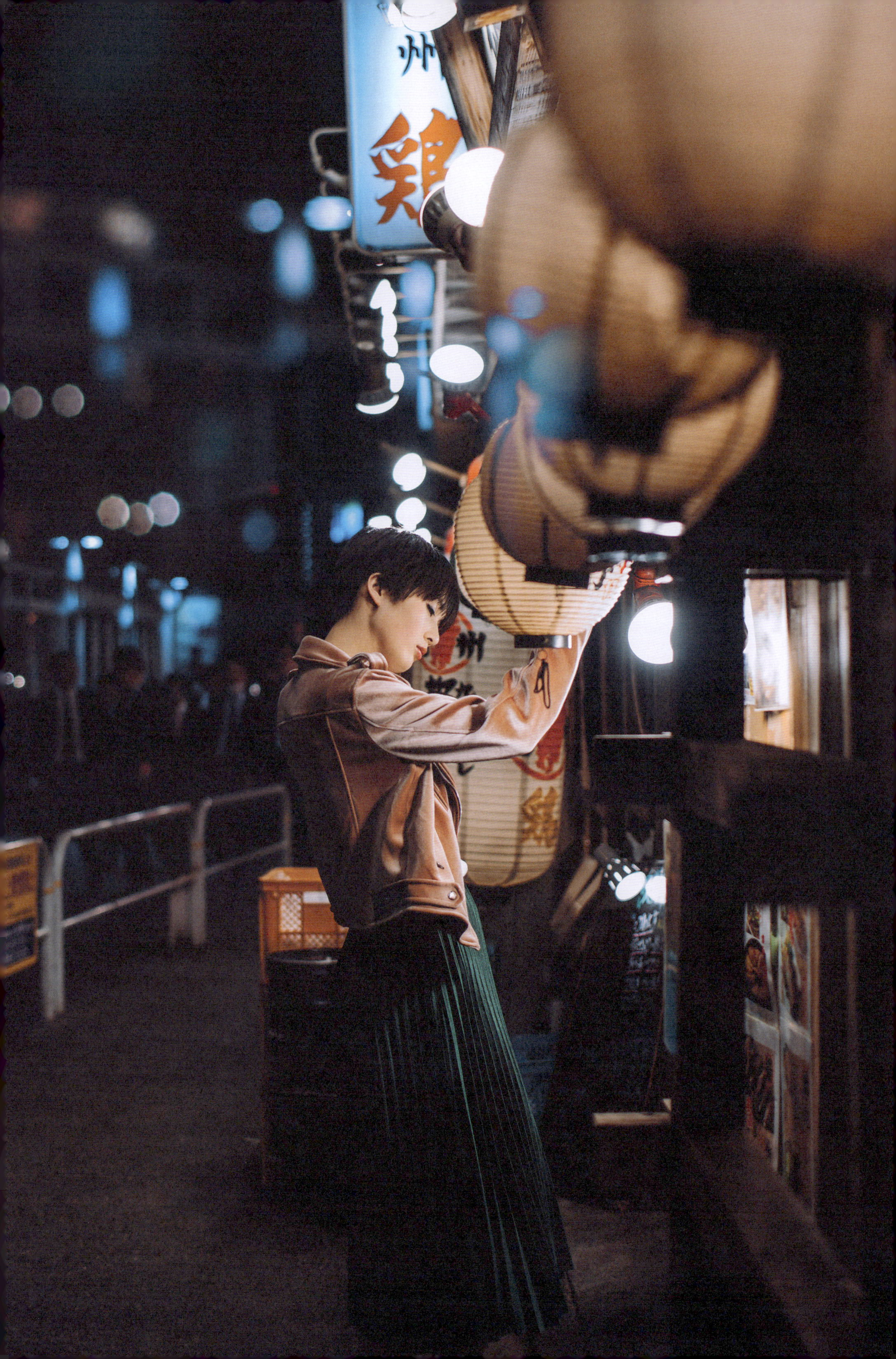

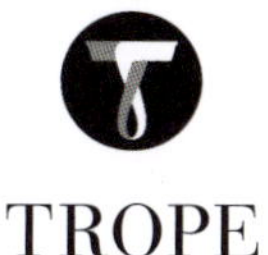

TROPE

VIVIEN LIU

Being There

TROPE EDITION

VOLUME IV

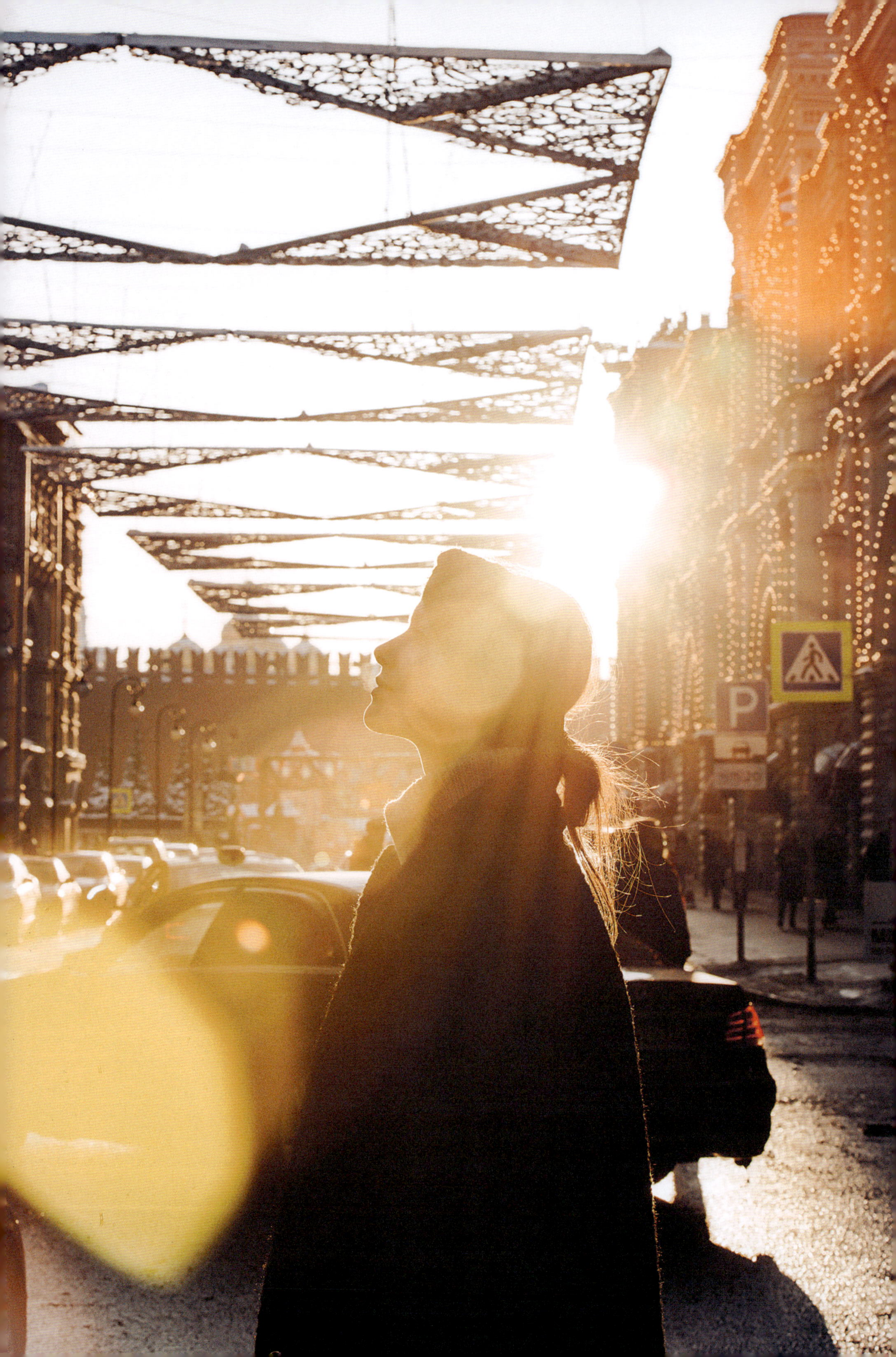

INTRODUCTION

"Architecture is about making space. Photography is about capturing space. And architects are trained to see space before it's realized."

Vivien Liu has worked in architecture and photography for over a decade in the United States, Canada, the United Kingdom, China and Hong Kong, where she now resides. Inspired but not constrained by her training, Vivien quickly developed a strong sensibility for portraying space as seen through the first person, which now defines her photographic style.

There's no escaping the architectural influence in her photography. While seemingly effortless and serendipitous, her images are inherently precise, measured and composed; powerfully telling a story of the way Vivien sees and captures the world around her.

Being There explores the dialogue and tension between people and spaces through portraiture, landscapes, and street photography, from the urban density of Hong Kong and Tokyo to epic natural landscapes in Zhangjiajie, China. With an architect's artful eye, Ms. Liu showcases this juxtaposition in the most beautiful way, sharply highlighting her eye for patterns and symmetry across settings.

Let Vivien Liu transport you to see the places she's traveled and meet the people she's encountered in her first solo publication, *Being There*, the fourth volume in the Trope Editions Emerging Photographers Series.

Sam Landers

Editor

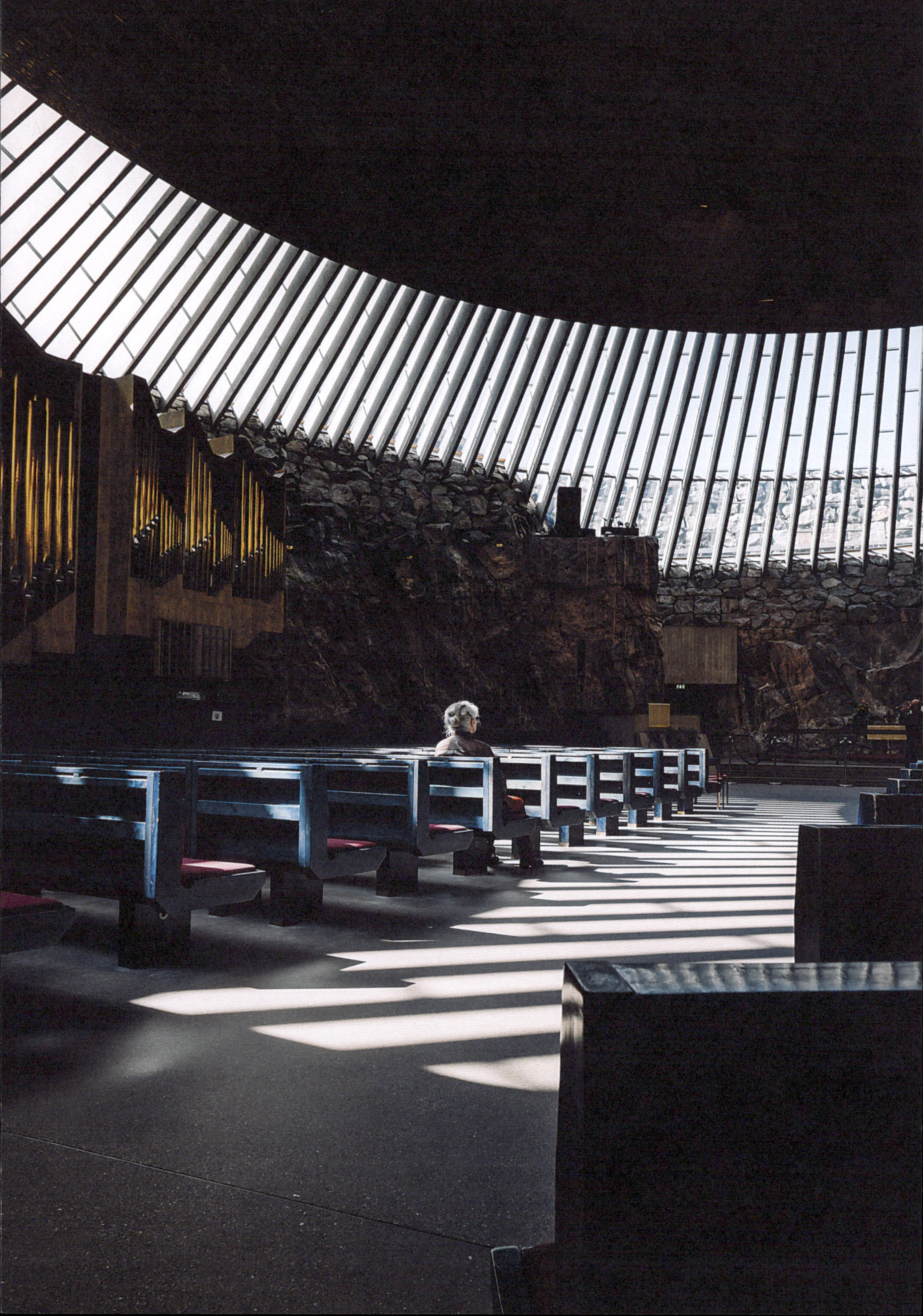

ARCHITECTURE IS THE VERY MIRROR OF LIFE.
YOU ONLY HAVE TO CAST YOUR EYES ON BUILDINGS TO
FEEL THE PRESENCE OF THE PAST, THE SPIRIT OF A PLACE;
THEY ARE THE REFLECTION OF SOCIETY.
I.M. PEI

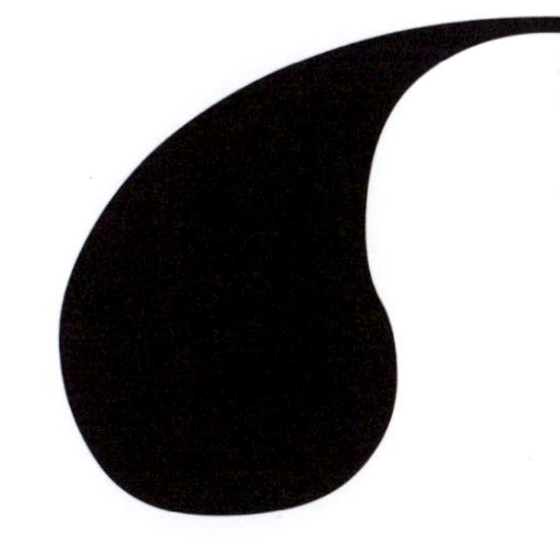

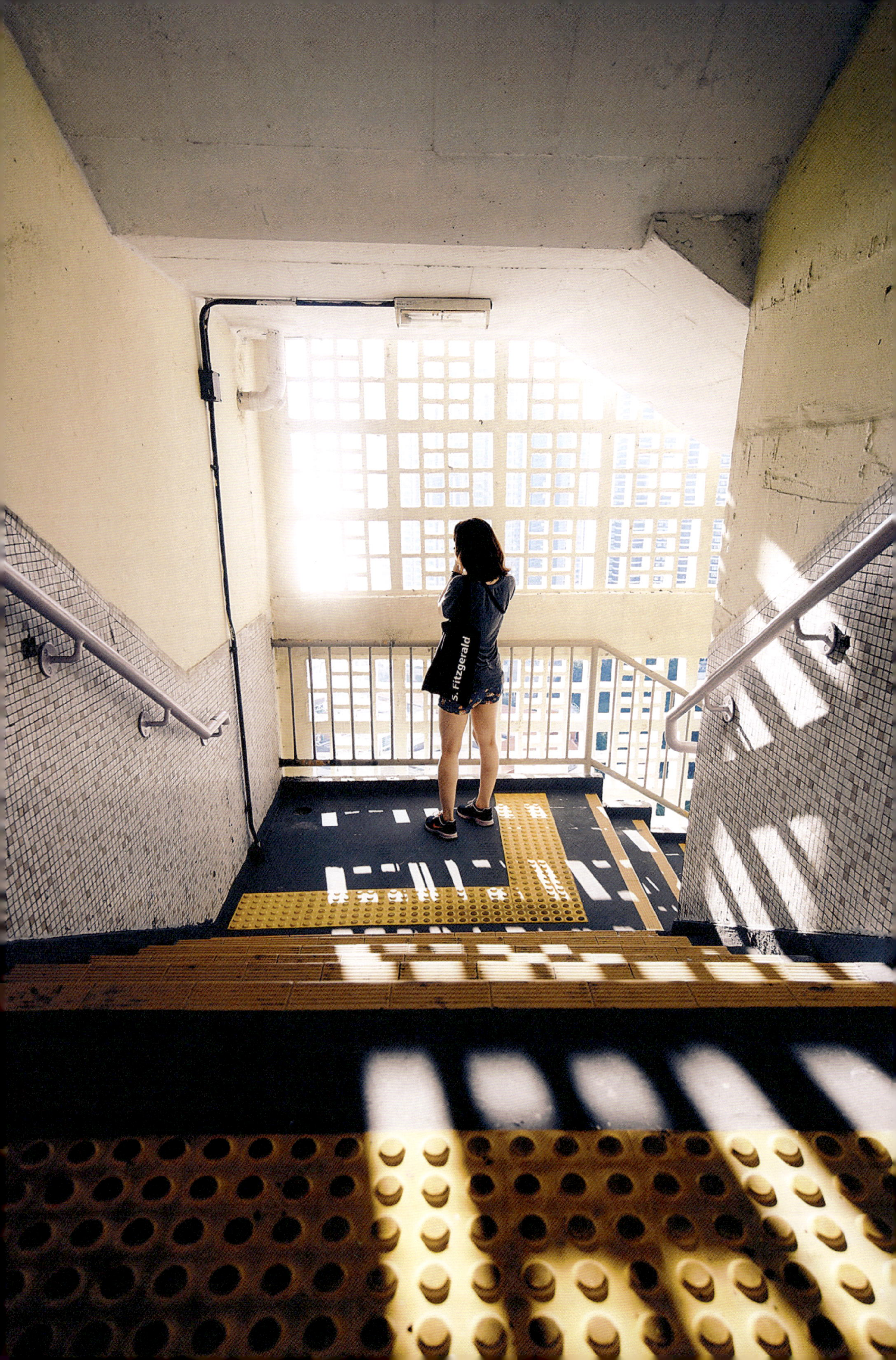
S. Fitzgerald

BEING THERE

The built environment is shaped by the people who live in it and reflects our way of life. The city and its people are dependent on one another and therefore the two are inseparable in the photos I take. Through photographing something, we document it in a particular state during a particular period of time. I chose this reason as a drive to photograph the spaces in which I live, and which I love. I want to use images as a medium to communicate a personal perspective of the things I see and live around. And I want to use these images as something I can look at in the future and celebrate, lament or feel nostalgic about.

In portraits, the dynamic between the subject and how they interact with the environment are recurring themes. Perhaps this originated from having a background in architecture - the context is never neglected and is synergetic with any character who appears in the work. It depicts a moment where the subject self-indulgently dances on a busy street, or is pensive under a warm ray of sunshine, or is slowly walking under the orange tone of fluorescent lights.

More than just the physical context, these images also capture emotion and connection. I shoot what is important for me, and I live and travel for the experience. With the images I create, I try to convey the essence of that experience, which may or may not appeal with the visual impact of something staged, but perhaps also with the spontaneity of living and feeling a particular moment of love, joy, melancholy, sadness, exhilaration or happiness.

Ever since I started photography, I have become more in touch with my senses. The sights and sounds which I used to know and couldn't previously describe materialized into one image after another. Through photography I was made aware of the details and the ingredients from which my memories were made, especially of places like Hong Kong where I grew up: the smell of incense burning against a bustling street, the humidity of the summer air, the color temperature of street market lights and the ambient glow of a red and green neon sign. The photographs I take of these little things become memorabilia for the future. They remind me of the places and faces I have encountered, just like 'being there' all over again.

Vivien Liu

being there

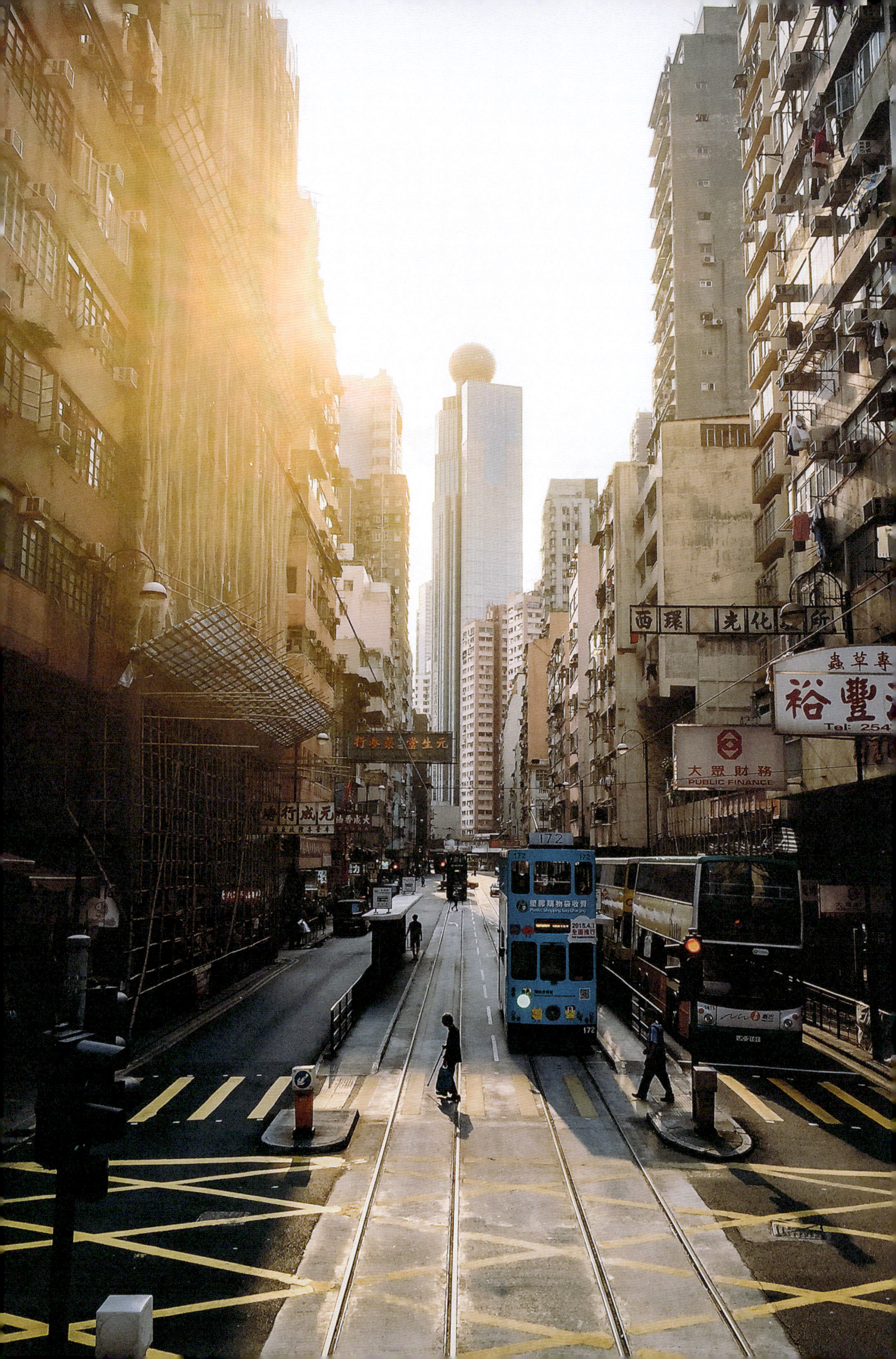

西環 光化 ☐ 所
蟲草專
裕豐☐
Tel: 254☐
大眾財務
PUBLIC FINANCE
元生堂 業參行
元成行
大歲香陽
172
塑膠購物袋收費
Plastic Shopping Bag Charging
2015.4.1
全國推行
嘉喬

EARLY STAGES

I studied architecture for eight years and practiced for six before
I ventured into photography. As a beginner I was naturally drawn
to shooting architecture. Because of my training, I saw space in a
very technical order. Like architectural drawings, I was particularly
interested in framing geometry, symmetry, repetition and strong
lines in my composition. The results were dynamic, almost abstract
portrayals of utilitarian, modernist architecture.

In contrast to this early work, street photography portrays a more
humane side of a city. With the camera poised to shoot a fleeting
moment at any time, I became fascinated by the spontaneous nature
of not knowing what to capture next. Sporting a telephoto lens,
I walk the city with eyes like a hunter to capture people in their
environment. The outcomes are unexpected, and getting something
extraordinary is incredibly satisfying. This fascination motivated me
to move into portraiture. Shooting my subjects provides a degree
of the unknown, which allows for the creative input of two or more
people. I started with a few friends until I began to work with models,
but regardless of who, what you see in the end is the result of great
connection and teamwork.

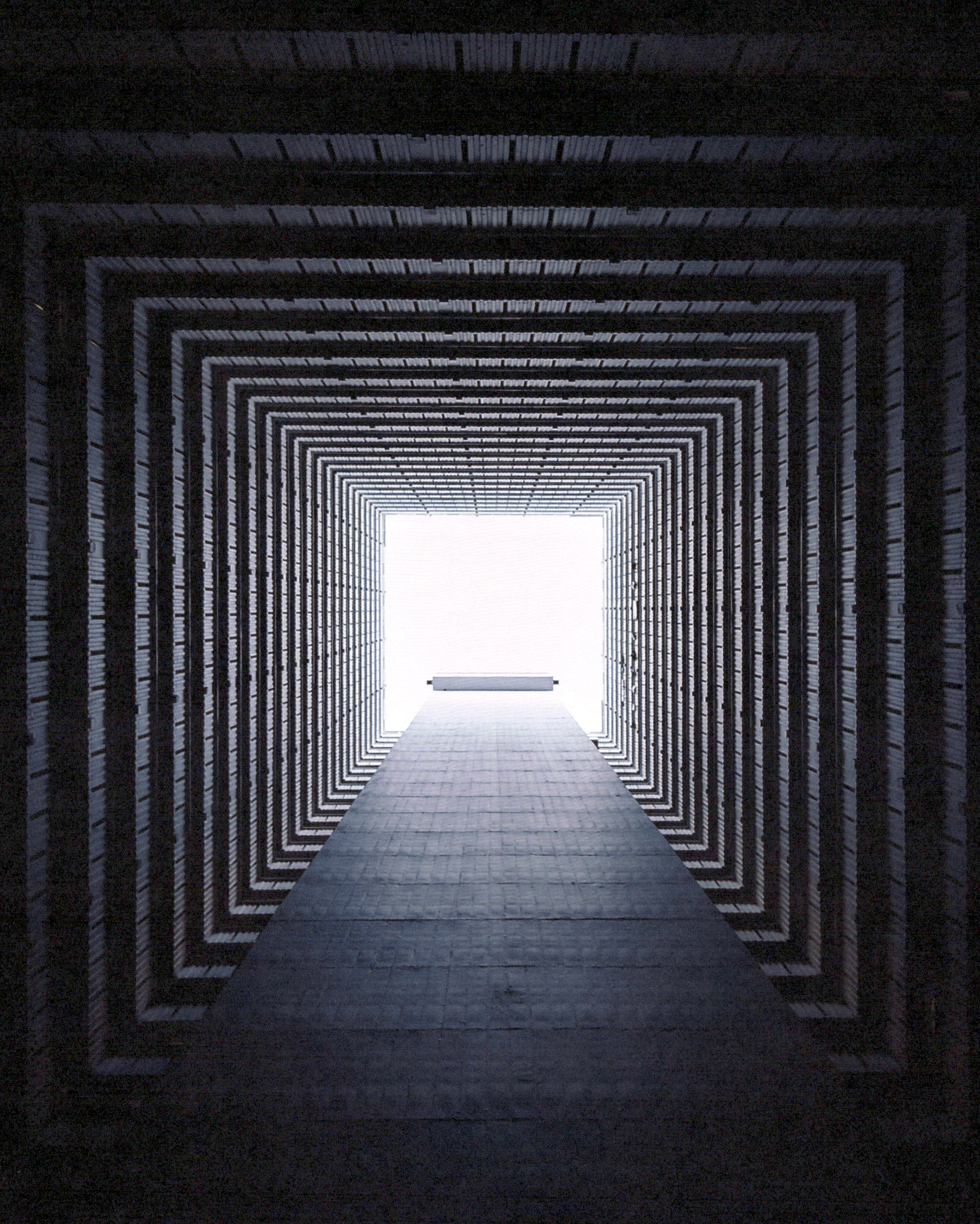

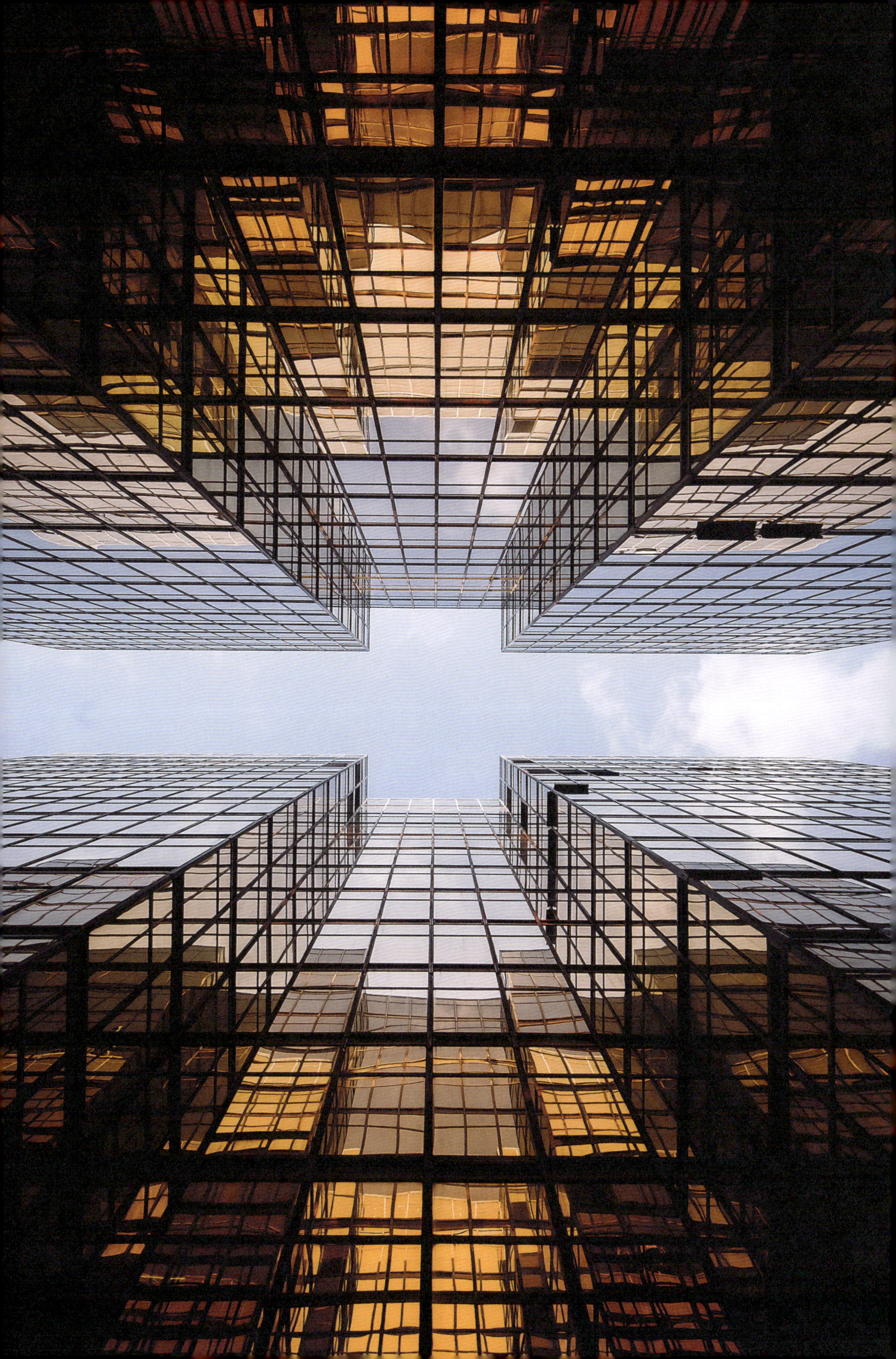

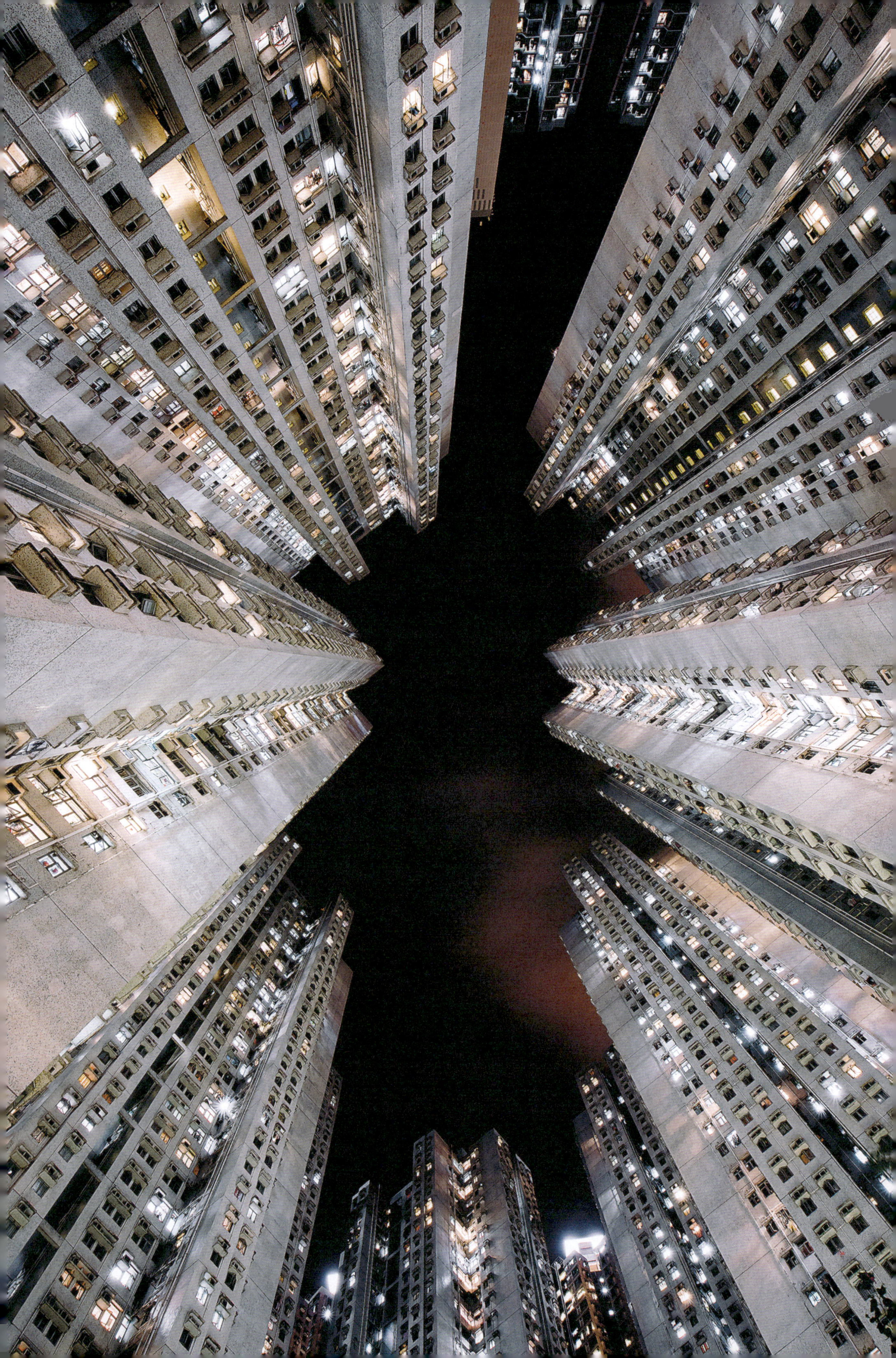

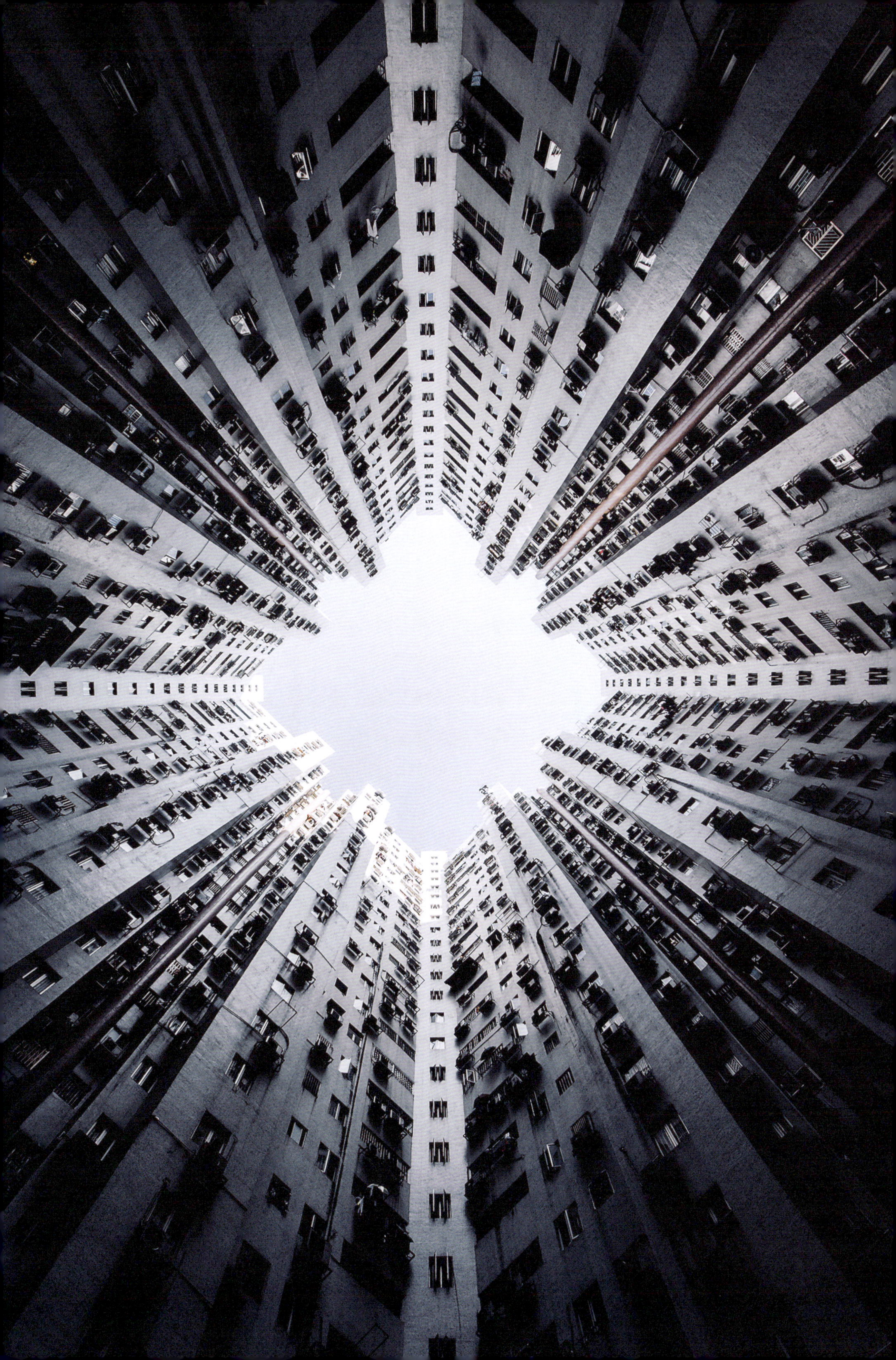

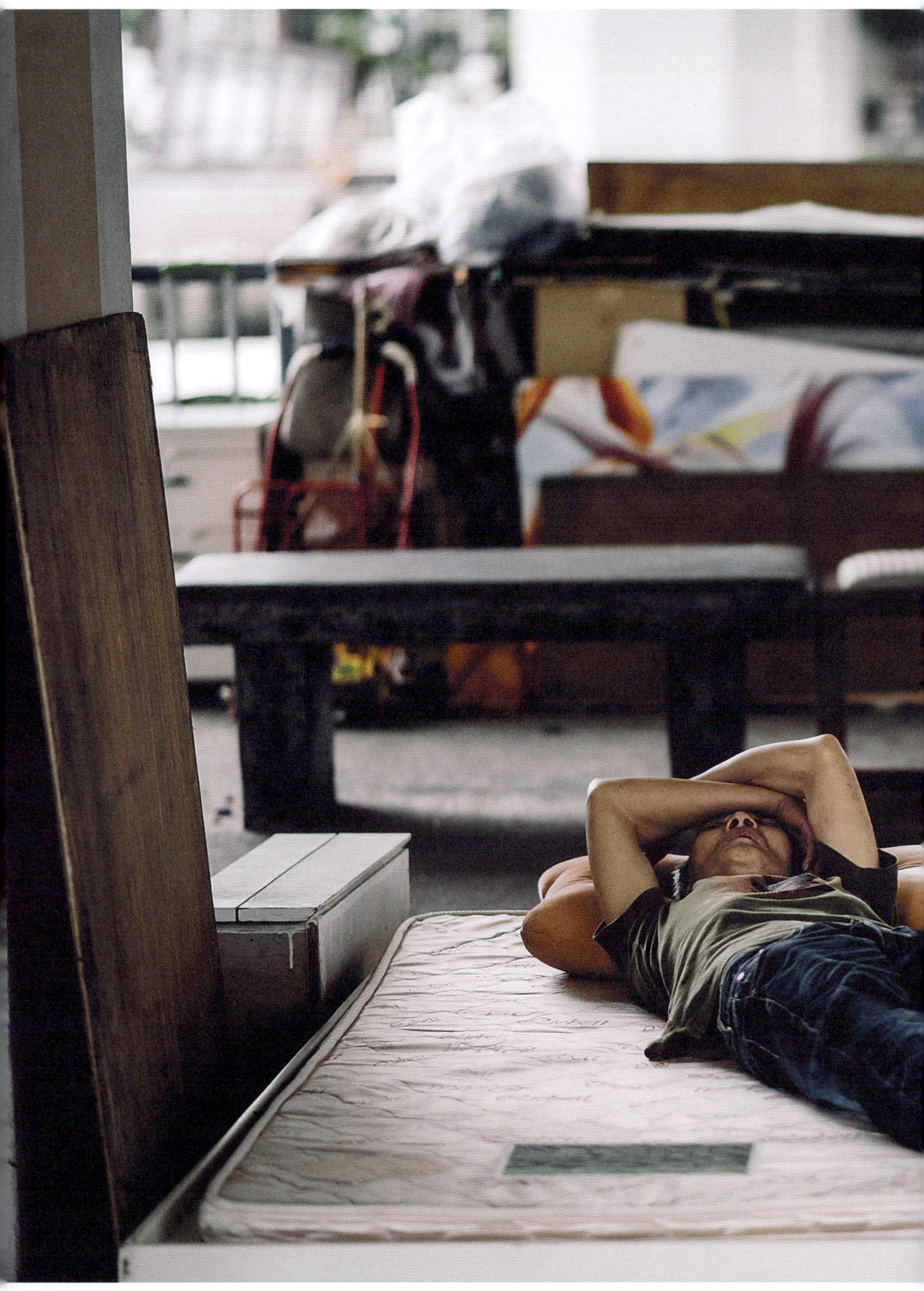

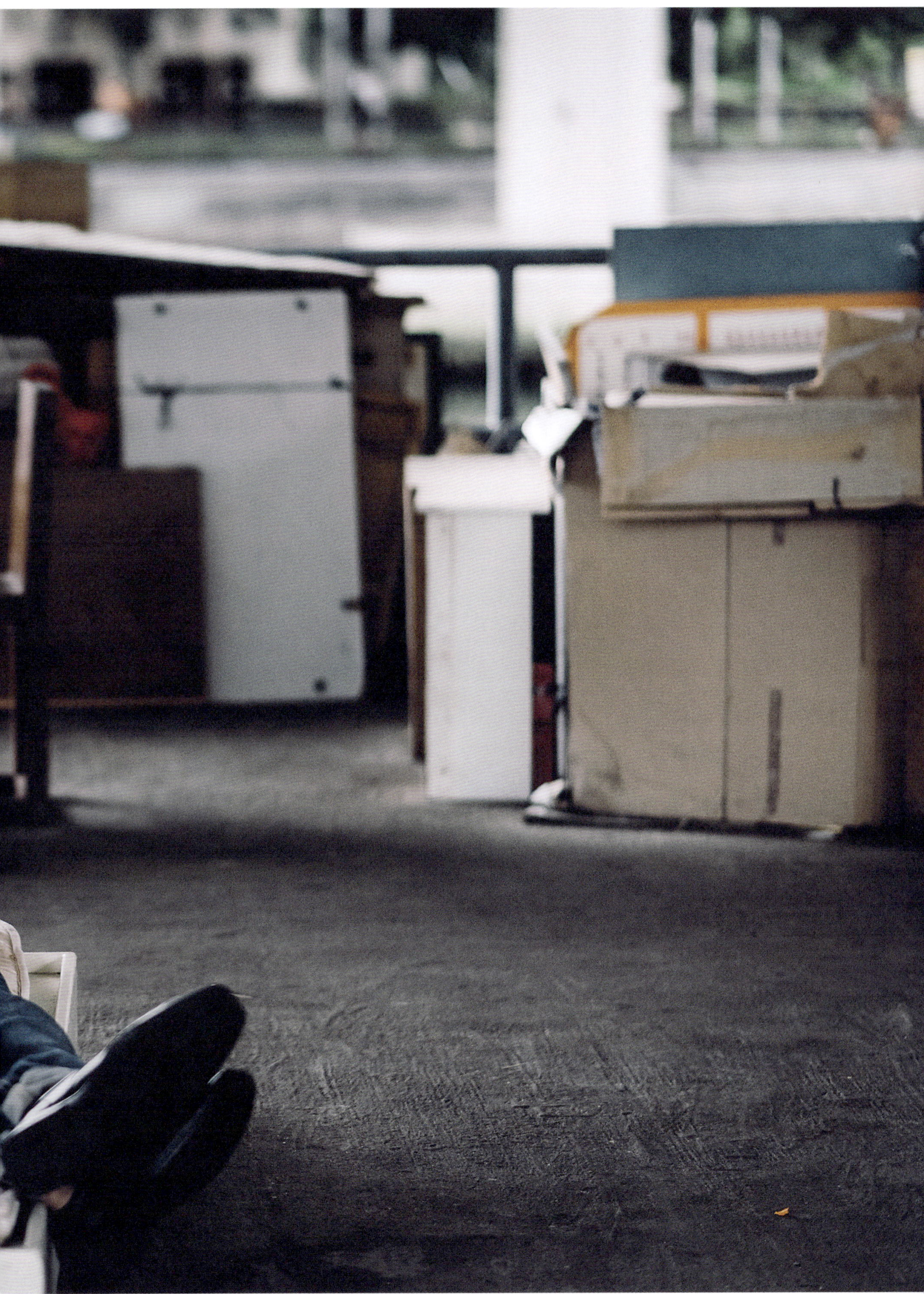

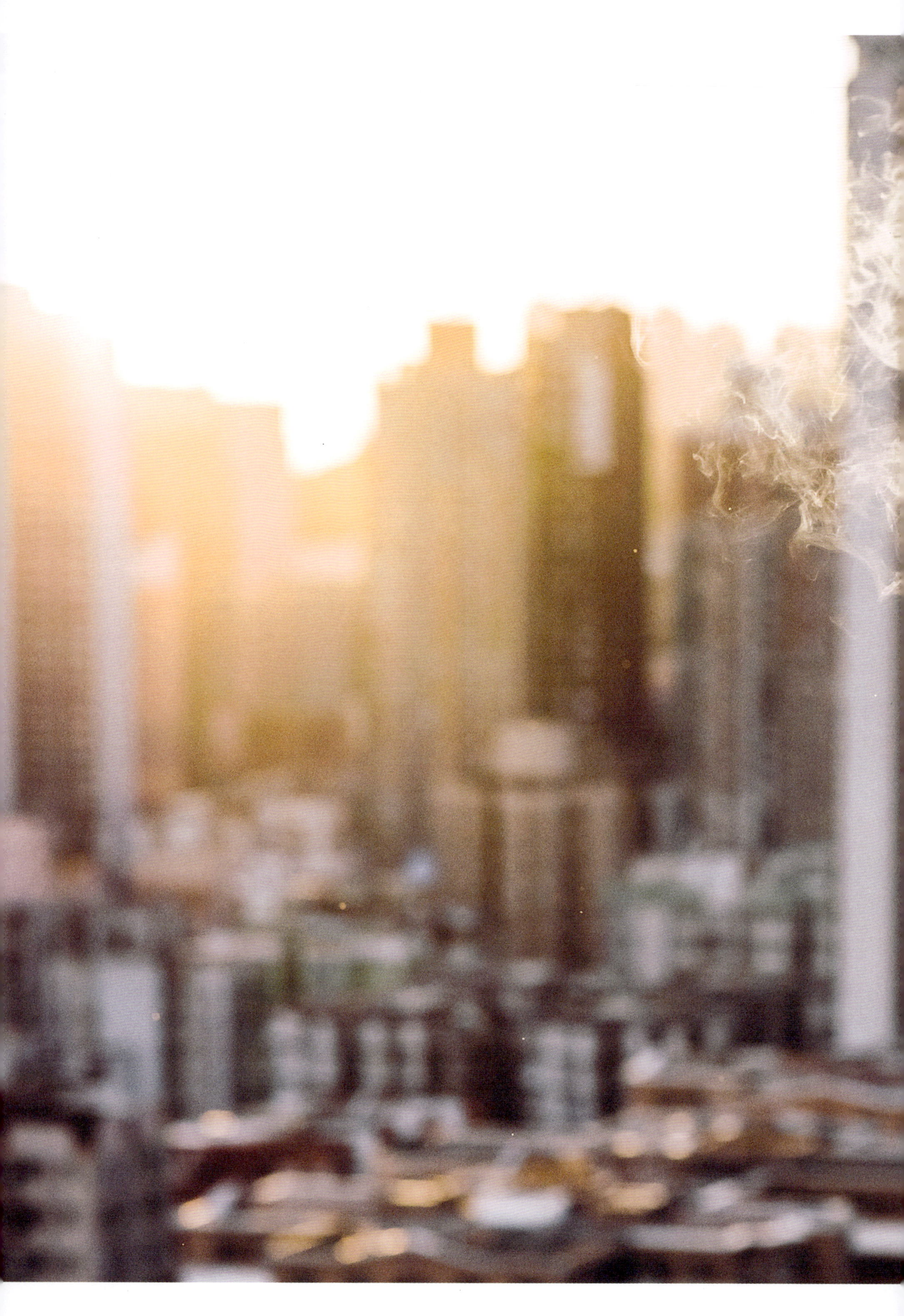

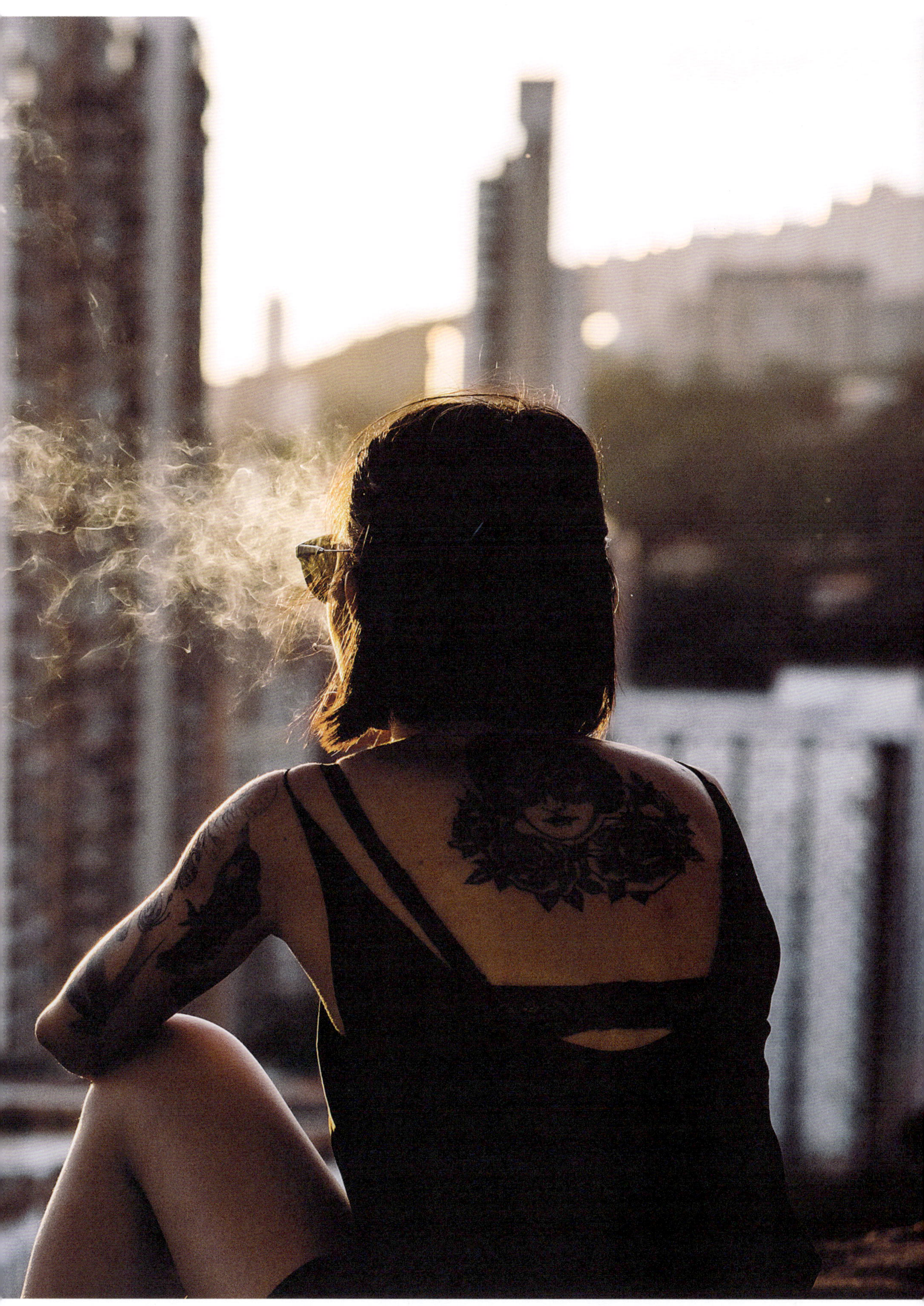

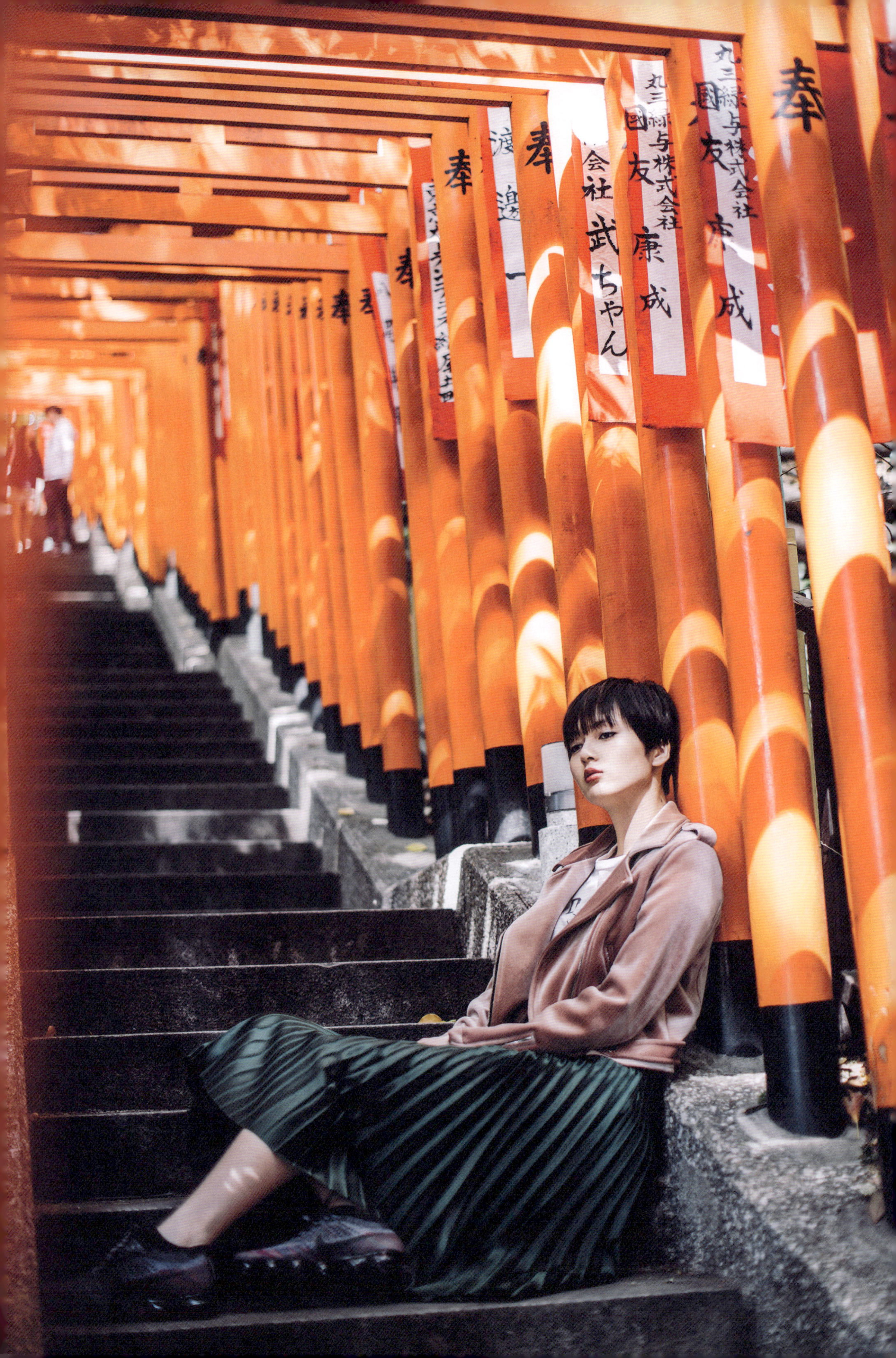

奉
奉
奉
渡邊一
丸三緑与株式会社
國友
会社 武ちゃん
丸三緑与株式会社
國友 康成
丸三緑与株式会社
國友 康成
奉

my places

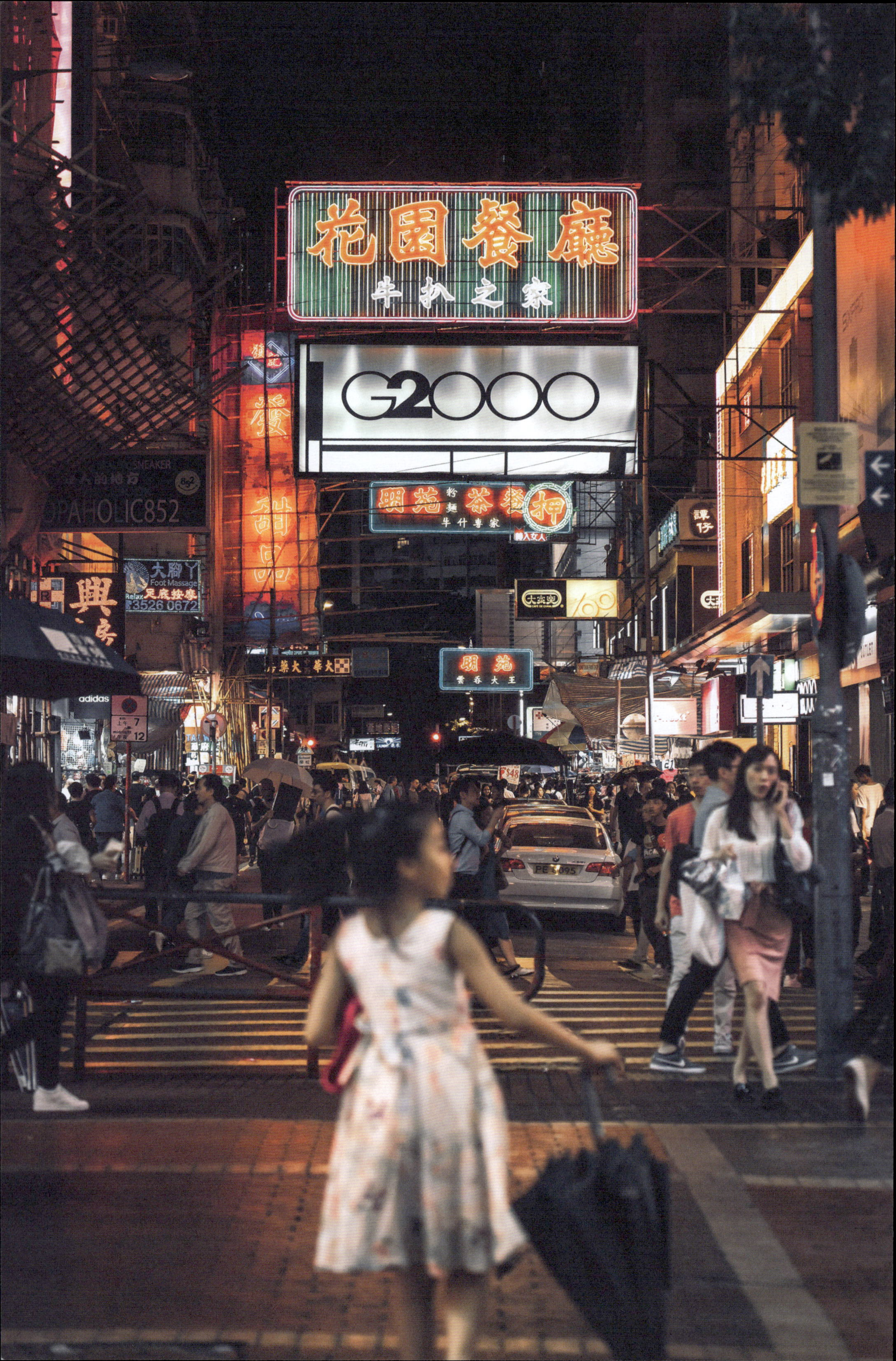

花園餐廳
牛扒之家
G2000
發
甜品
龍虹
SNEAKER
人的地方
OPAHOLIC852
8g2
大聯丫
Foot Massage
Relax
3526 0672
興房
adidas
7
12
明苑 粉麵 茶餐 押
牛什專家 婢入女人
大來遊
769
明苑
雲吞大王
譚仔
$48
PE 095

I was born in Vancouver, Canada, and spent a substantial number of years in North America before calling Hong Kong my current home. Being educated in the West while growing up with a traditional Chinese family, my identity was torn between the different cultural values of my social circle and at home. In hindsight, I do not complain because this allows me to see two cultures – one from the East, and one from the West – each through a different lens.

During my childhood in Hong Kong, the dense, urban jungle was nothing special. The soaring towers and endless, hive-like windows were ubiquitous, and I had accepted it as the typical way of life. It was not until I started taking photos that I realized what a different world I had been living in.

My architectural background provided a solid base to my way of perceiving the urban environment. In the photos, you can see an augmented version of places as I try my best to bring out what I see are its most beautiful qualities. My goal is to immerse the viewer into these augmented qualities so they can imagine what it is like to live within it.

For me, extracting the best strengths of a city and heightening these strengths by showing them to the rest of the world, has an impact on the way we shape our future cities.

For example, people are amazed by the way Hongkongers live in such high density, but for us who are so accustomed to it, it may be quite an unremarkable concept. High density living does not only provide astonishing visuals – it is actually a visionary and futuristic model of living that has merits of being extremely land- and energy-efficient, an ideal setup for sustainability.

Through showing the beauty of places to a wider audience, we bolster its best qualities, and hopefully we can proliferate these qualities by incorporating them into future city building. I give myself the mission as a curator of beautiful moments, urban qualities, ideas and culture, then act as a distributor of these images to raise the awareness of people locally and globally.

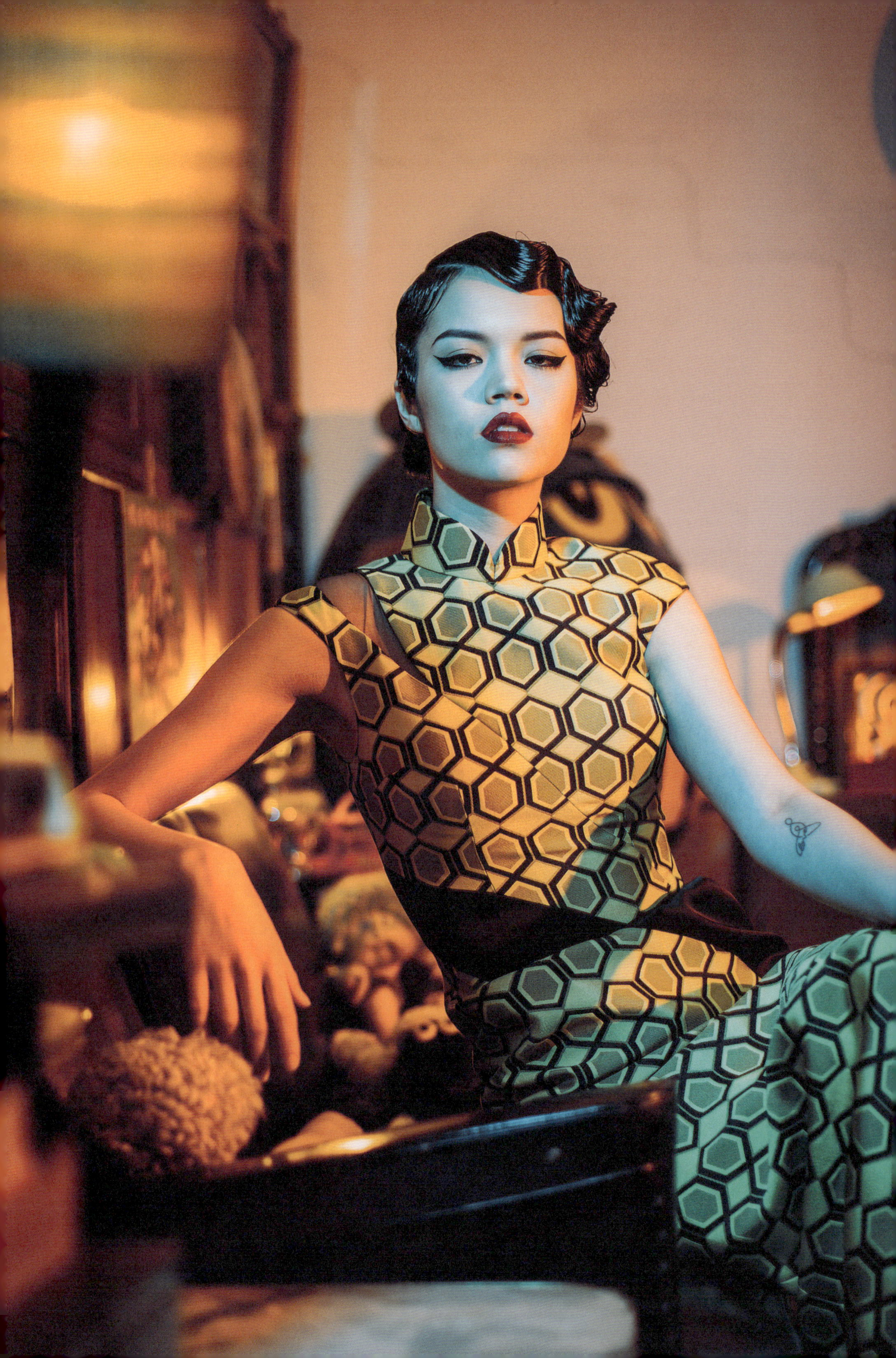

hong kong

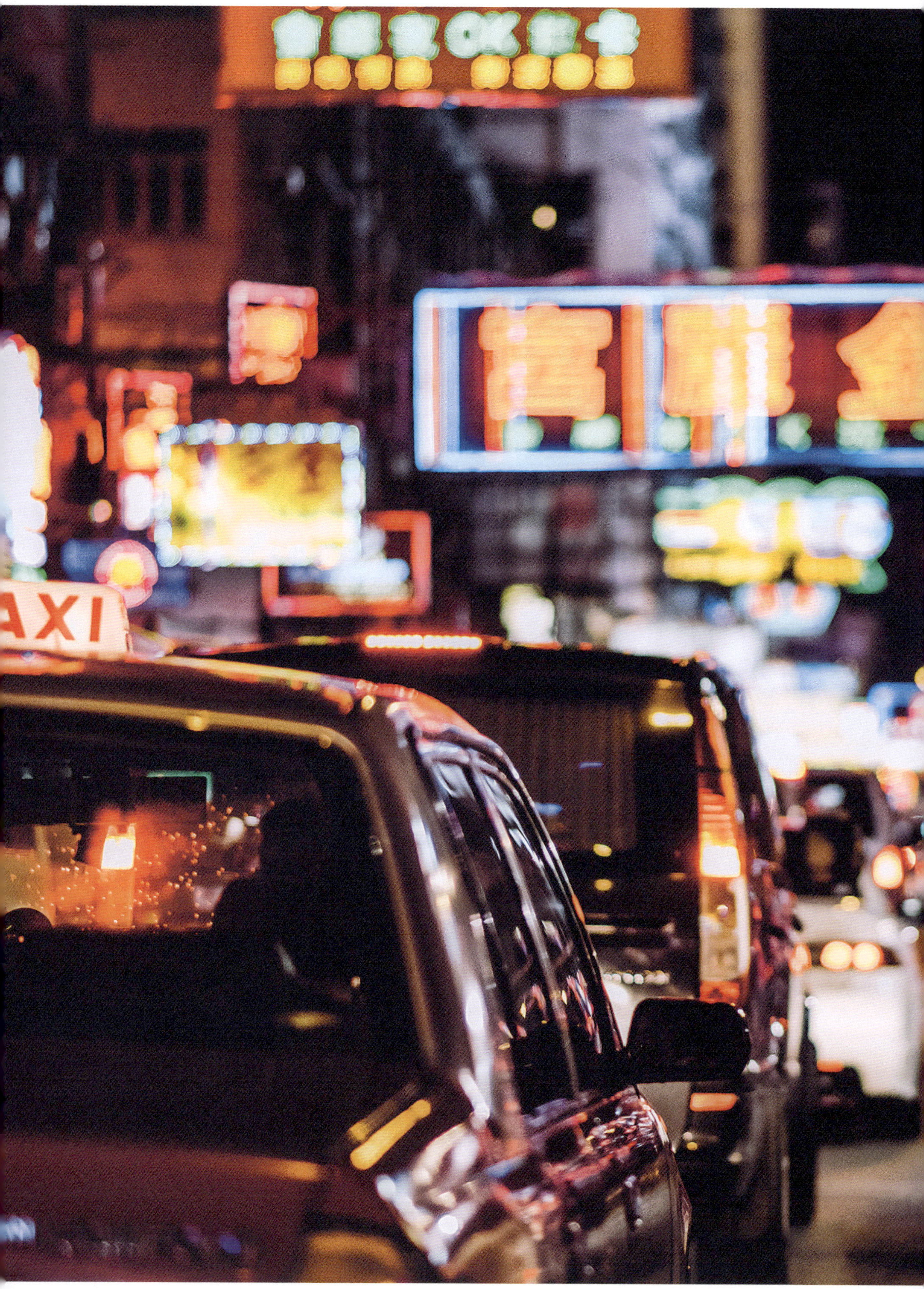

AXI

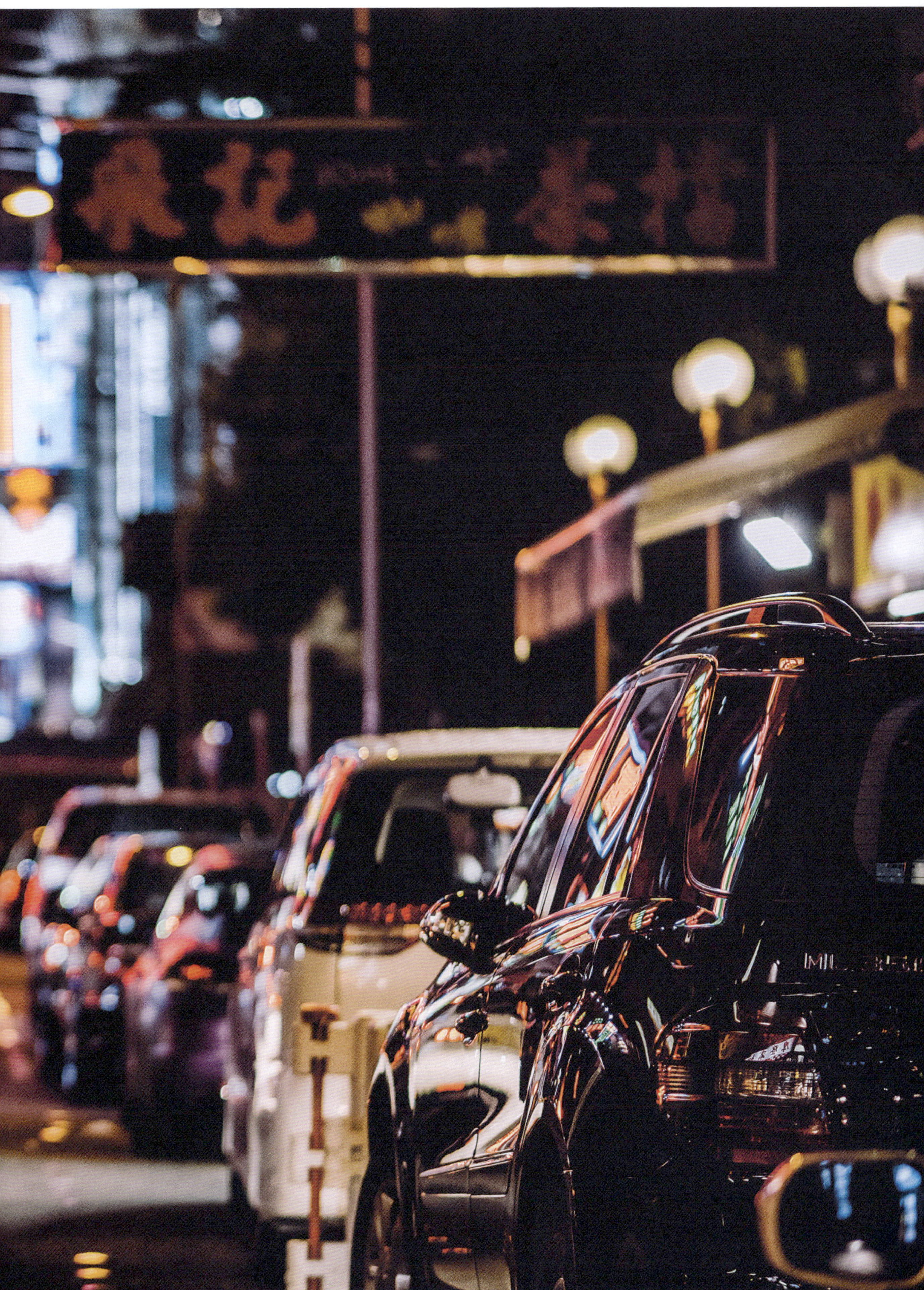

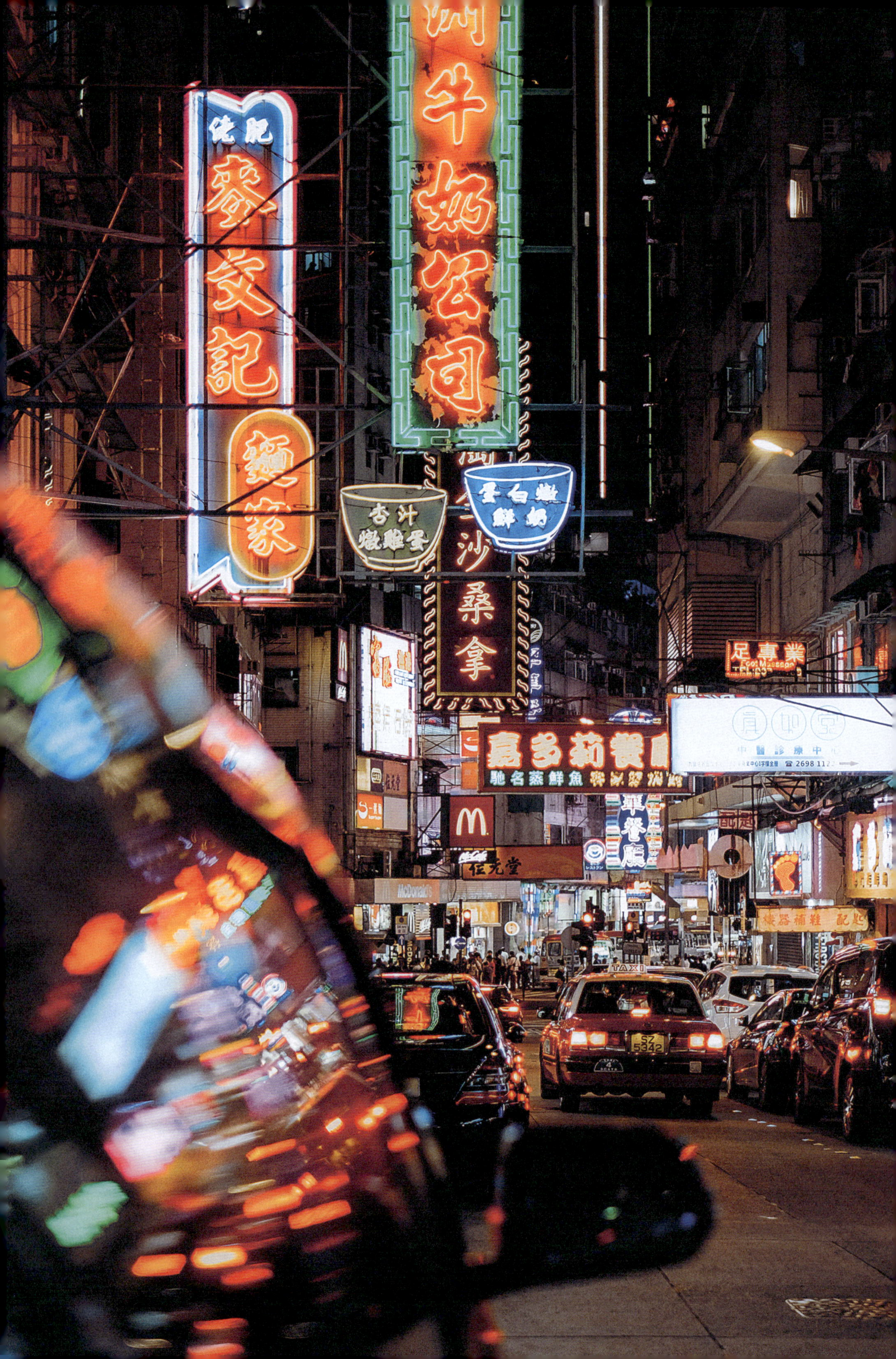
佳記
麥文記
麵家
洲
牛
奶
公
司
杏汁
燉雞蛋
蛋白鱉
鮮奶
沙
桑
拿
足車業
Foot Massage
中醫診療中心
2698 1122
嘉多新餐
馳名蒸鮮魚
M
McDonald's
任先堂
TAXI
SZ
5342
修整補鞋 記足

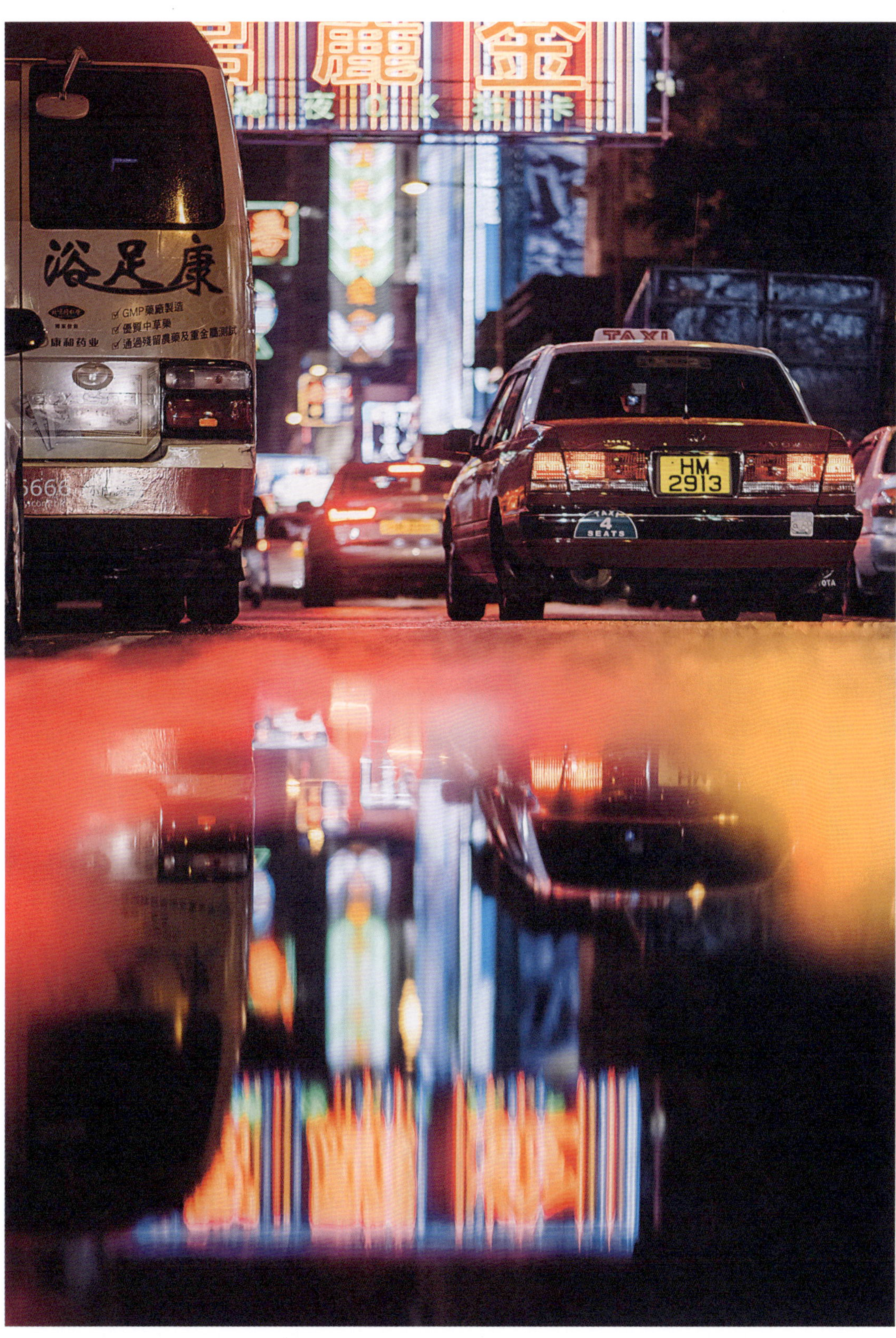
浴足康
GMP藥廠製造
優質中草藥
通過殘留農藥及重金屬測試
康和药业
TAXI
HM
2913
TAXI
4
SEATS
金麗高
夜 OK 新卡

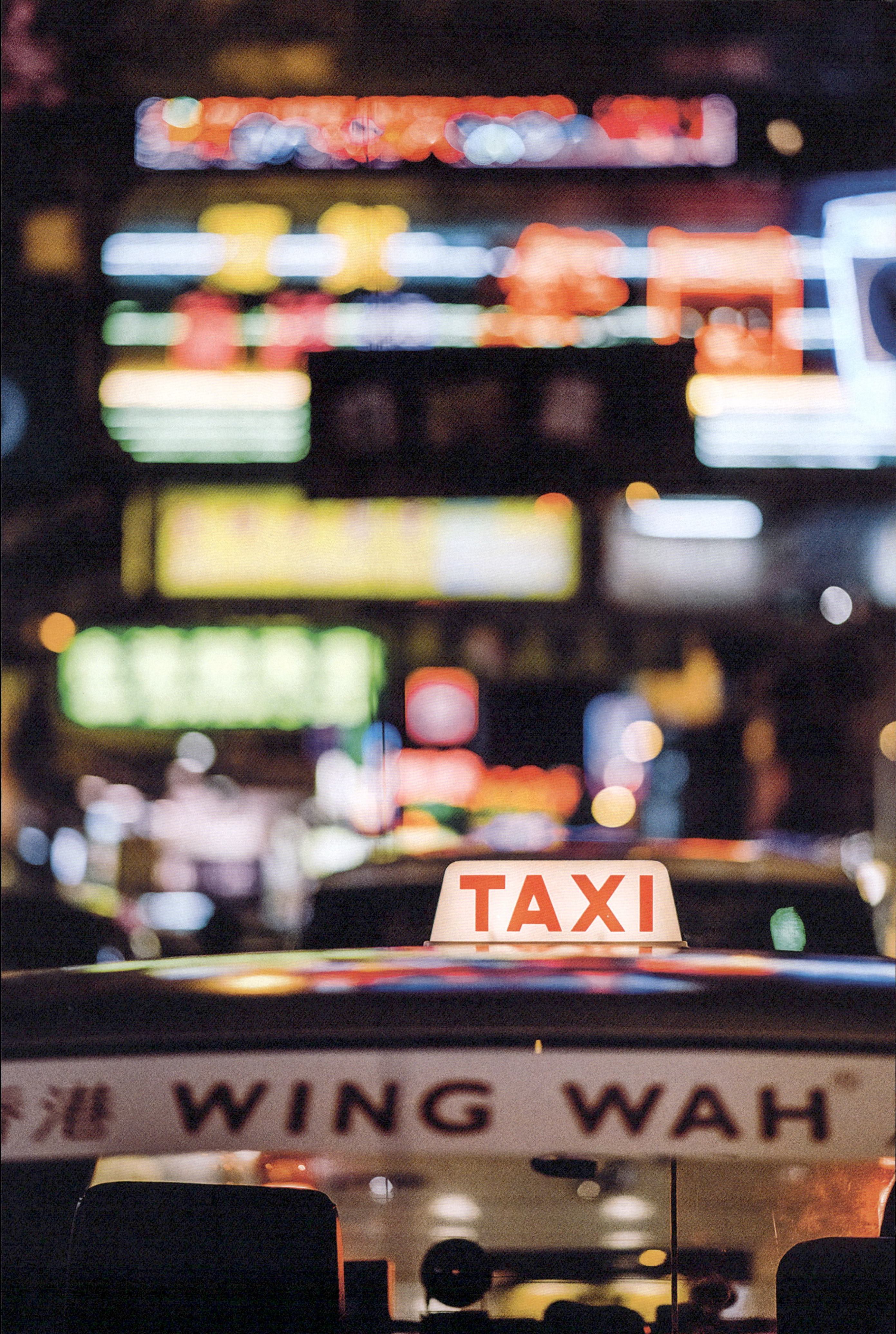
TAXI
香港 WING WAH

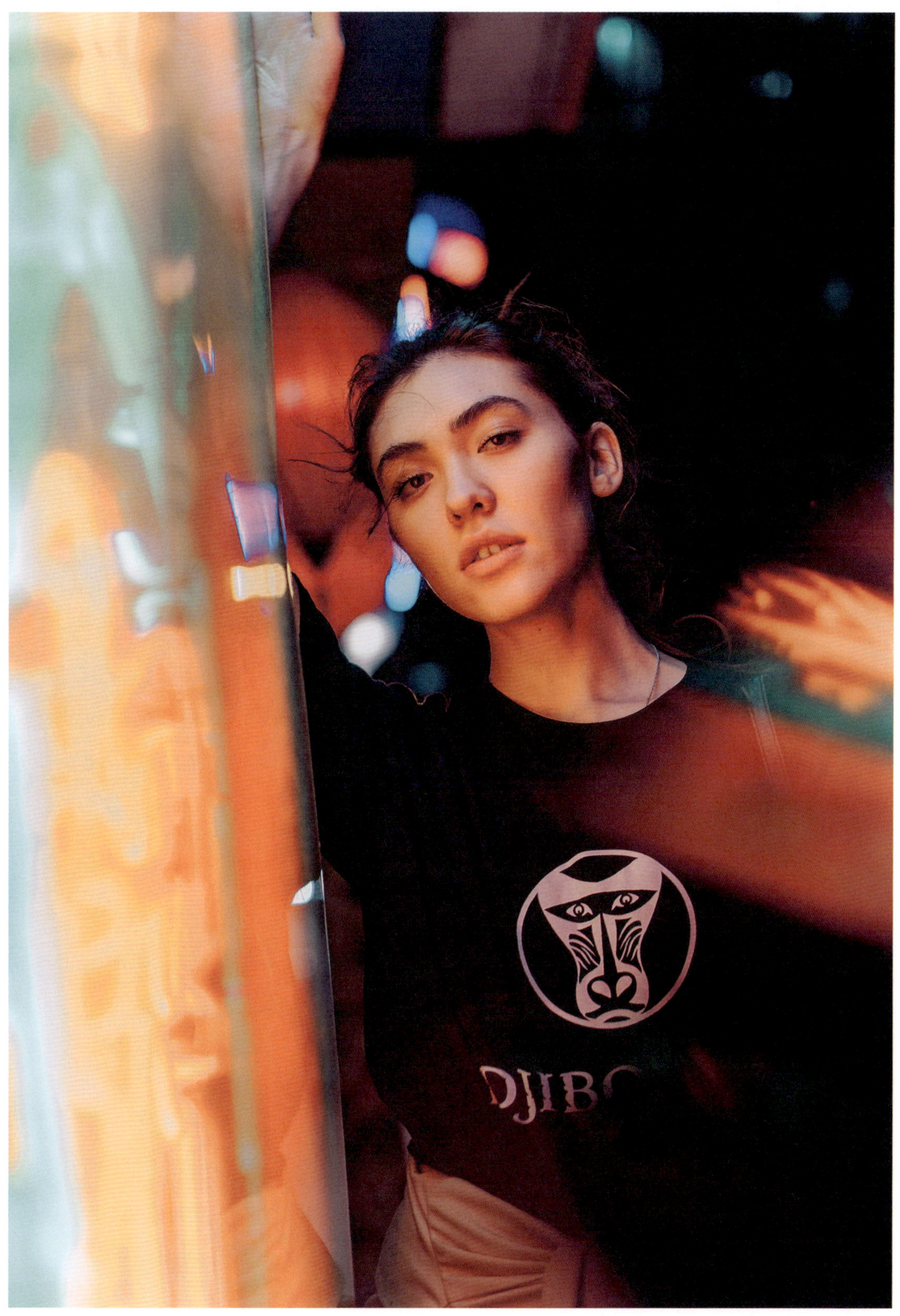
DJIBO

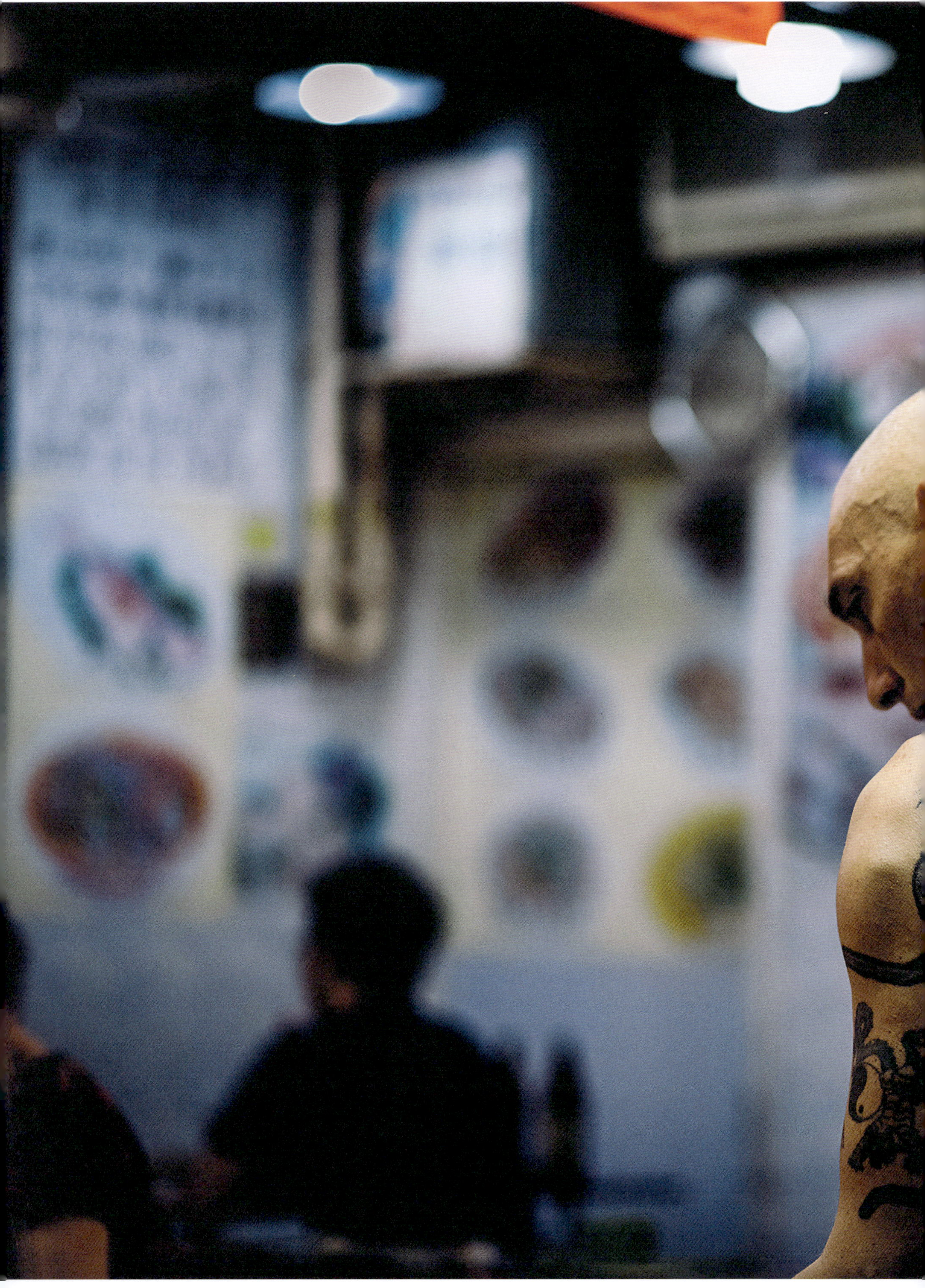

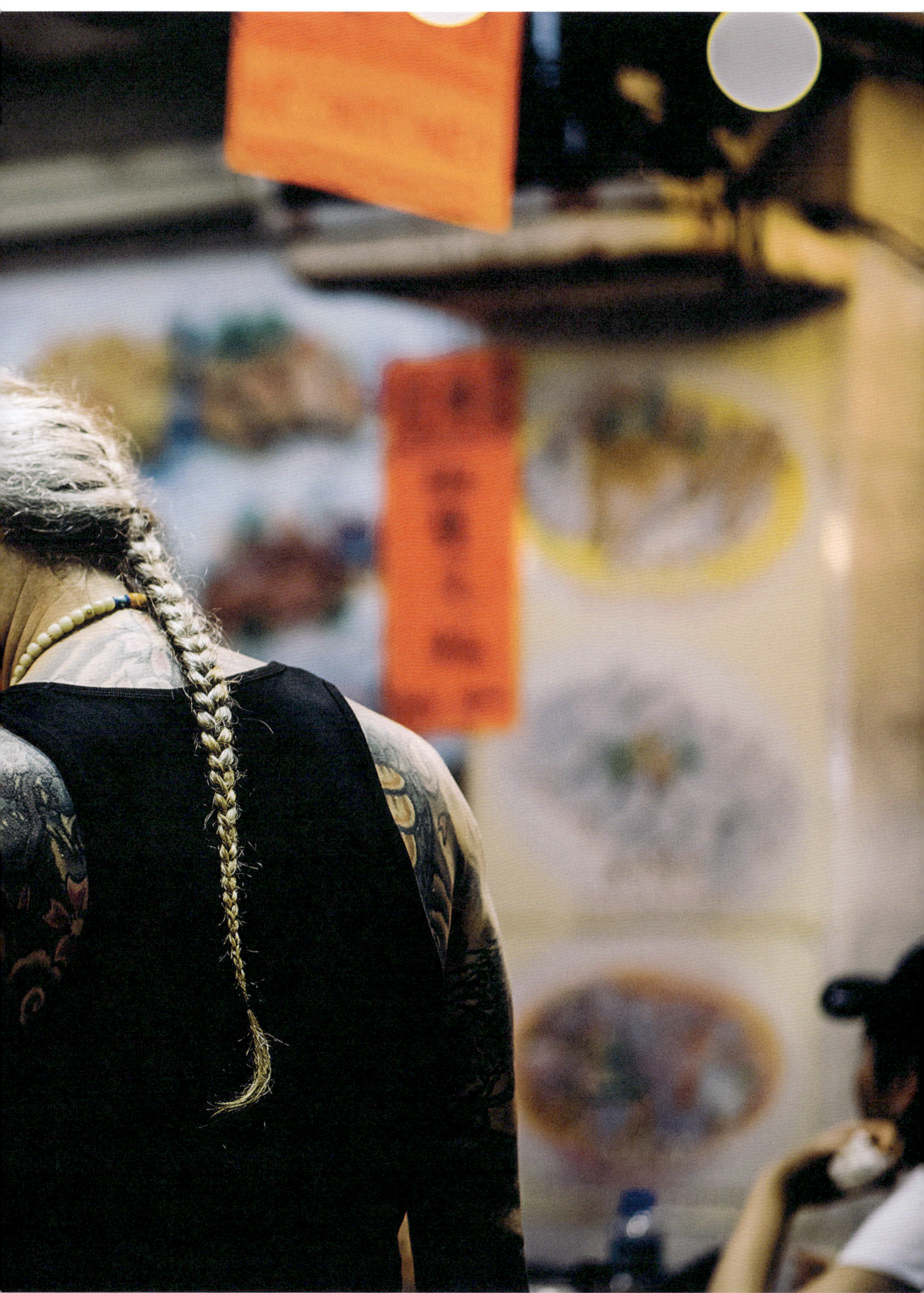

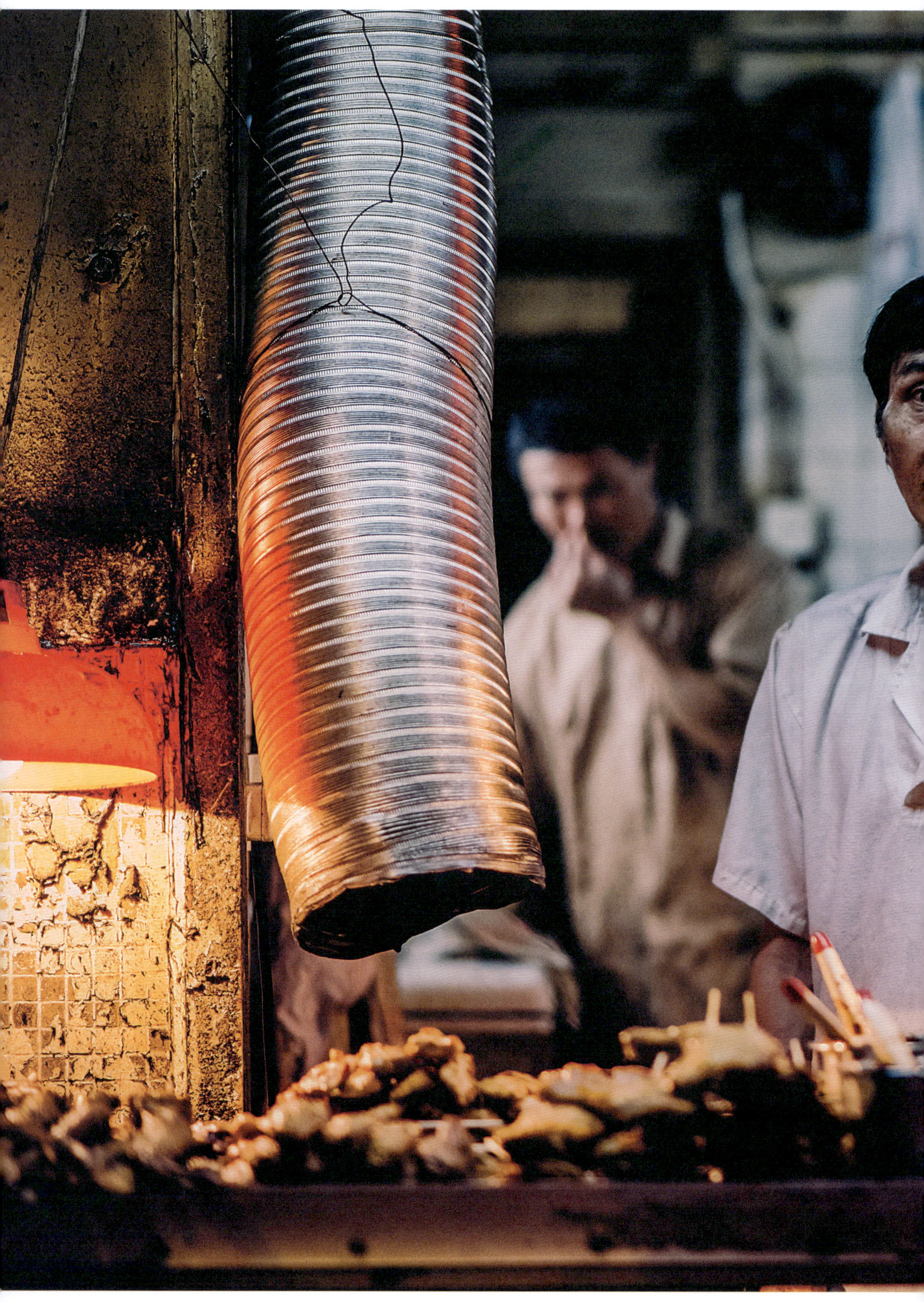

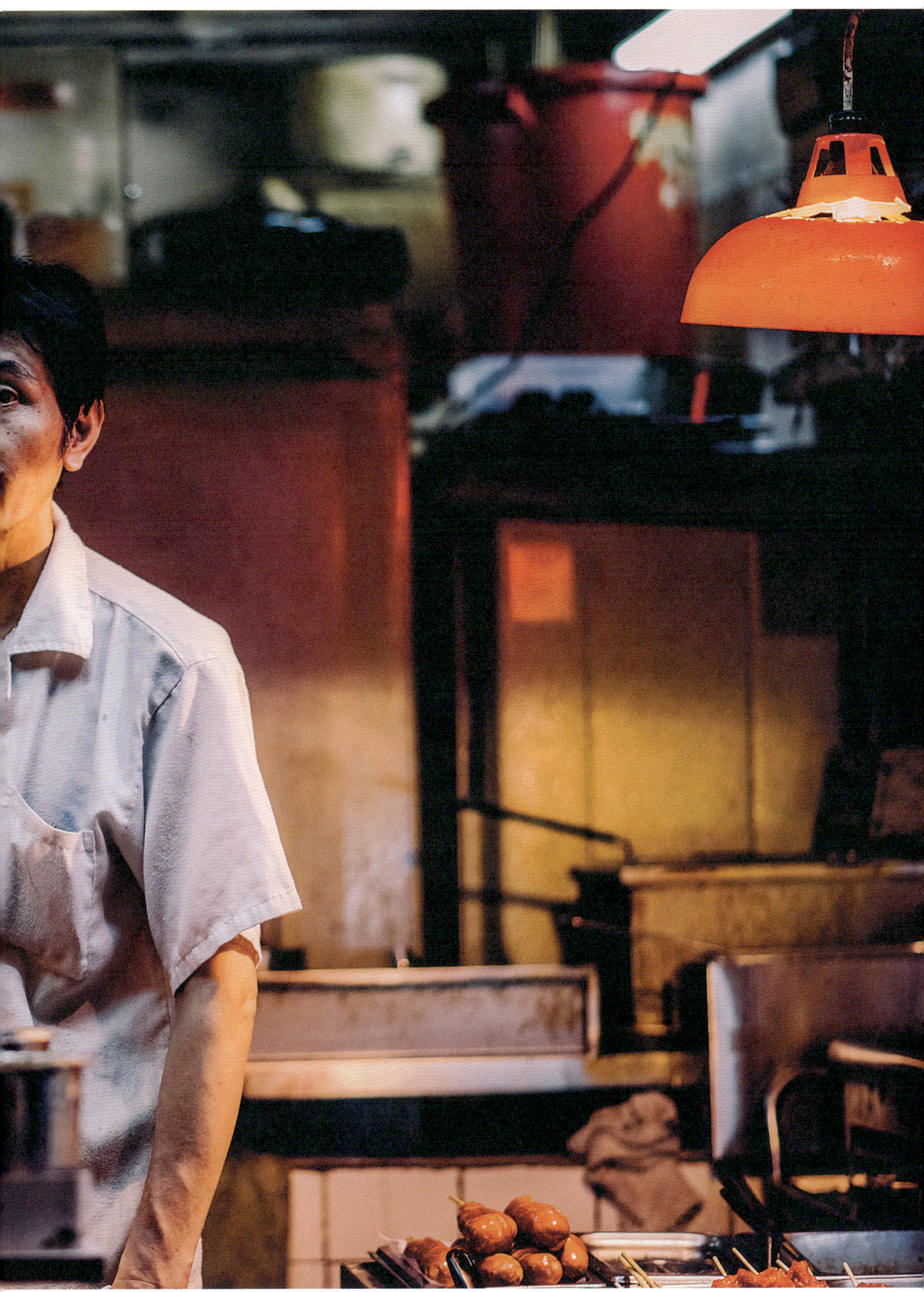

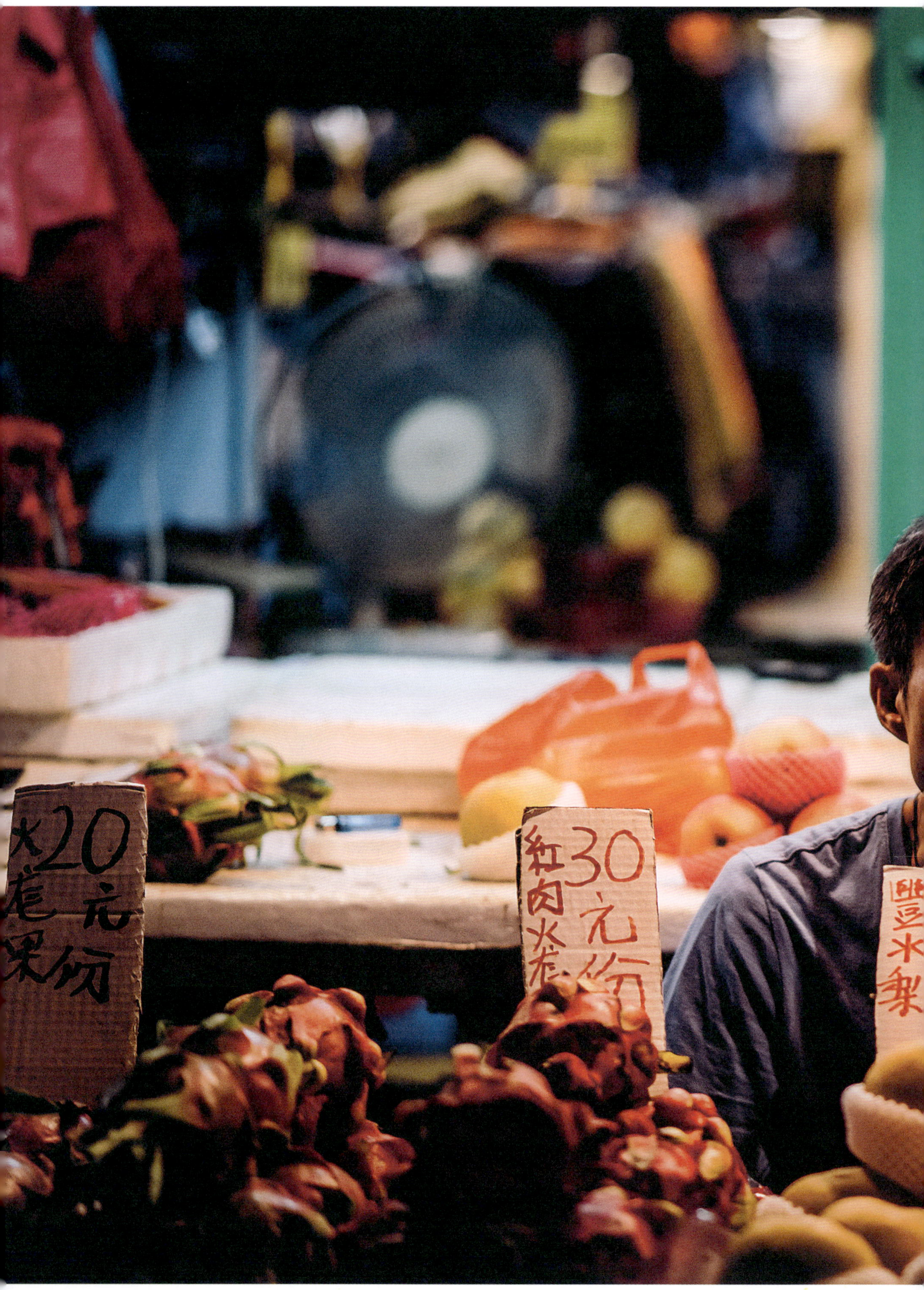
火龍果
20元份
紅肉火龍
30元份
豐水梨

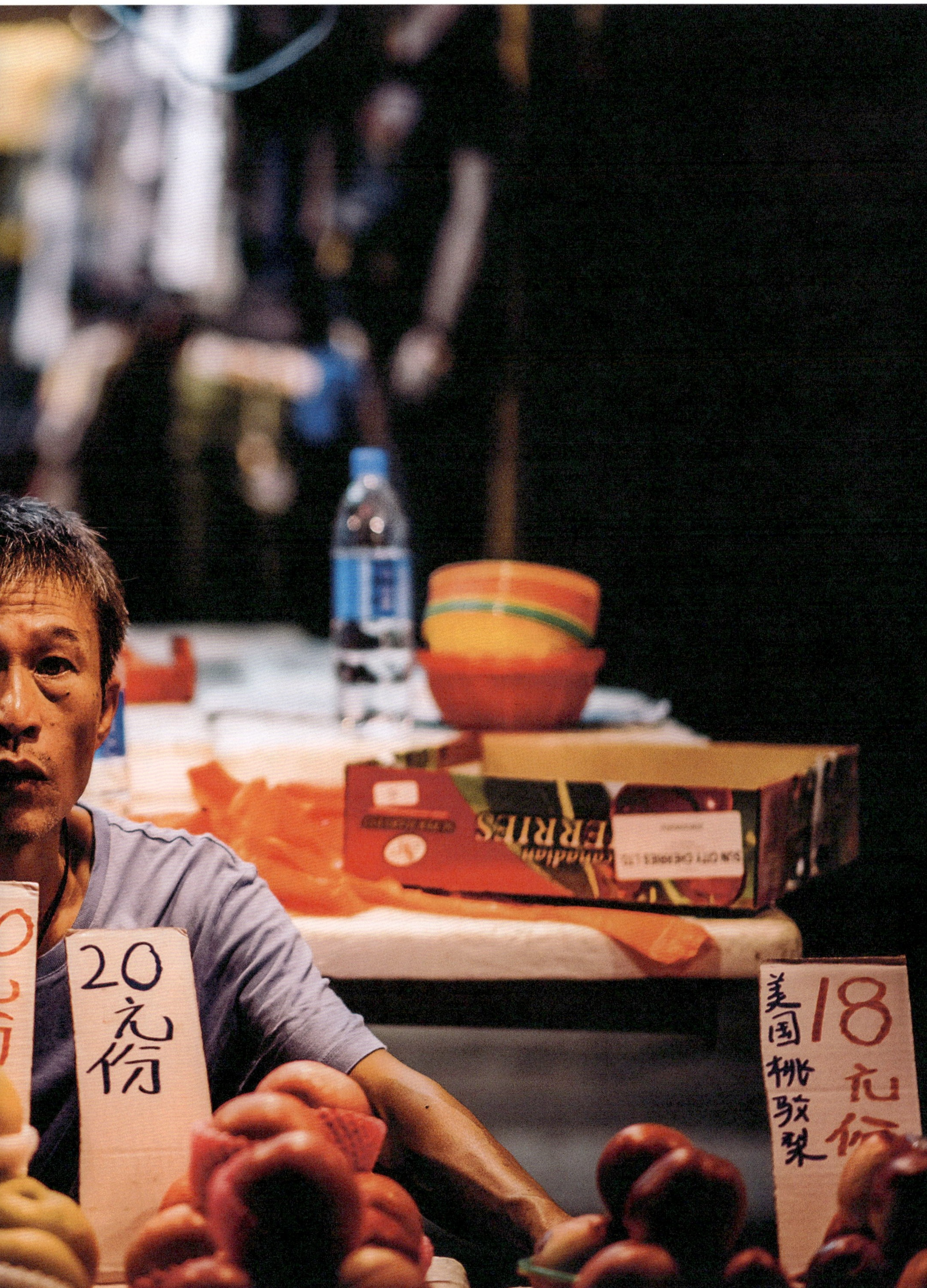

20
元斤
美国桃駁梨
18
元斤
Canadian
ERRIES
SUN CITY CHERRIES LTD

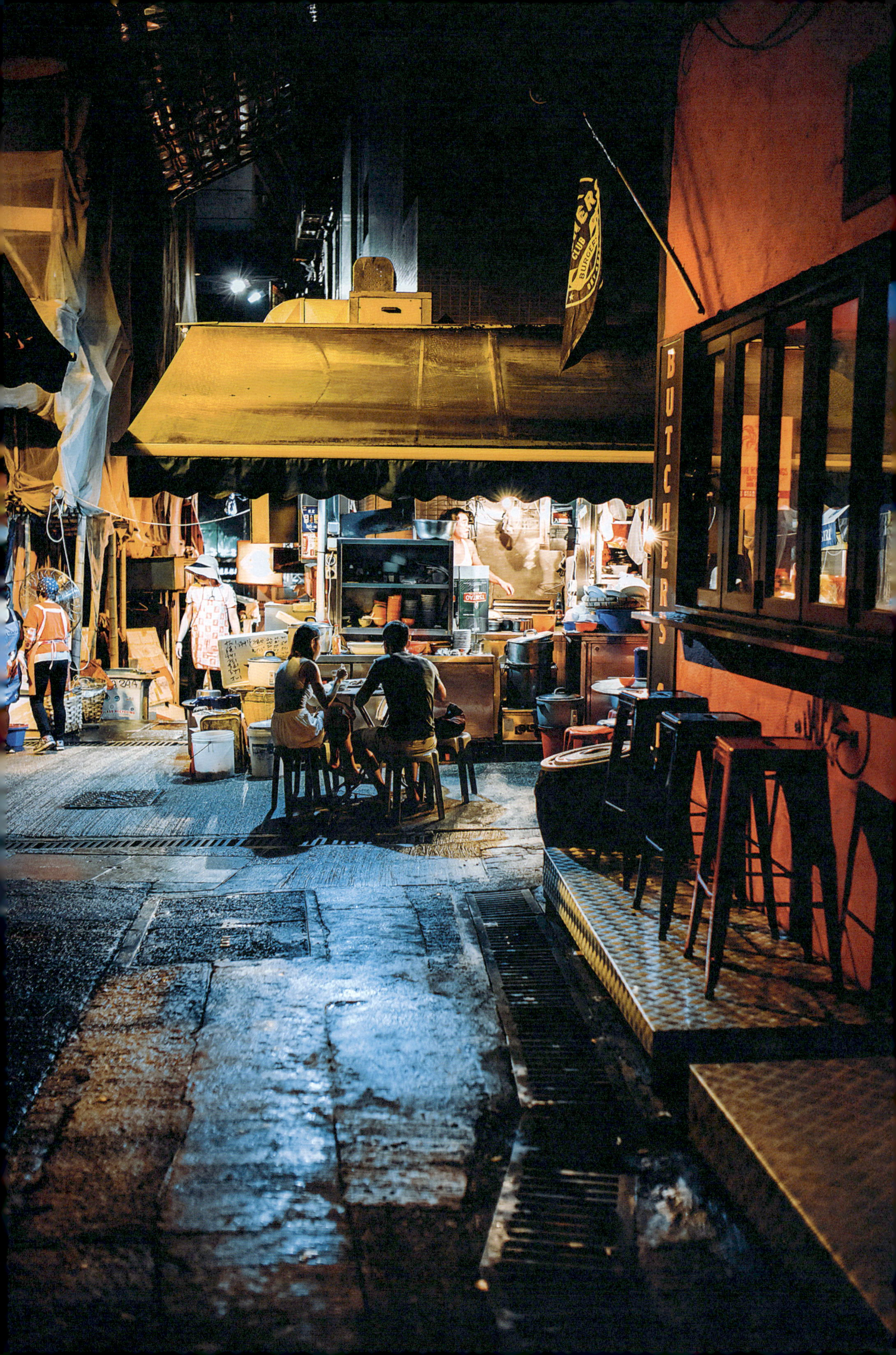

CLUB
BURGER
BUTCHERS

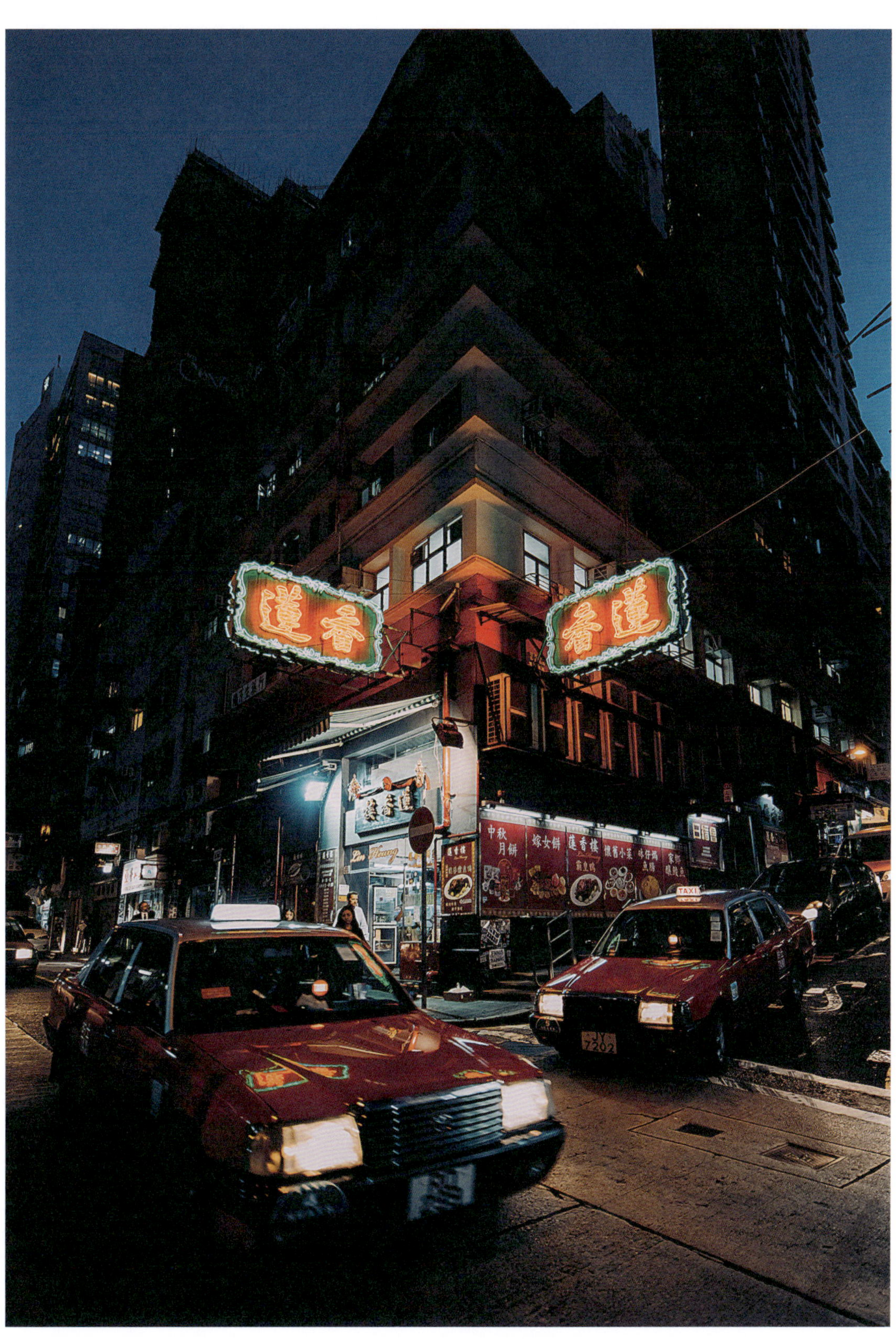
蓮香
香蓮
中秋月餅
嫁女餅
蓮香樓
禮餅小莱
咔仔嘅
食郡
TAXI
JX 7202

I STUDIED ARCHITECTURE FOR EIGHT YEARS AND PRACTICED

FOR SIX BEFORE I VENTURED INTO PHOTOGRAPHY.

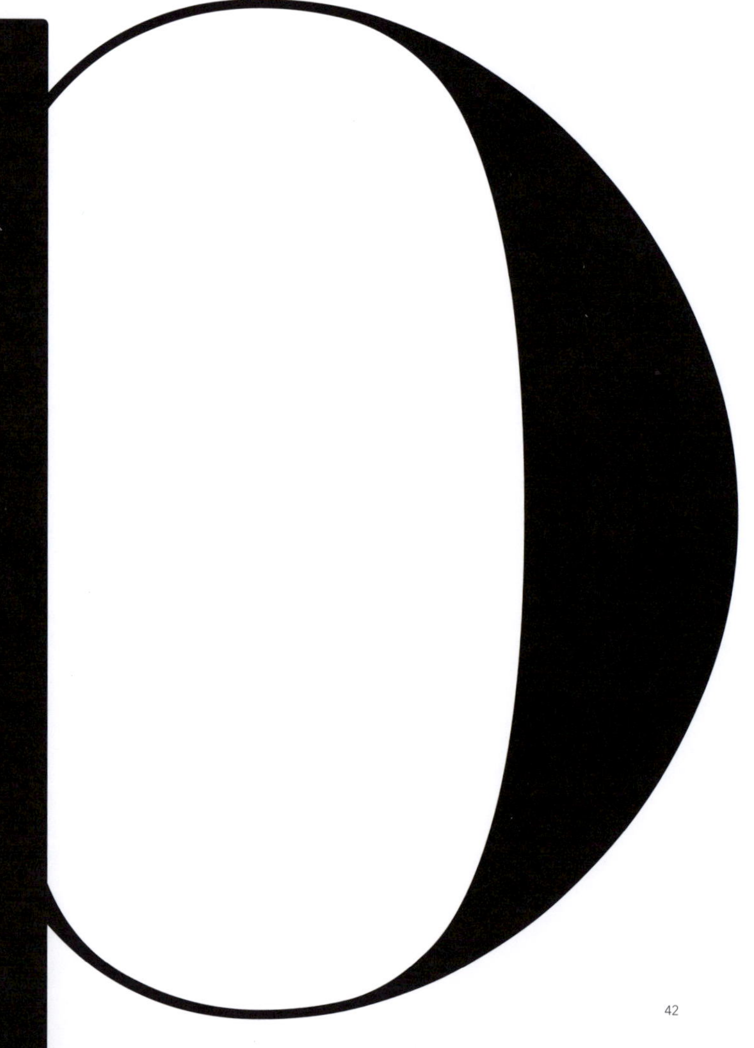

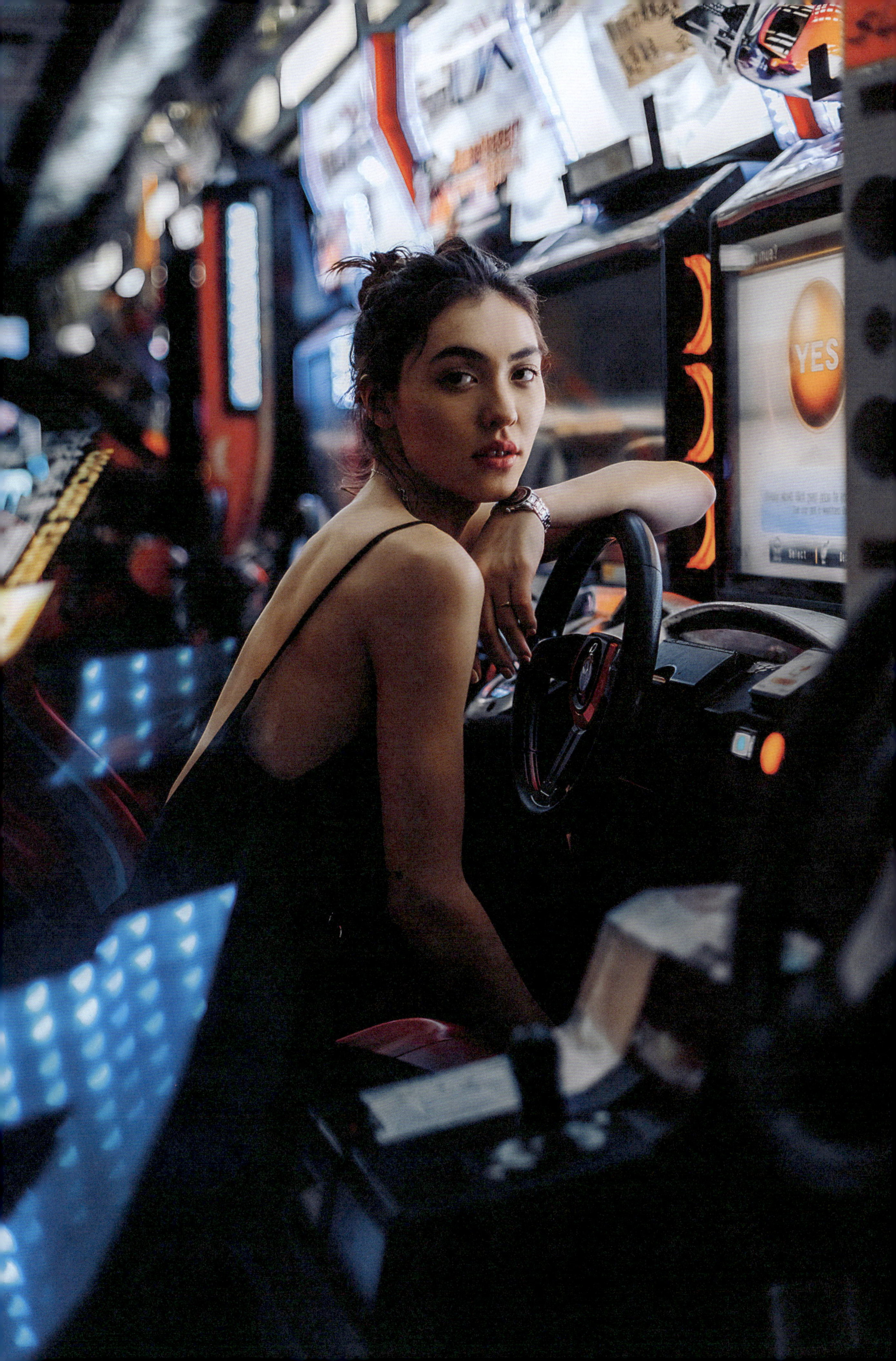

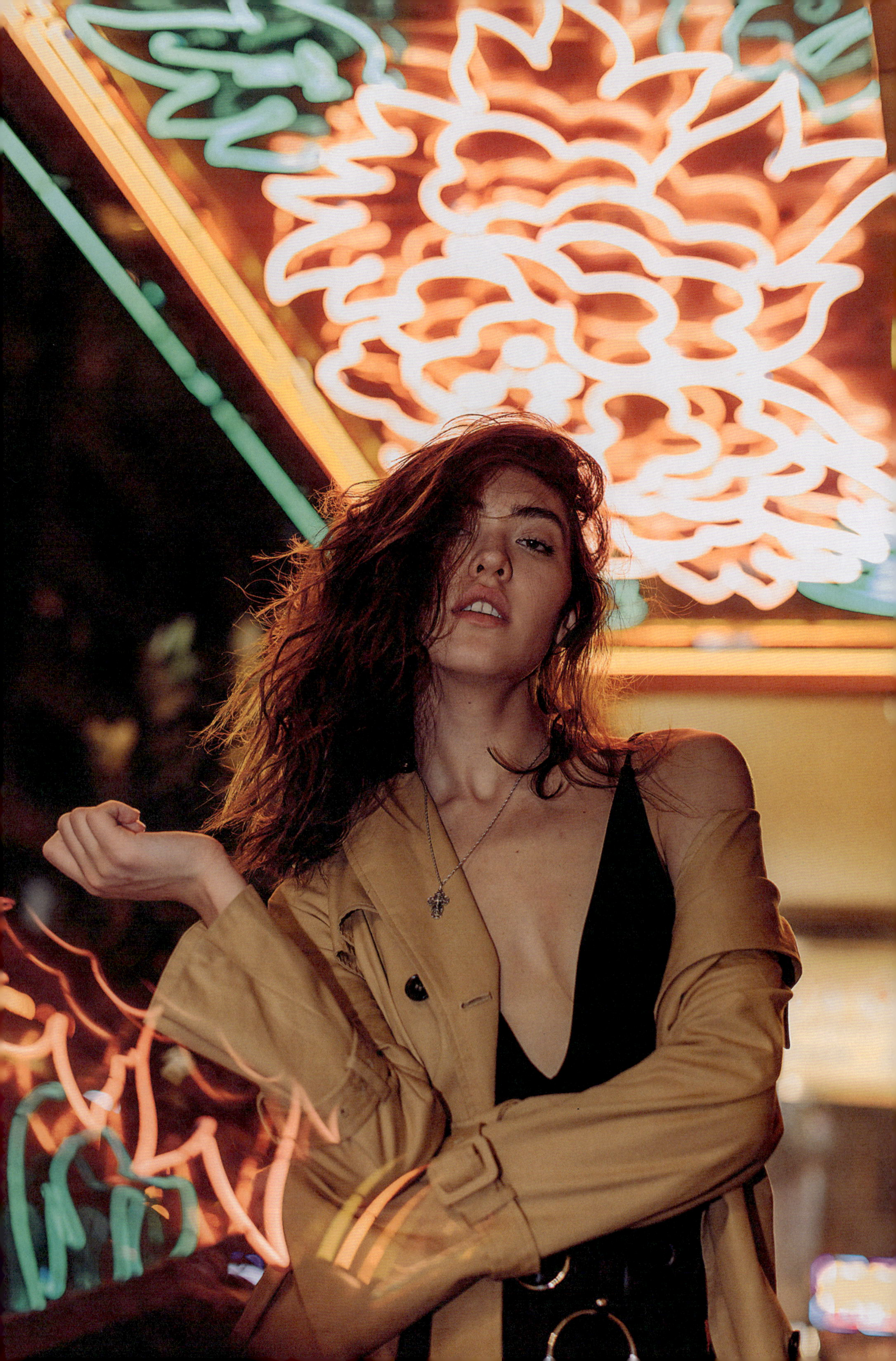

LIKE ARCHITECTURAL DRAWINGS, I WAS PARTICULARLY **INTERESTED IN FRAMING** GEOMETRY, SYMMETRY, REPETITION AND STRONG LINES IN MY COMPOSITION.

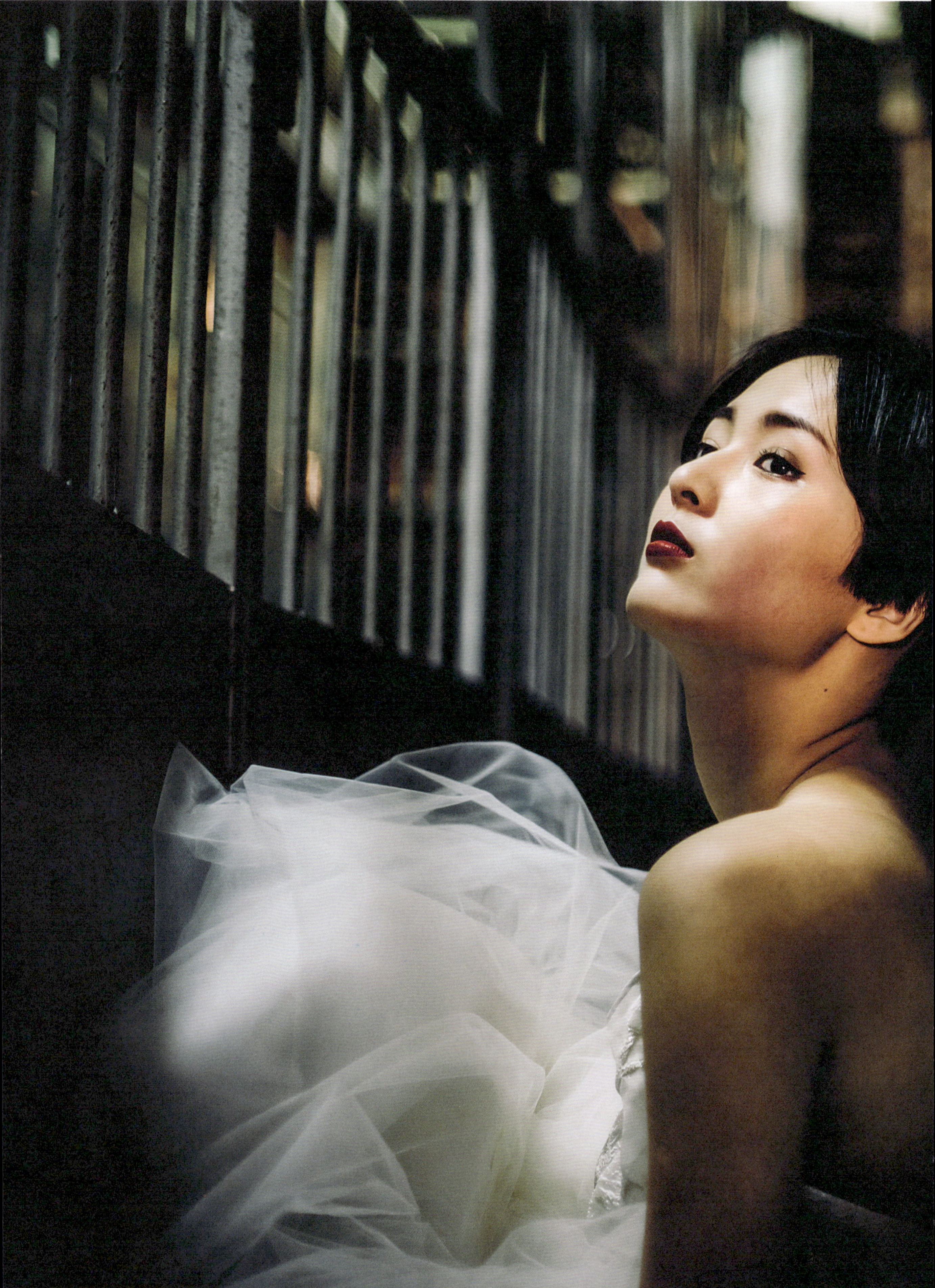

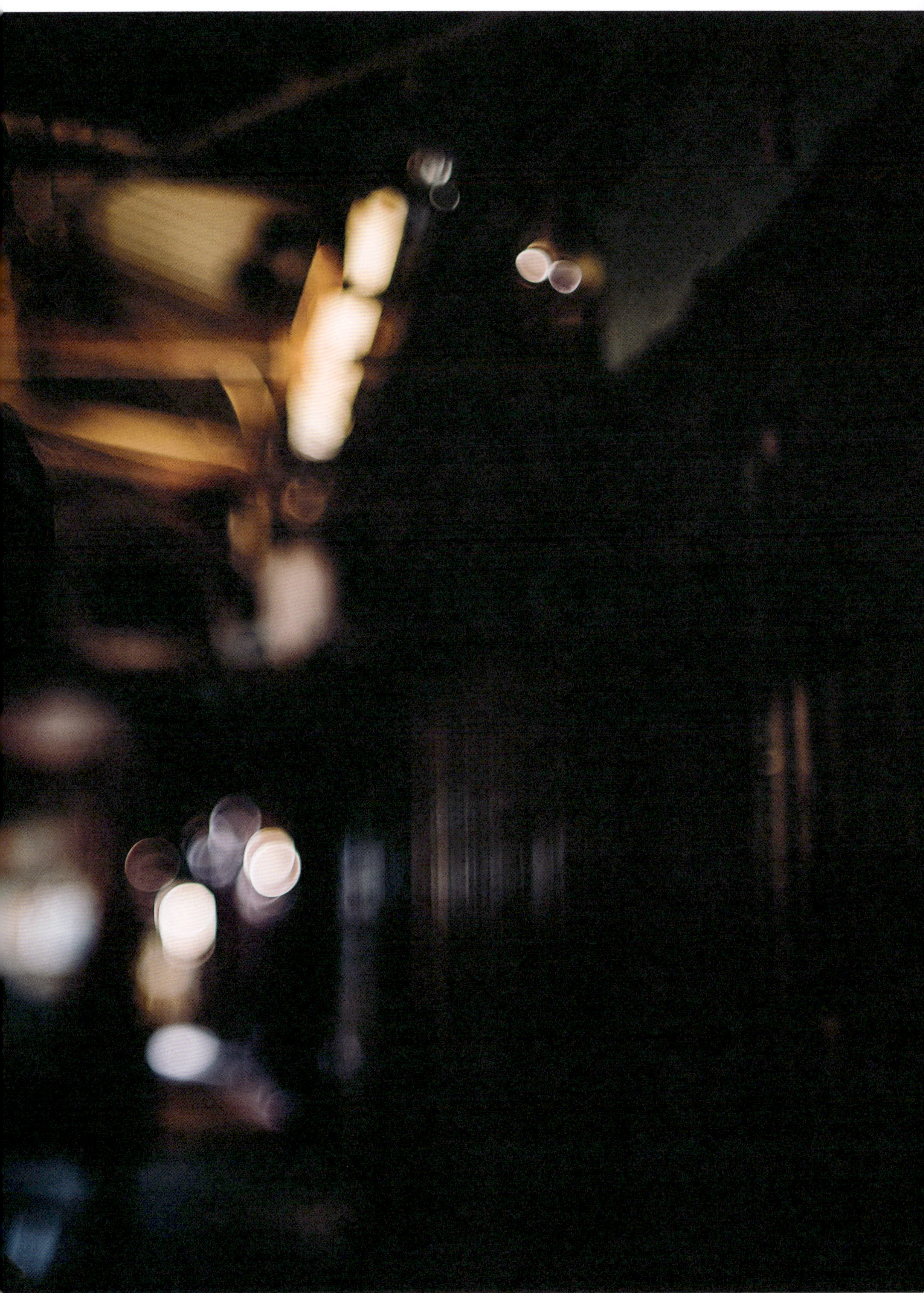

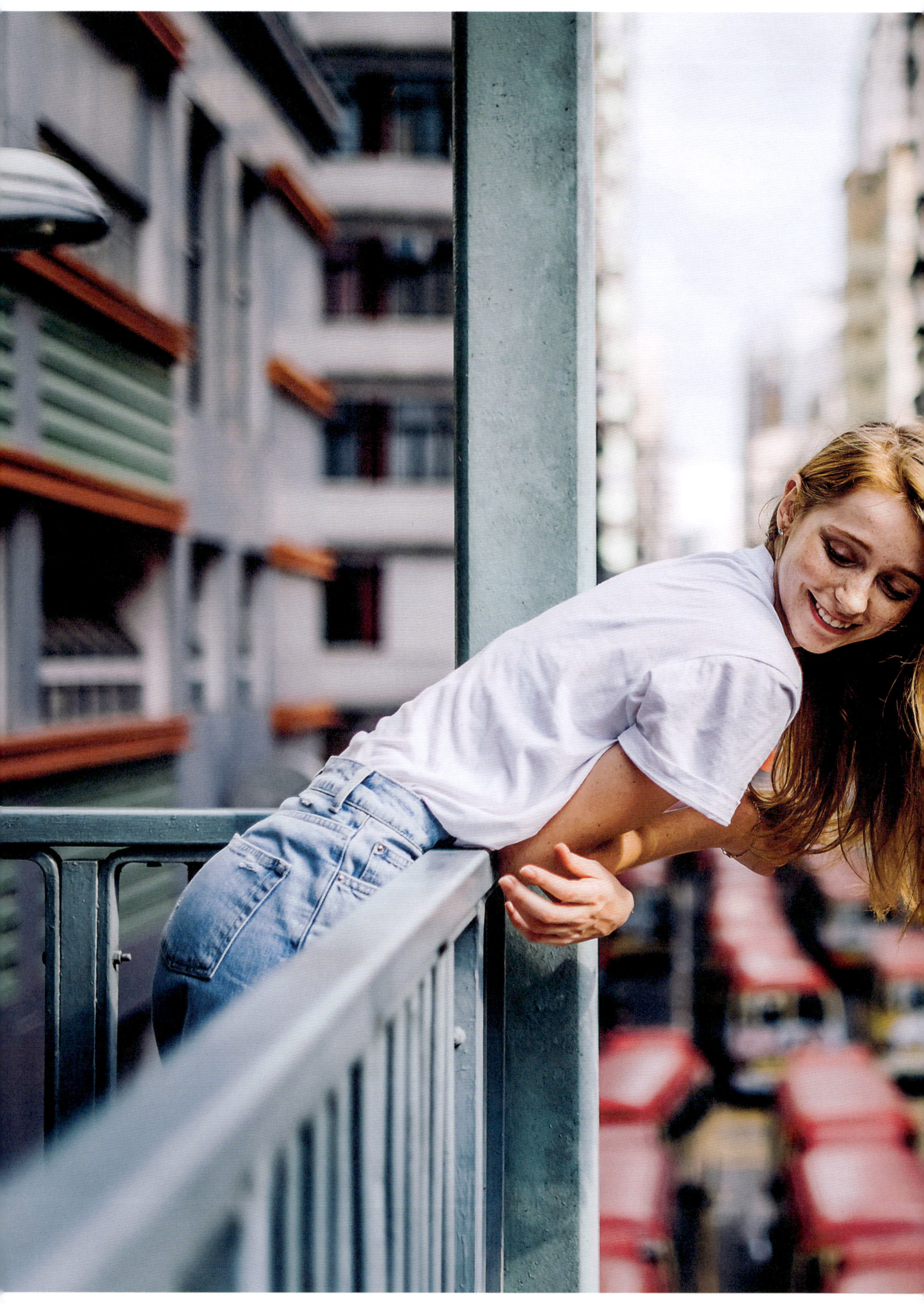

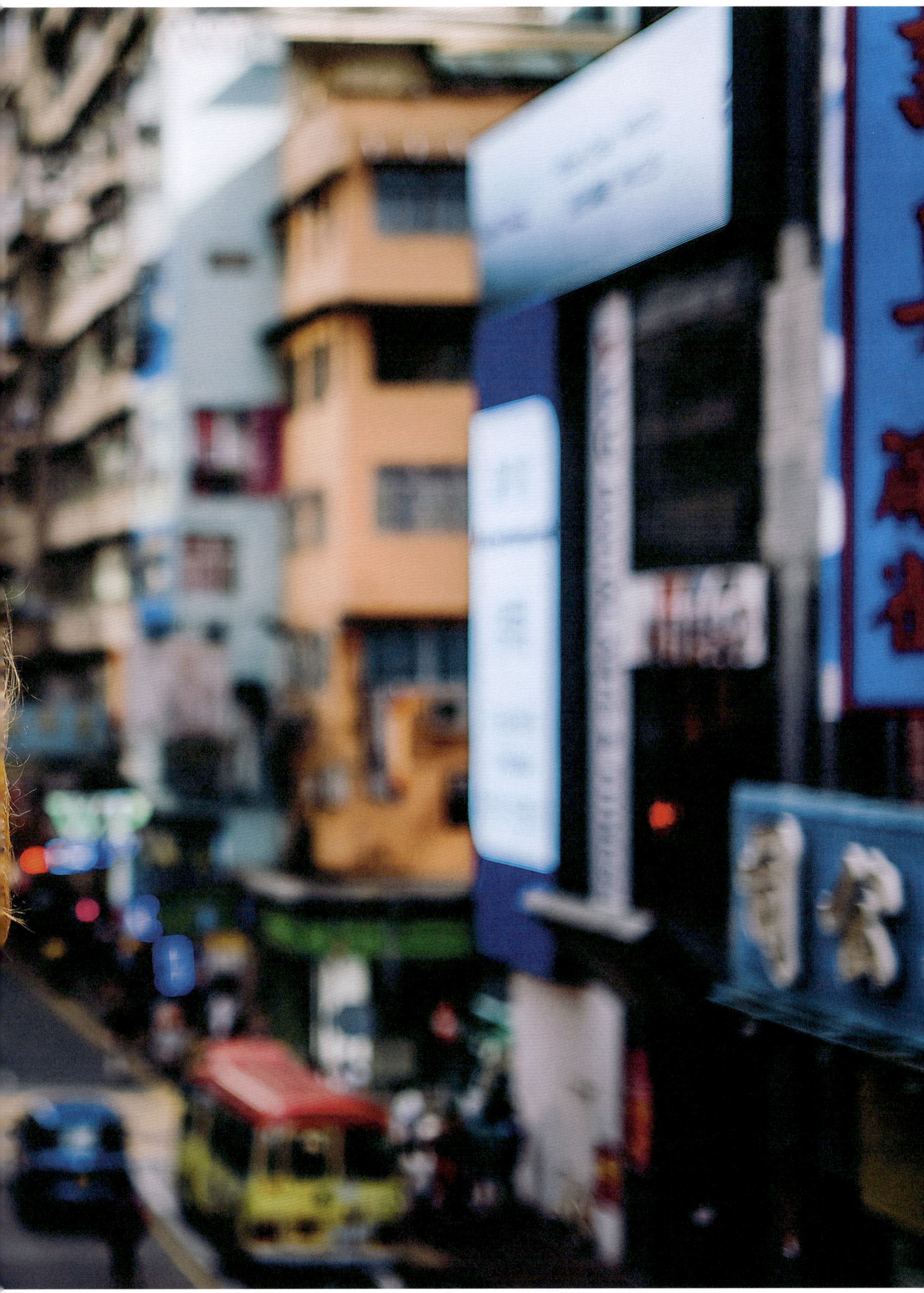

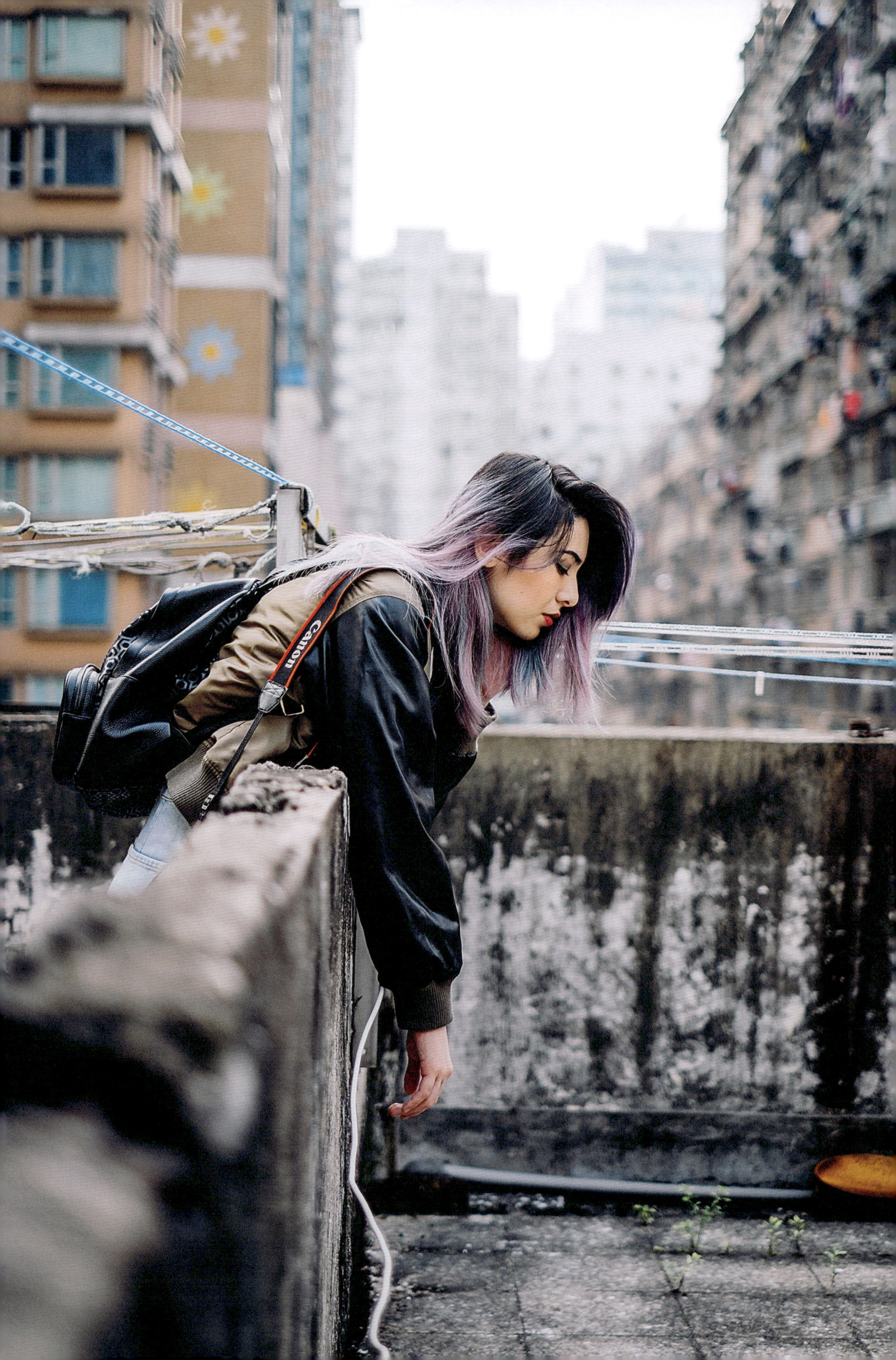

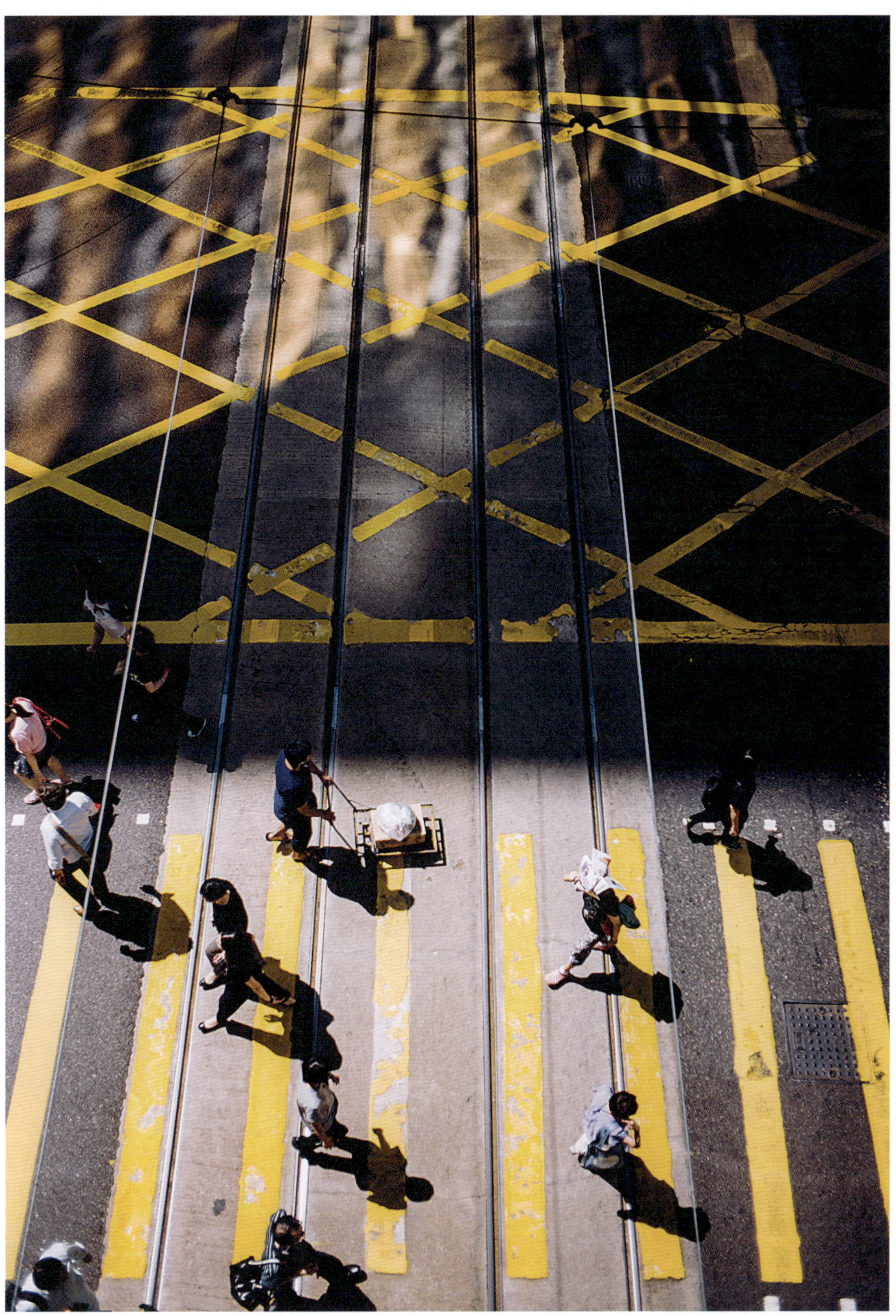

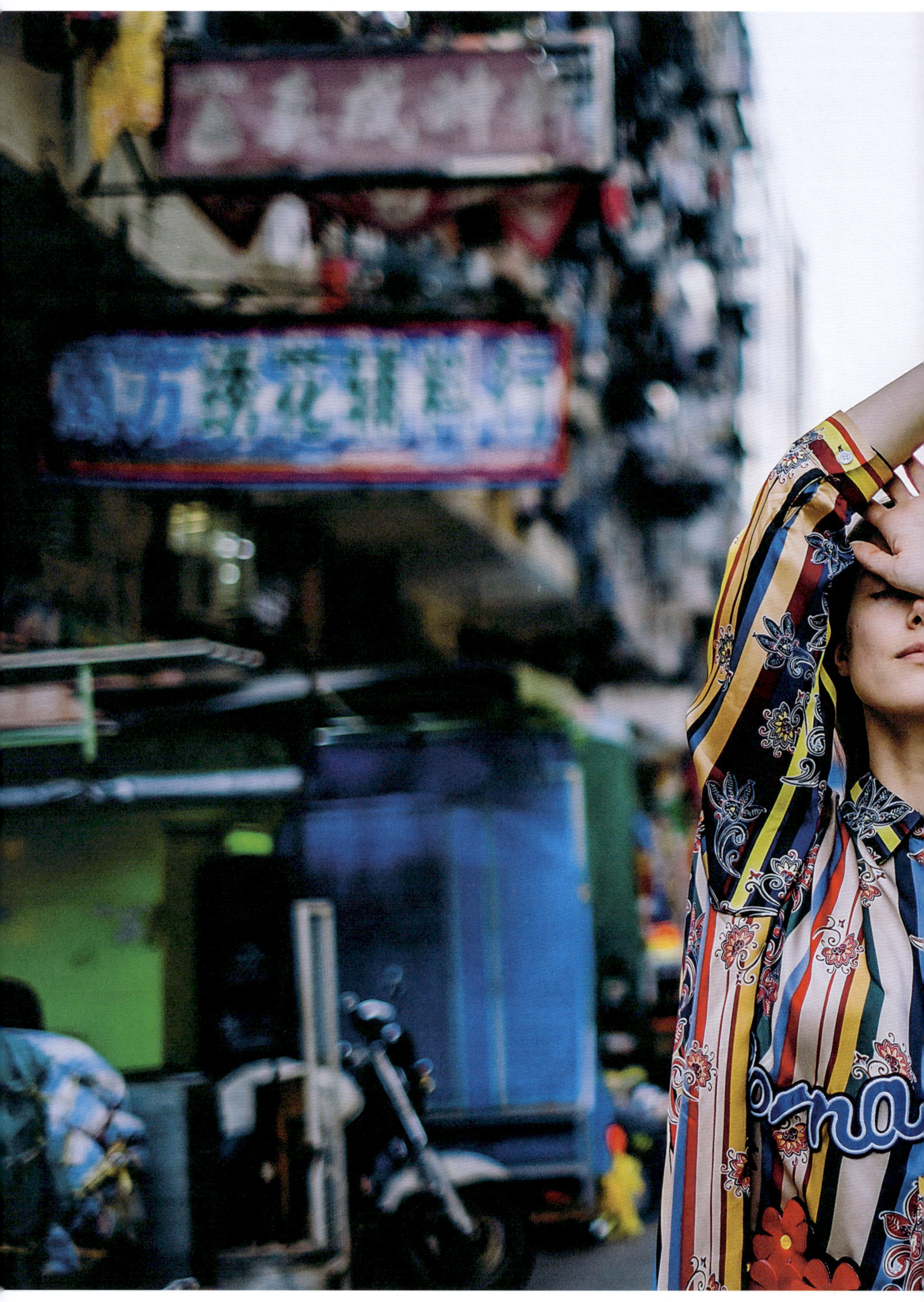

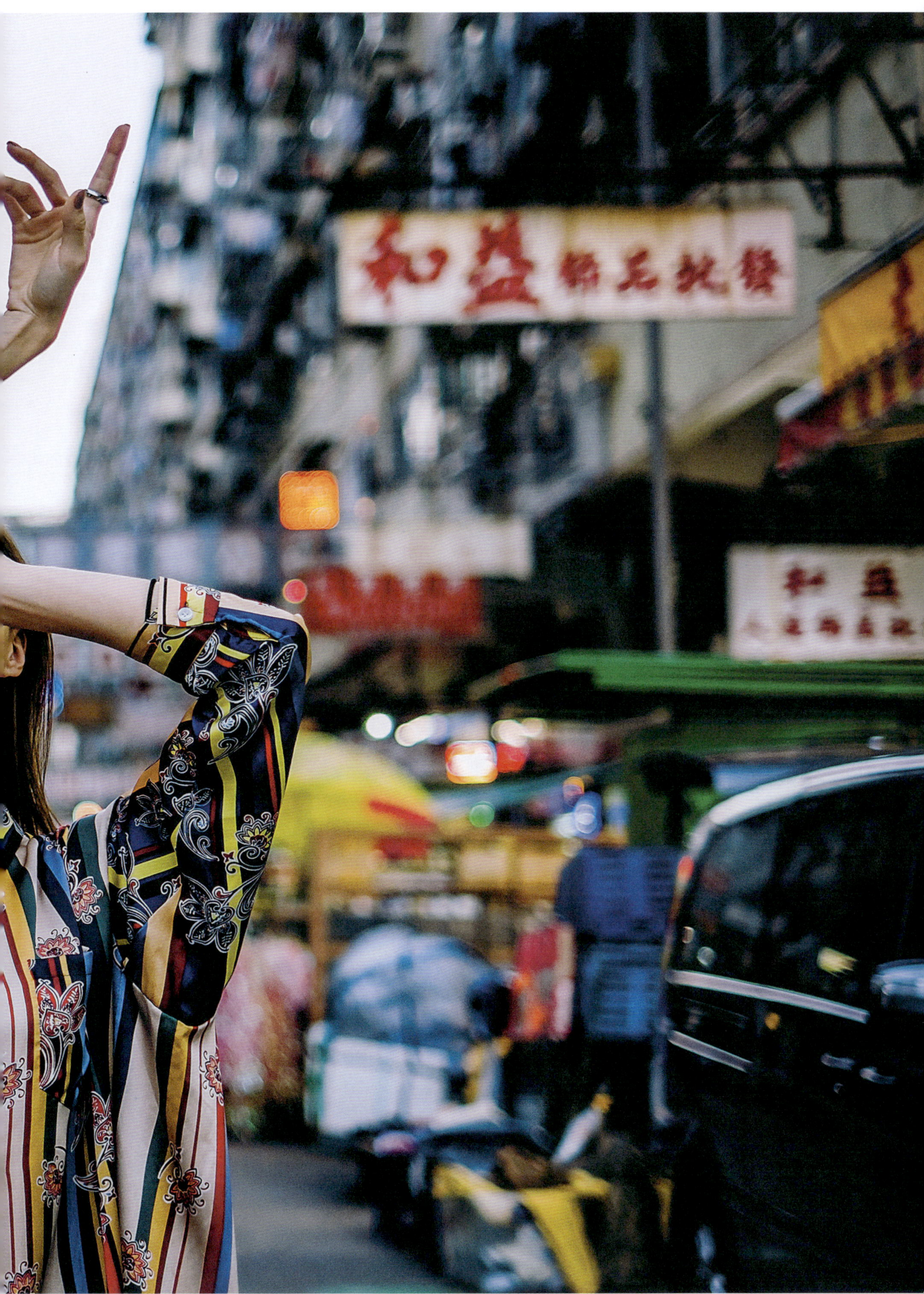

和益 棉毛批發
和益

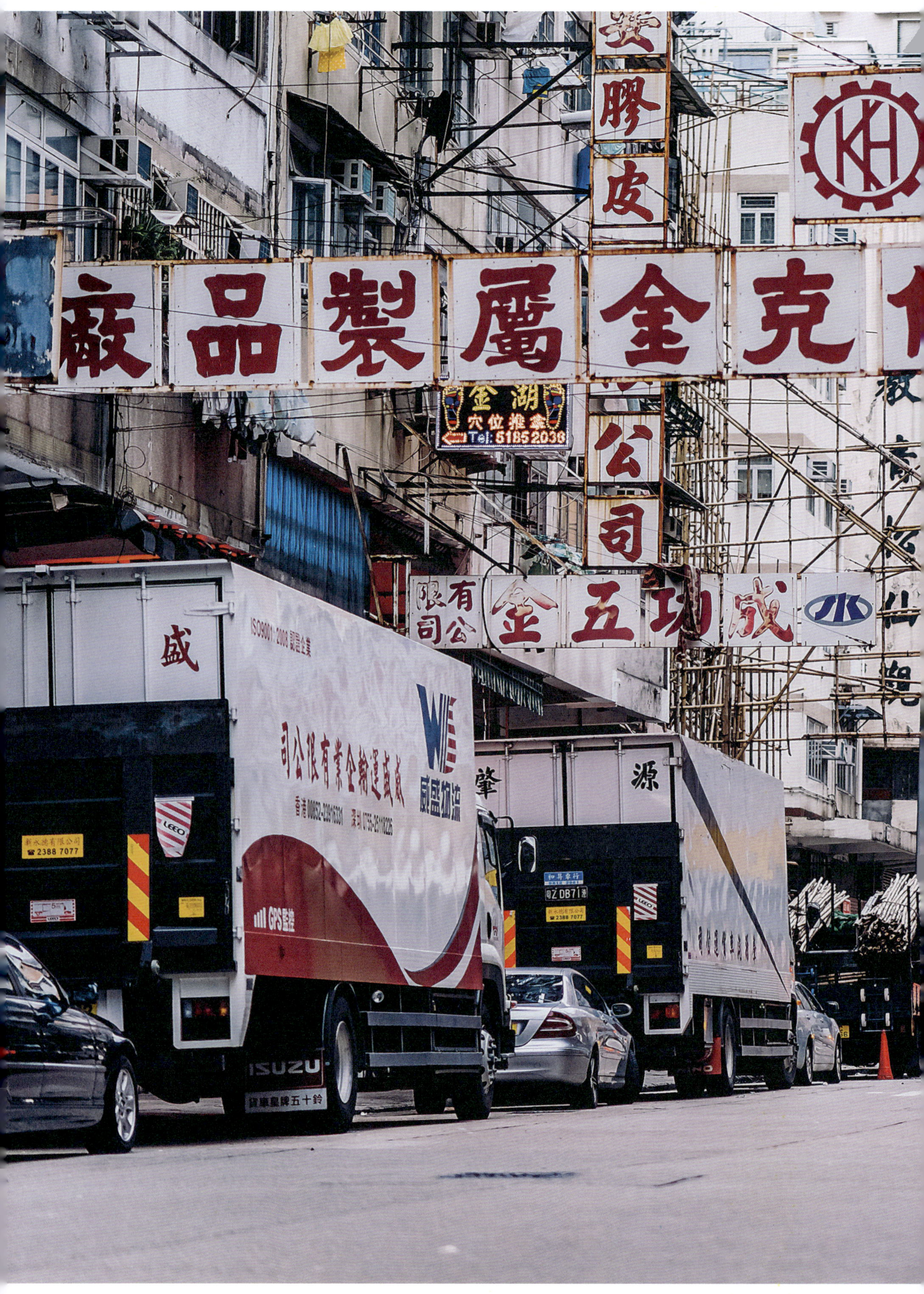

膠
皮
KKH
廠 品 製 屬 金 克
金湖
穴位推拿
Tel: 5185 2038
公
司
限有
司公
金 五 功 成
盛
ISO9001:2008 認證企業
司公限有金輸運盛威
威盛物流
香港 00852 29640
深圳 0755-26
GPS監控
LECO
2388 7077
ISUZU
肇
源
ZDB71
2388 7077

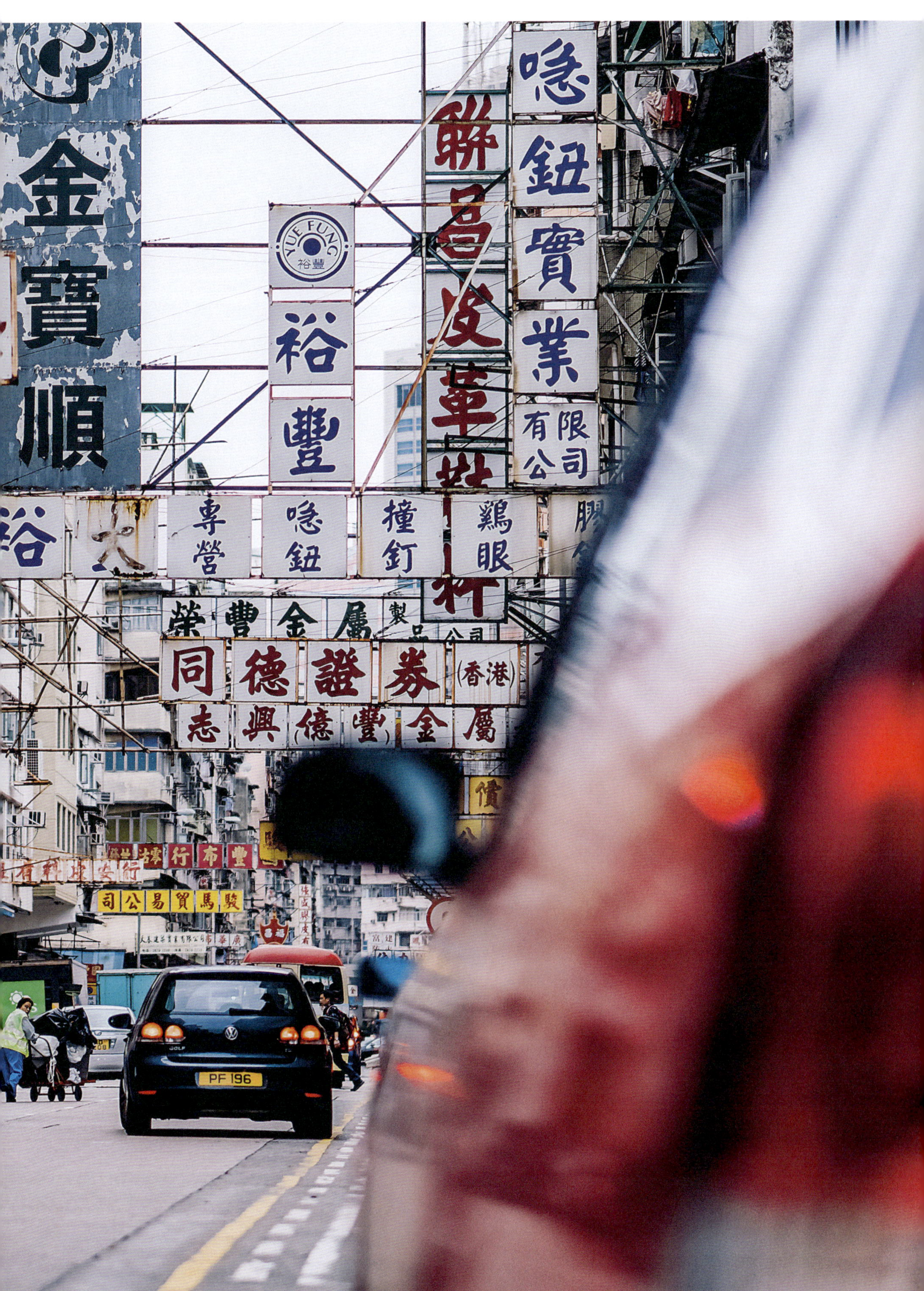

金寶順
裕
唔鈕寶業
聯昌發革社
有限公司
YUE FUNG
裕豐
專營
唔鈕
撞釘
鷄眼
榮豐金屬
同德證券 (香港)
志興 (德豐) 金屬
行布豐
司公易貿馬駿
VW
GOLF
PF 196

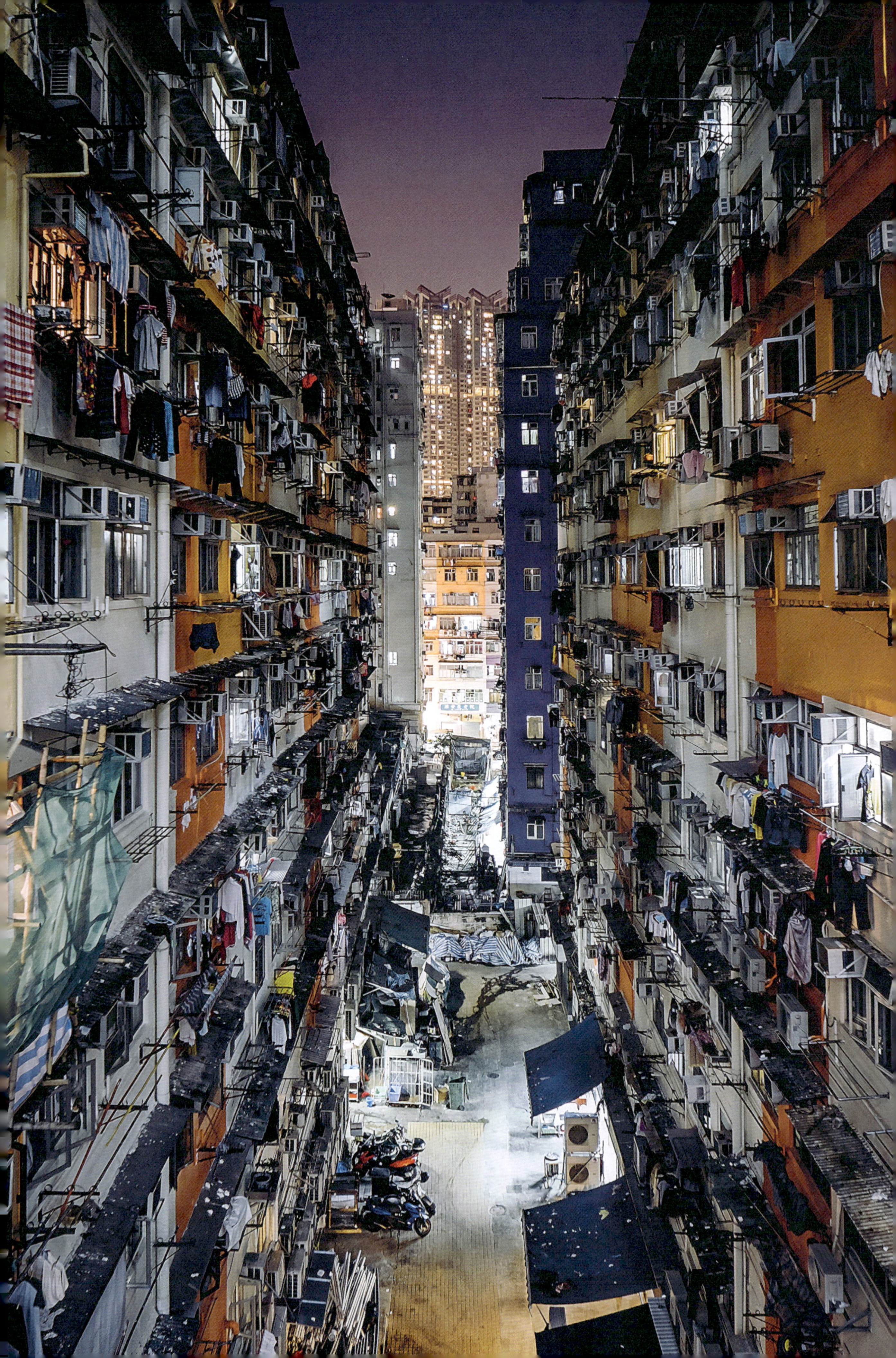

DURING MY CHILDHOOD IN HONG KONG, THE DENSE URBAN JUNGLE WAS NOTHING SPECIAL. THE SOARING TOWERS AND ENDLESS, HIVE-LIKE WINDOWS WERE UBIQUITOUS, AND I HAD ACCEPTED IT AS THE TYPICAL WAY OF LIFE.

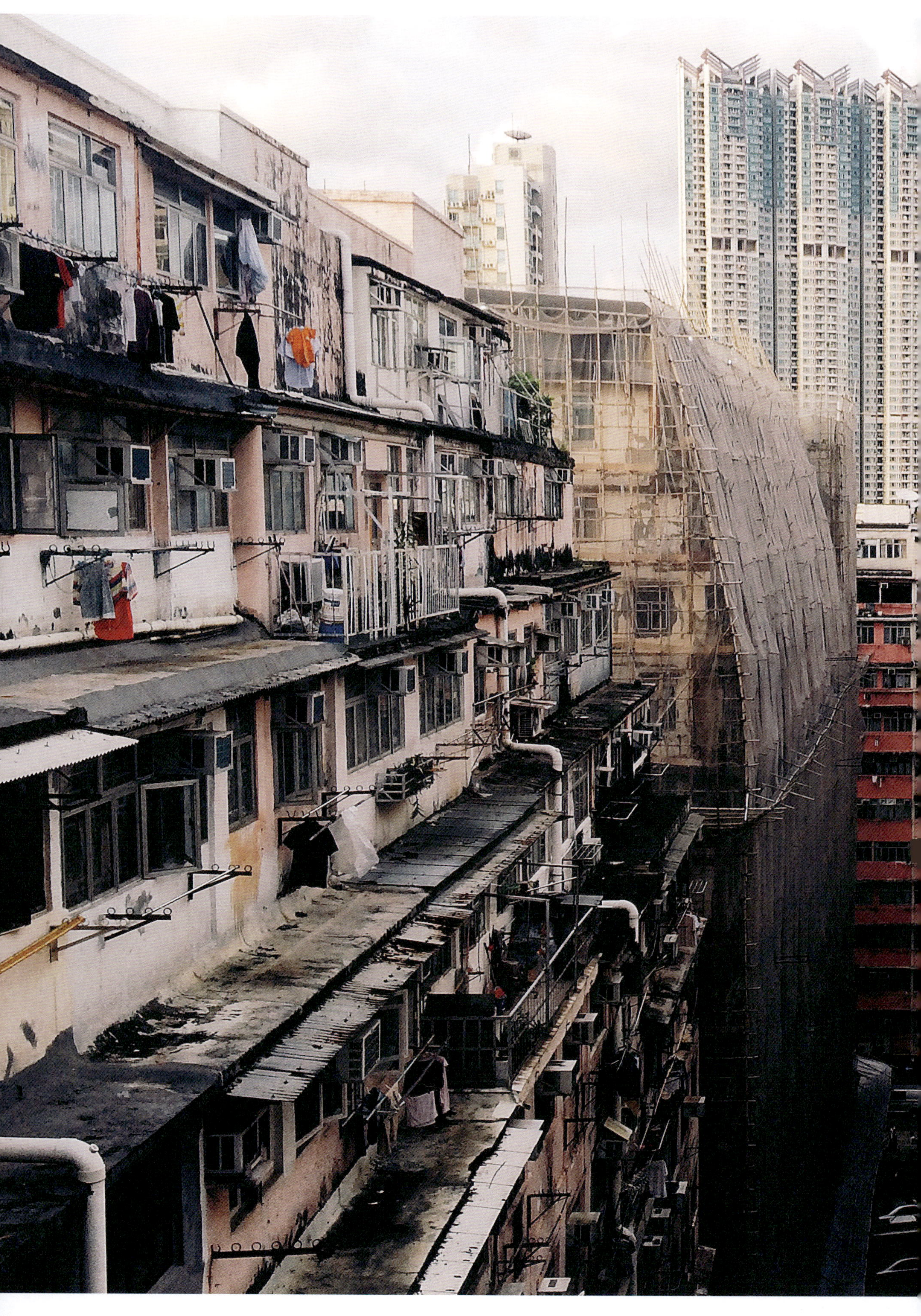

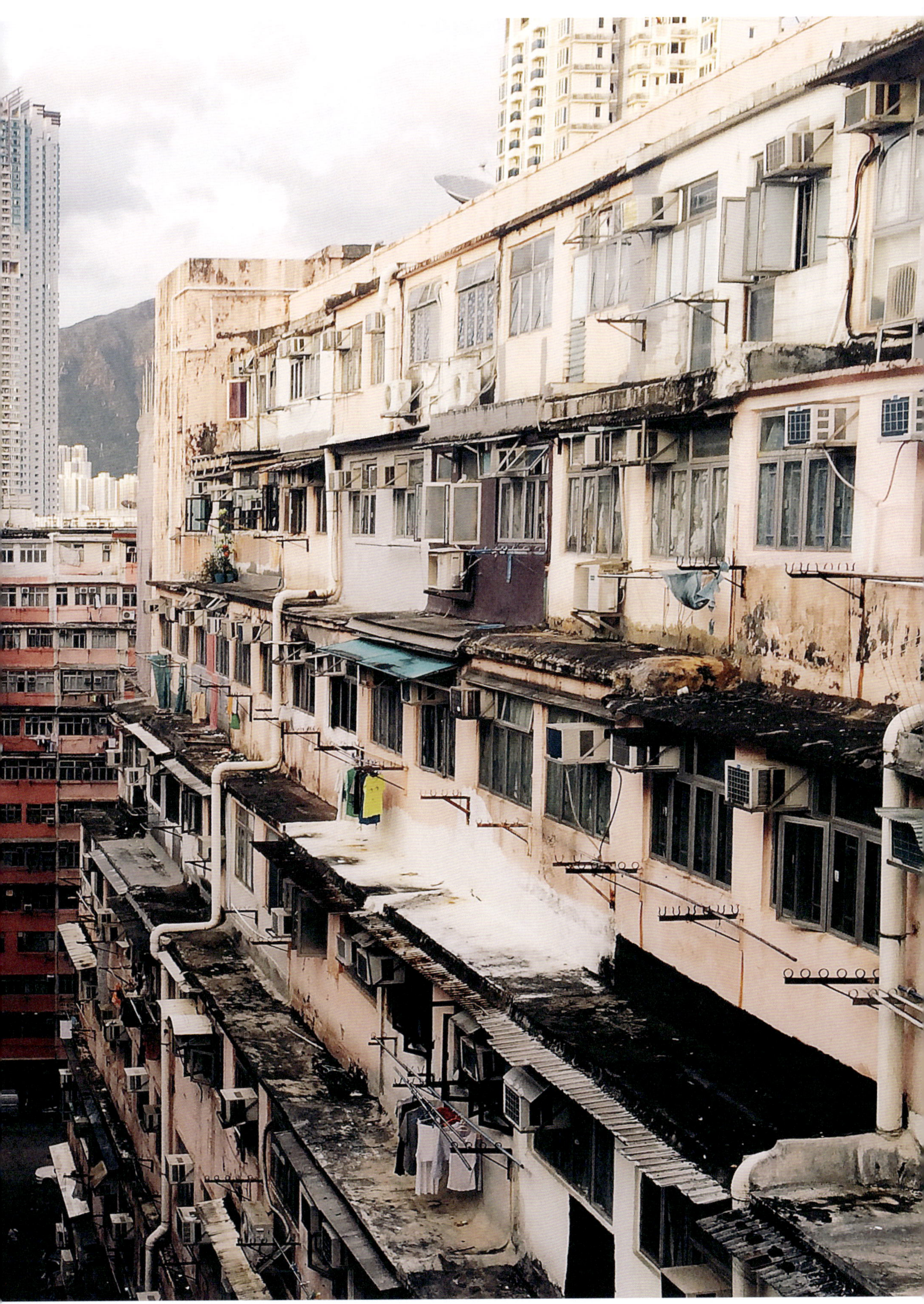

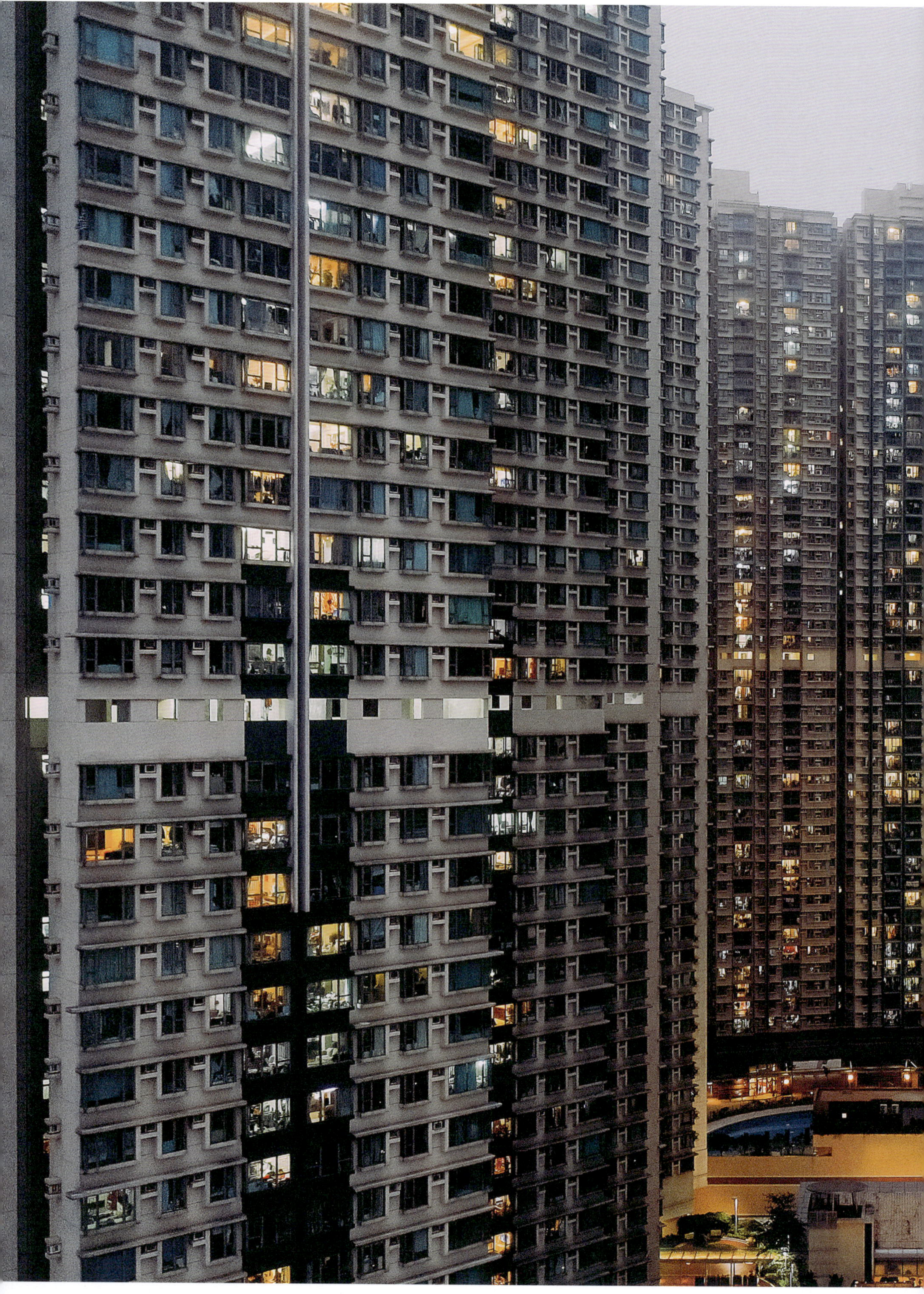

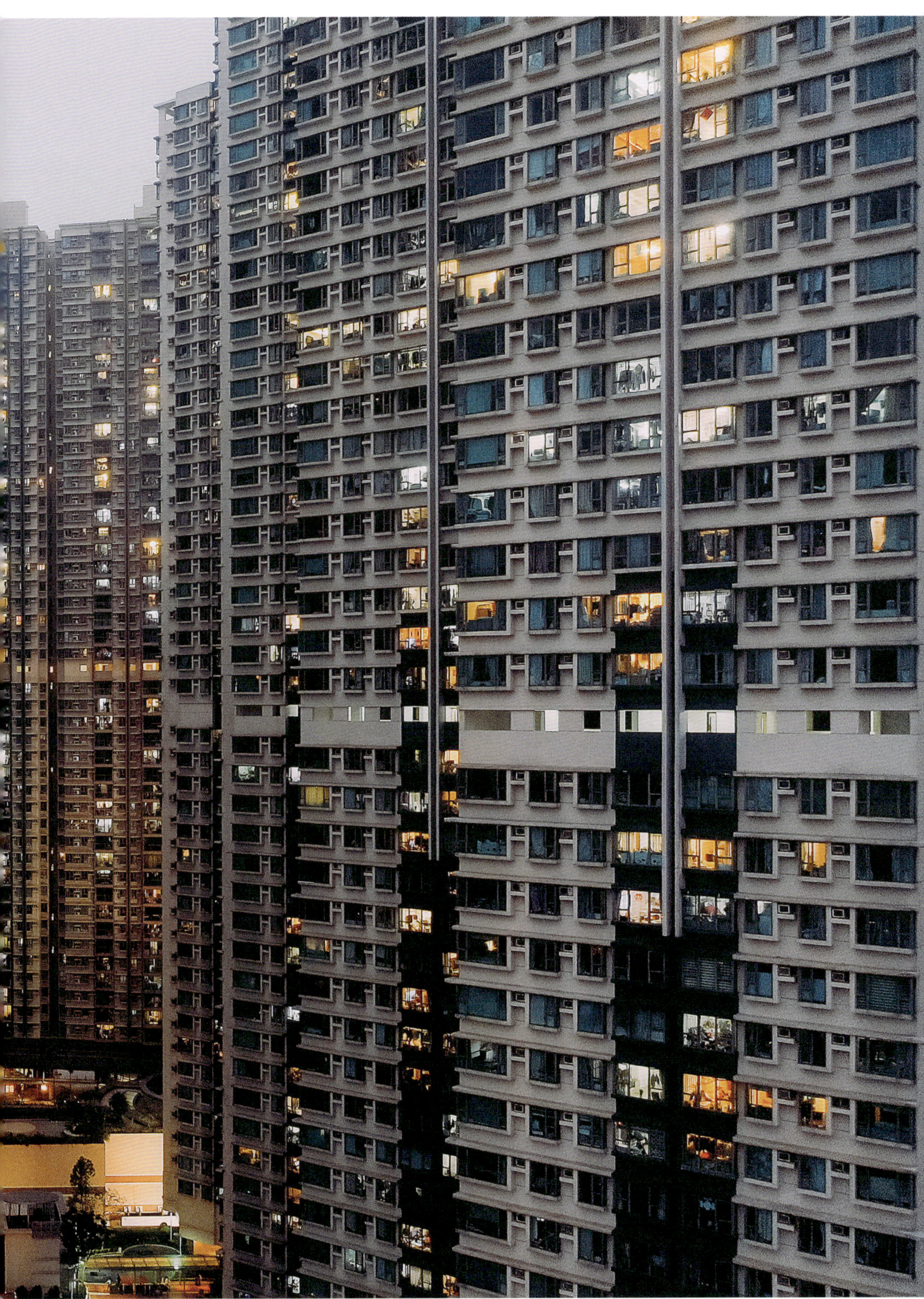

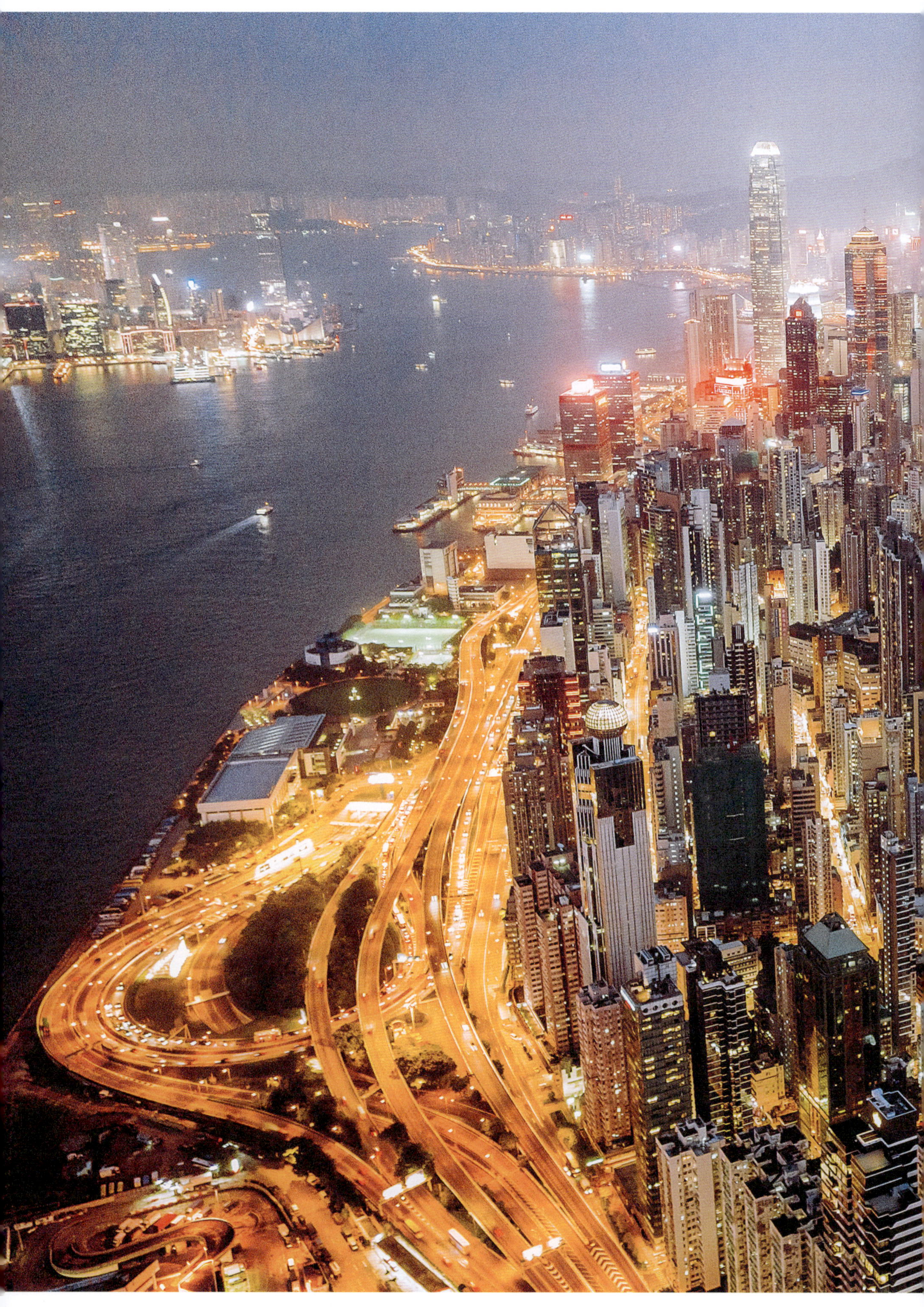

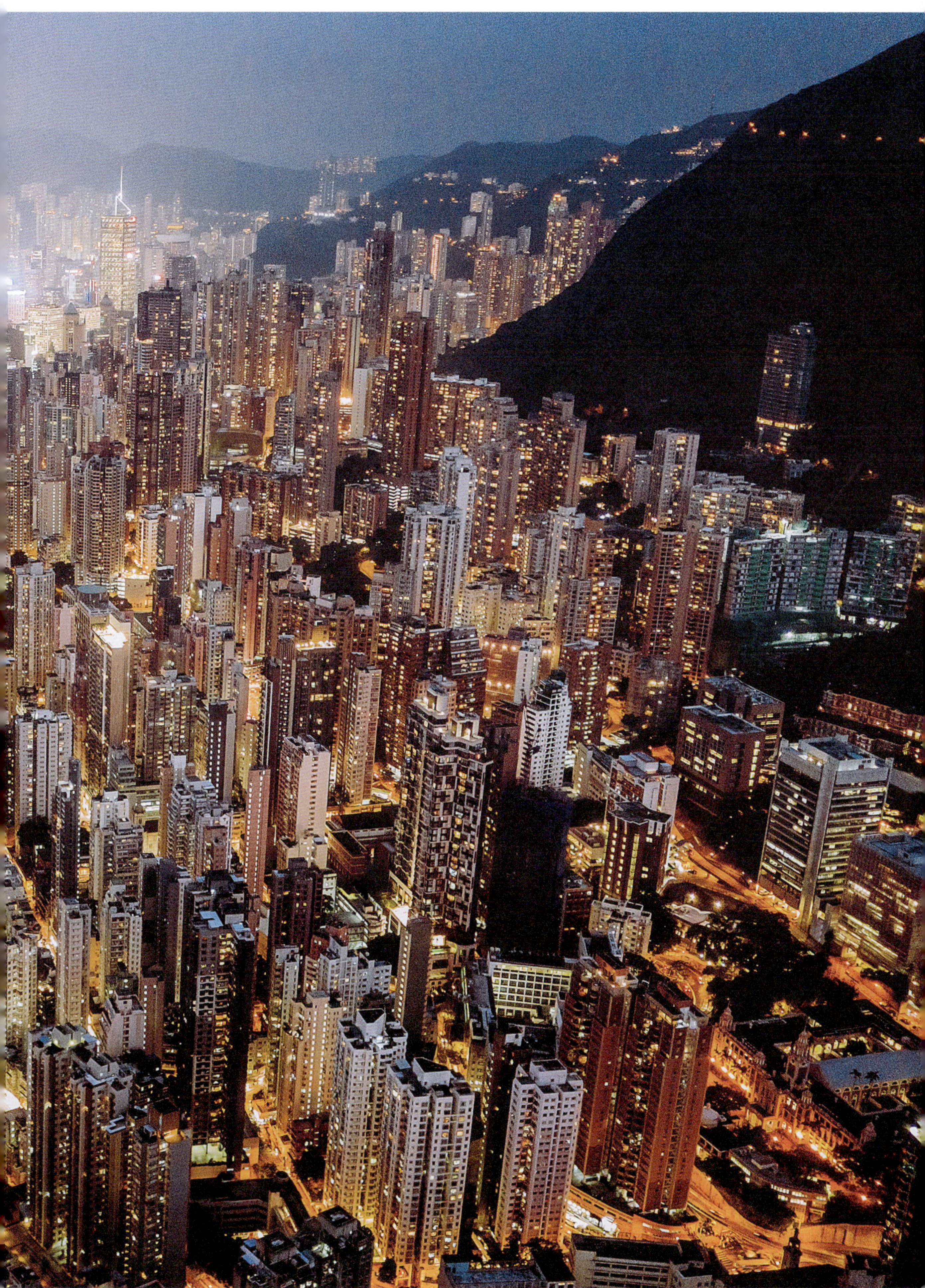

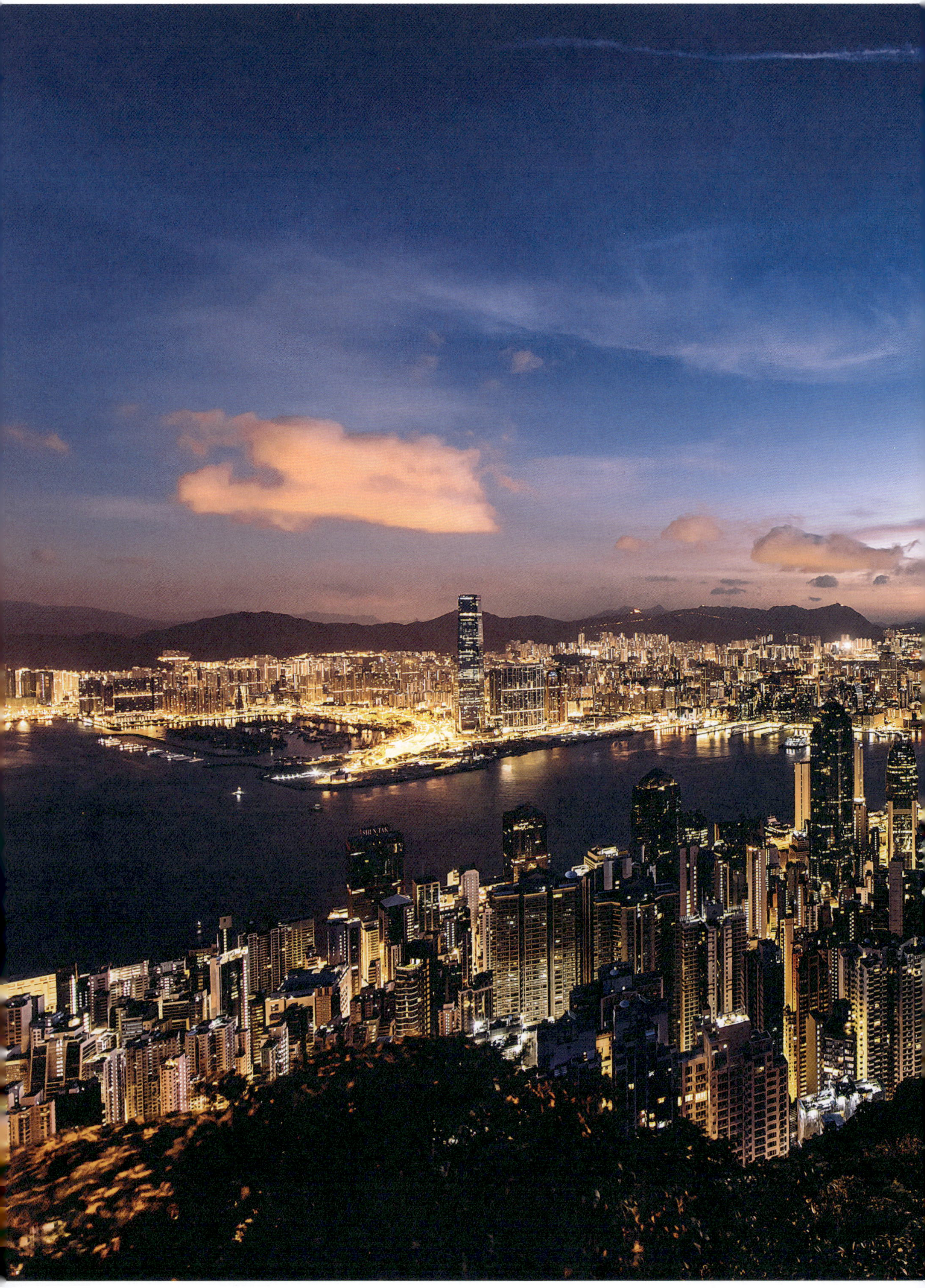

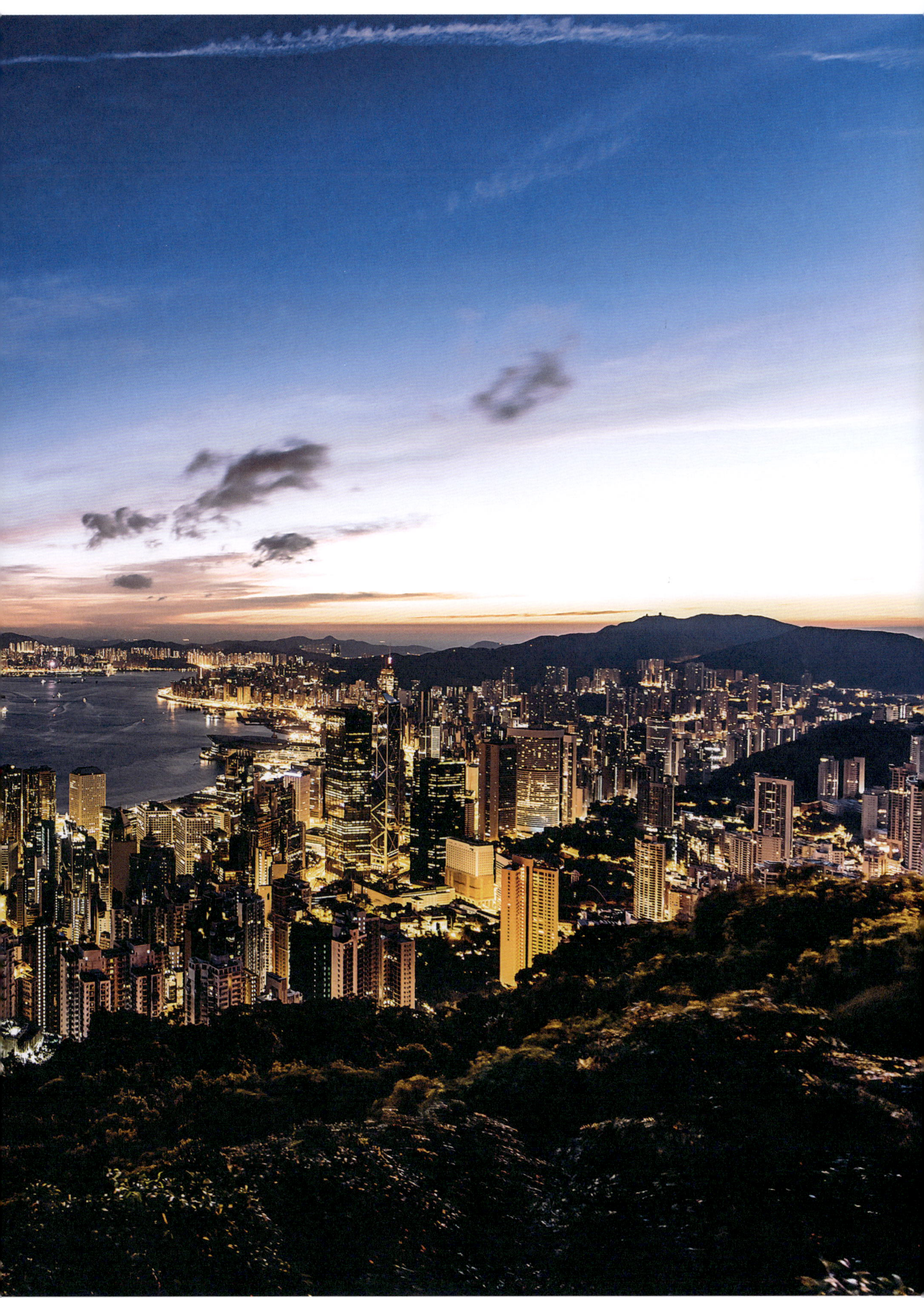

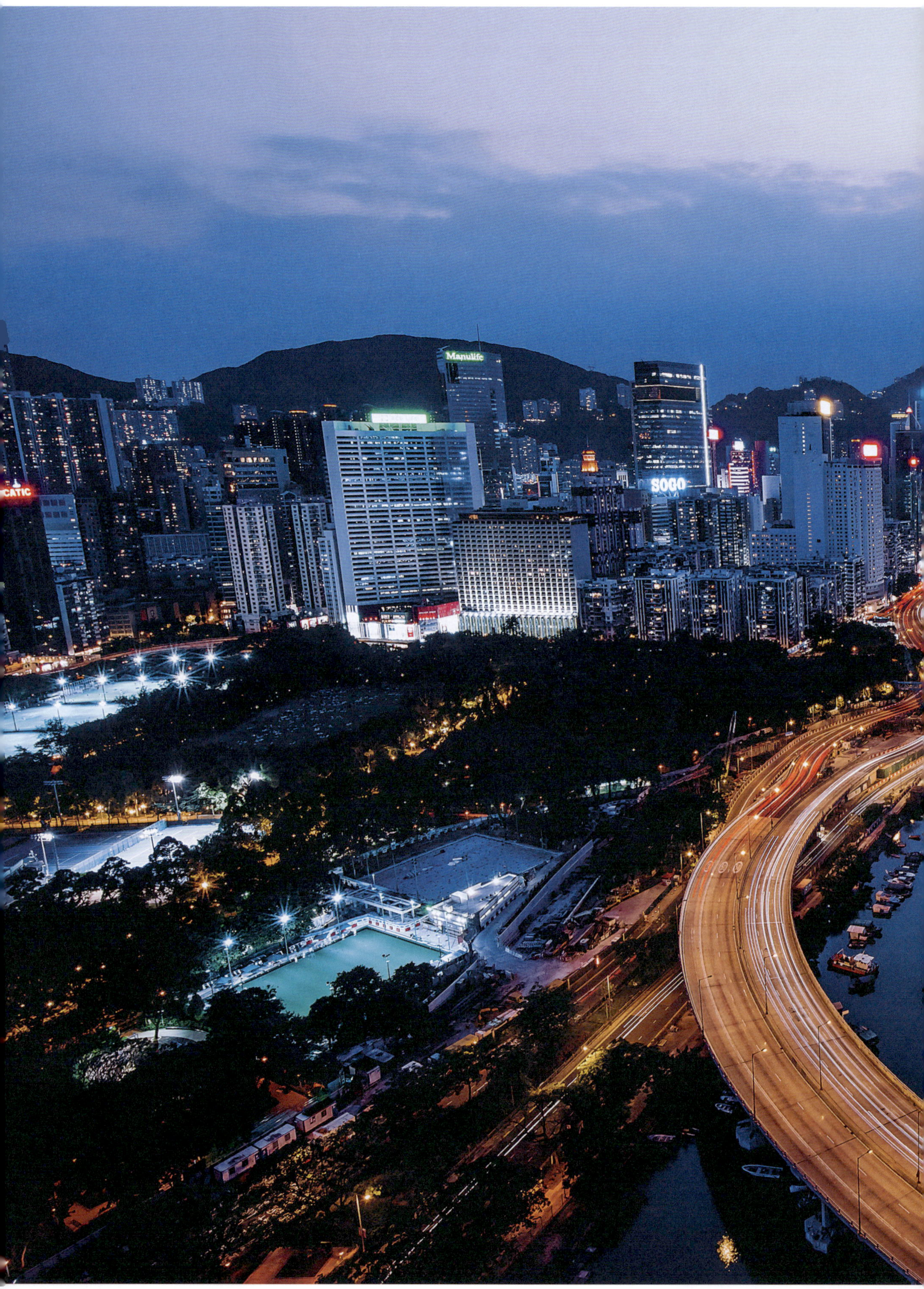

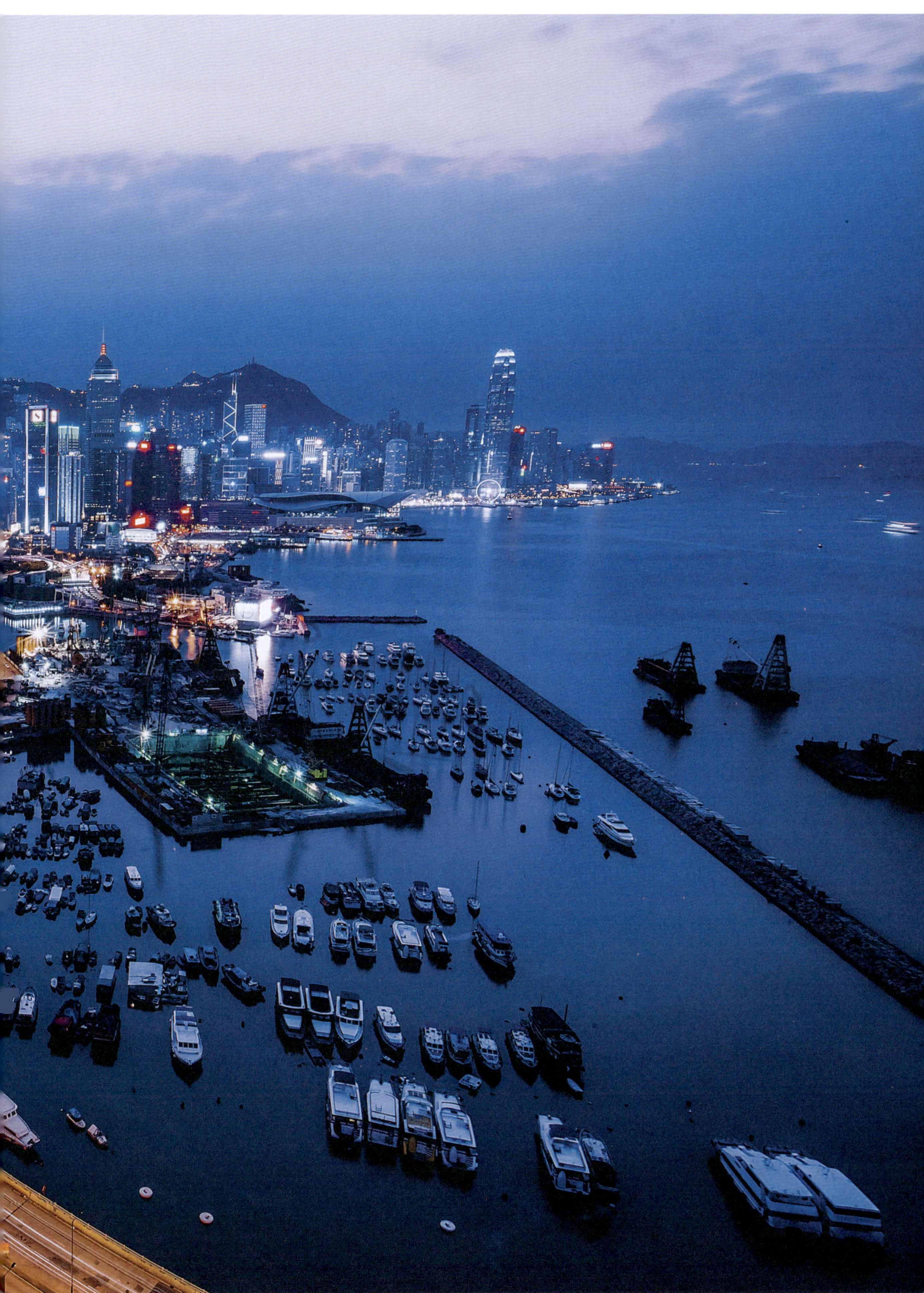

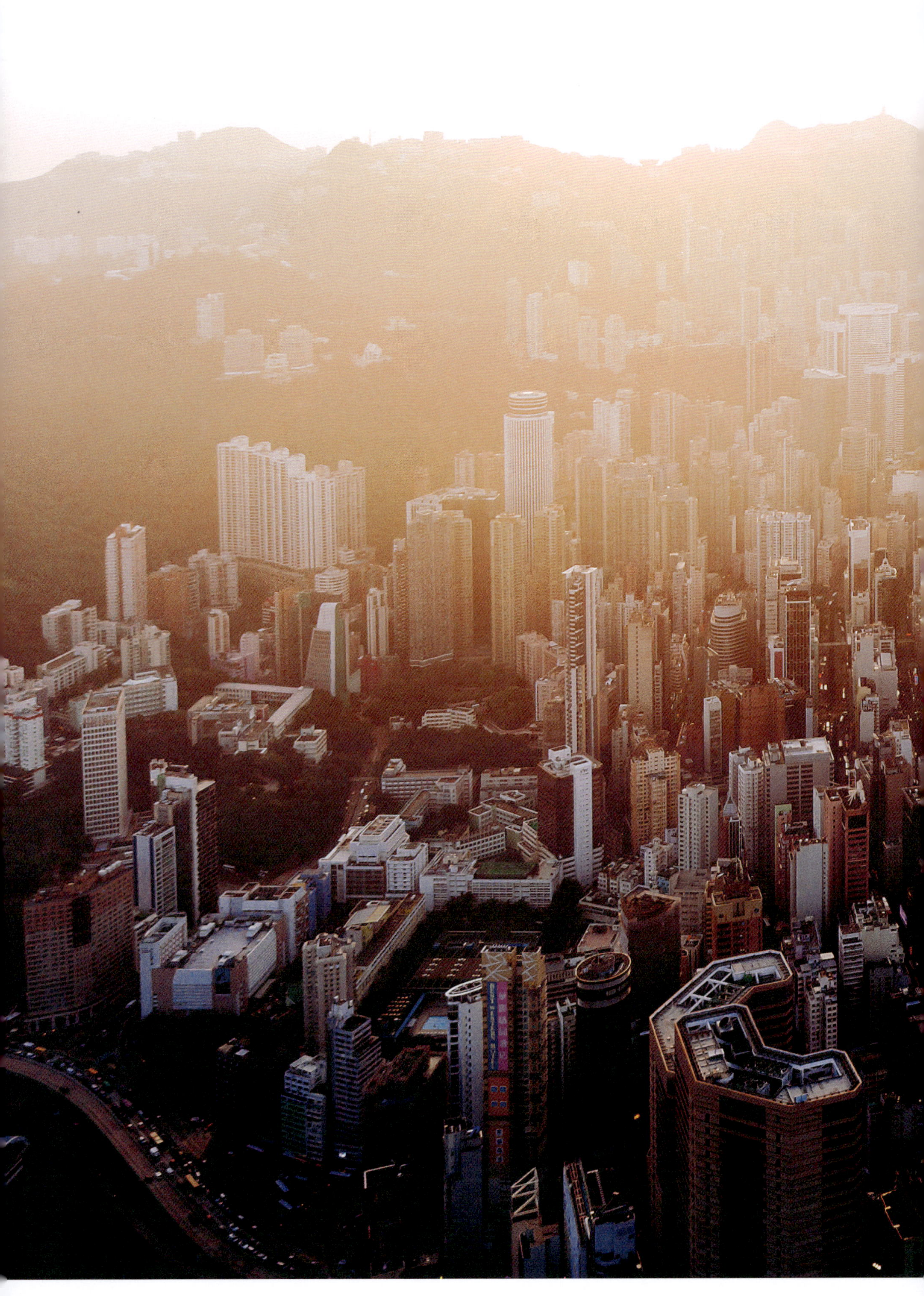

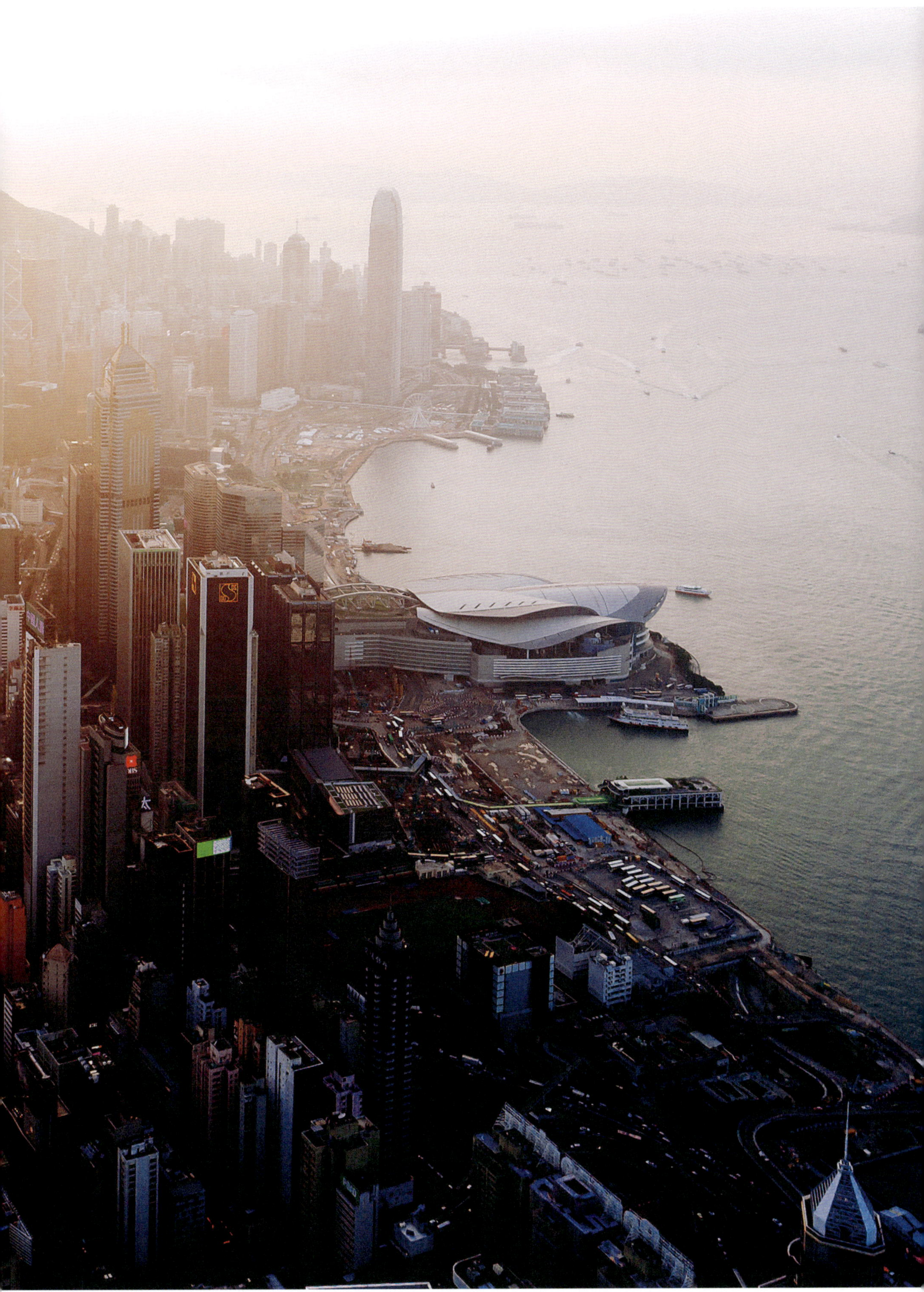

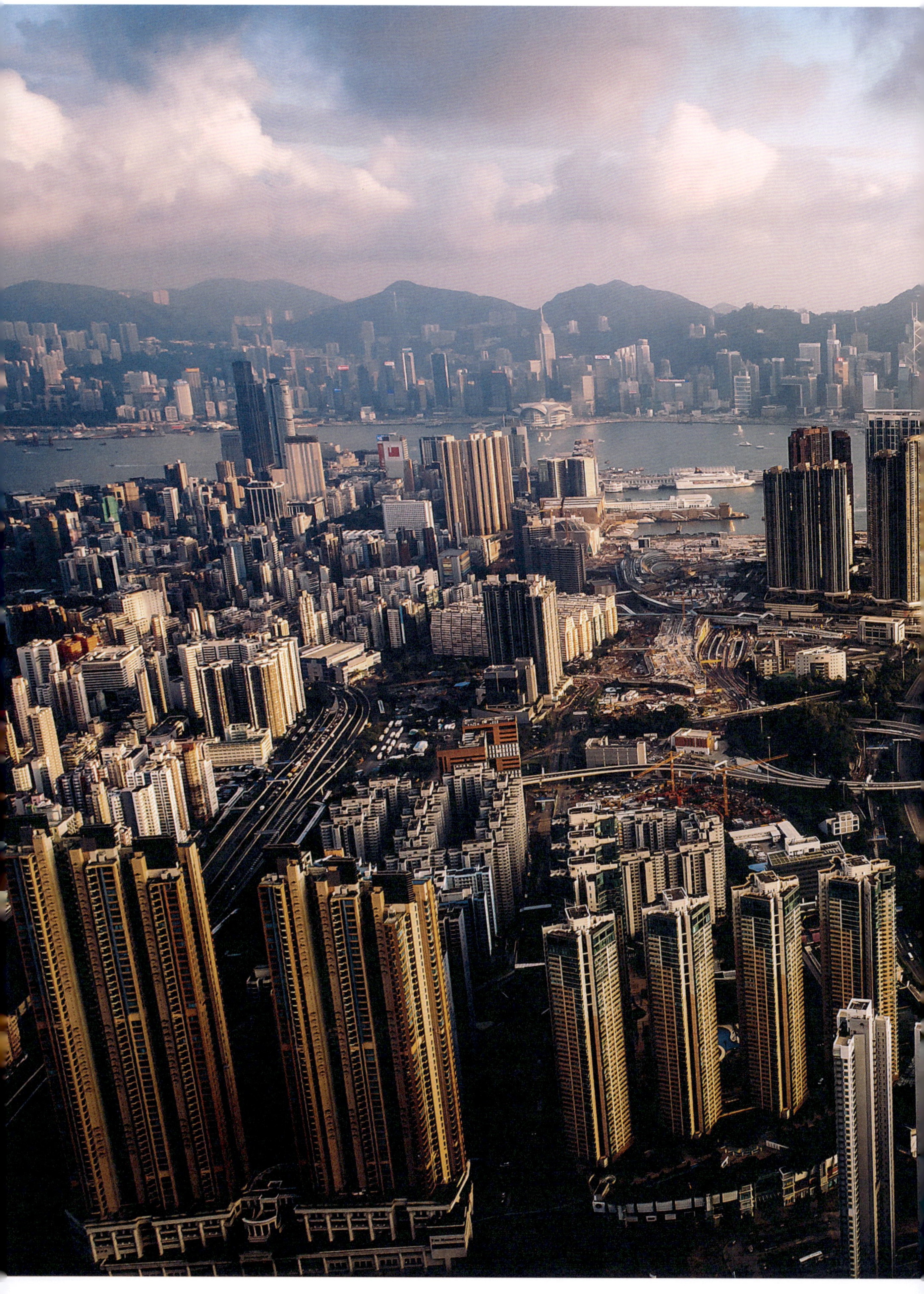

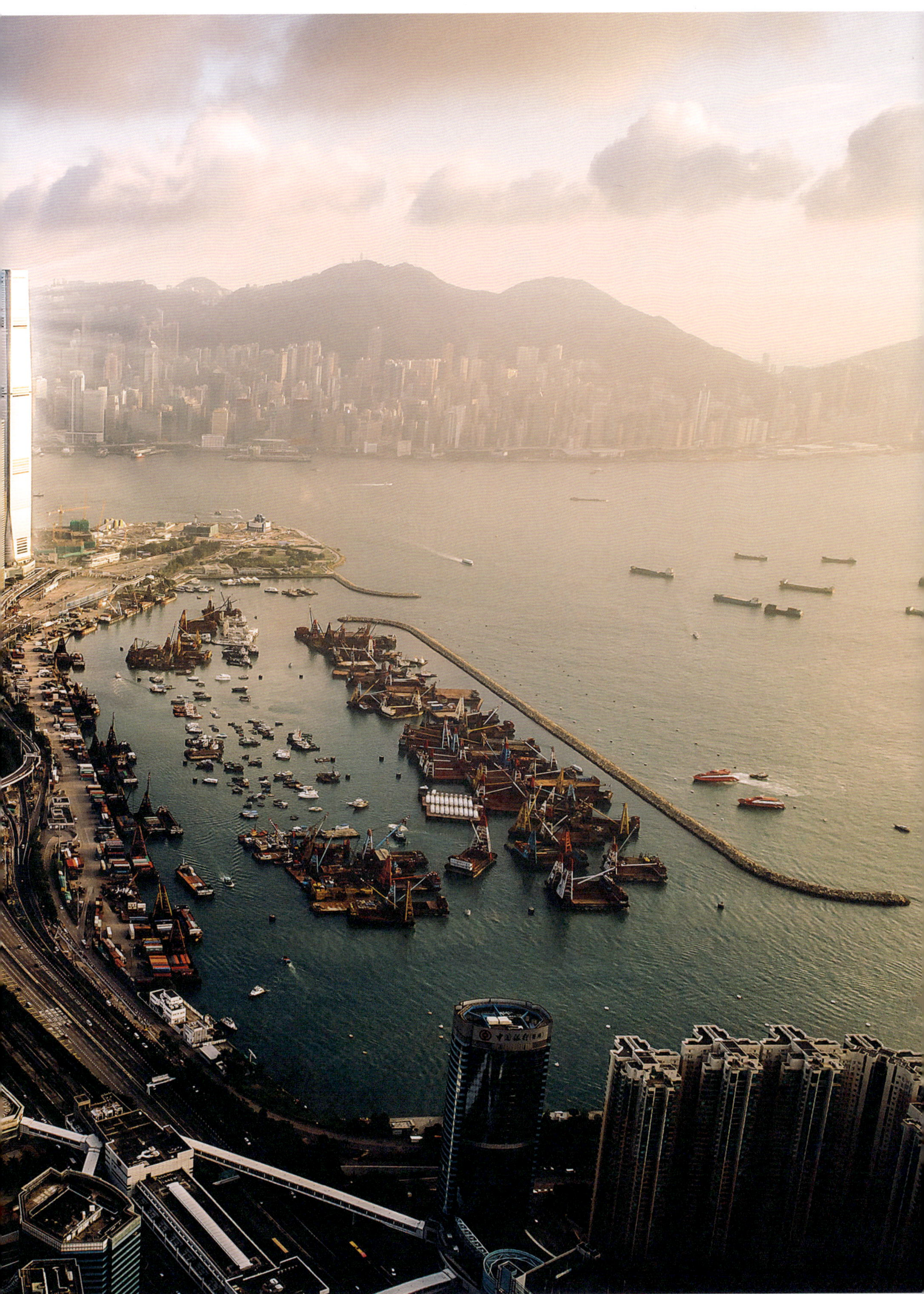

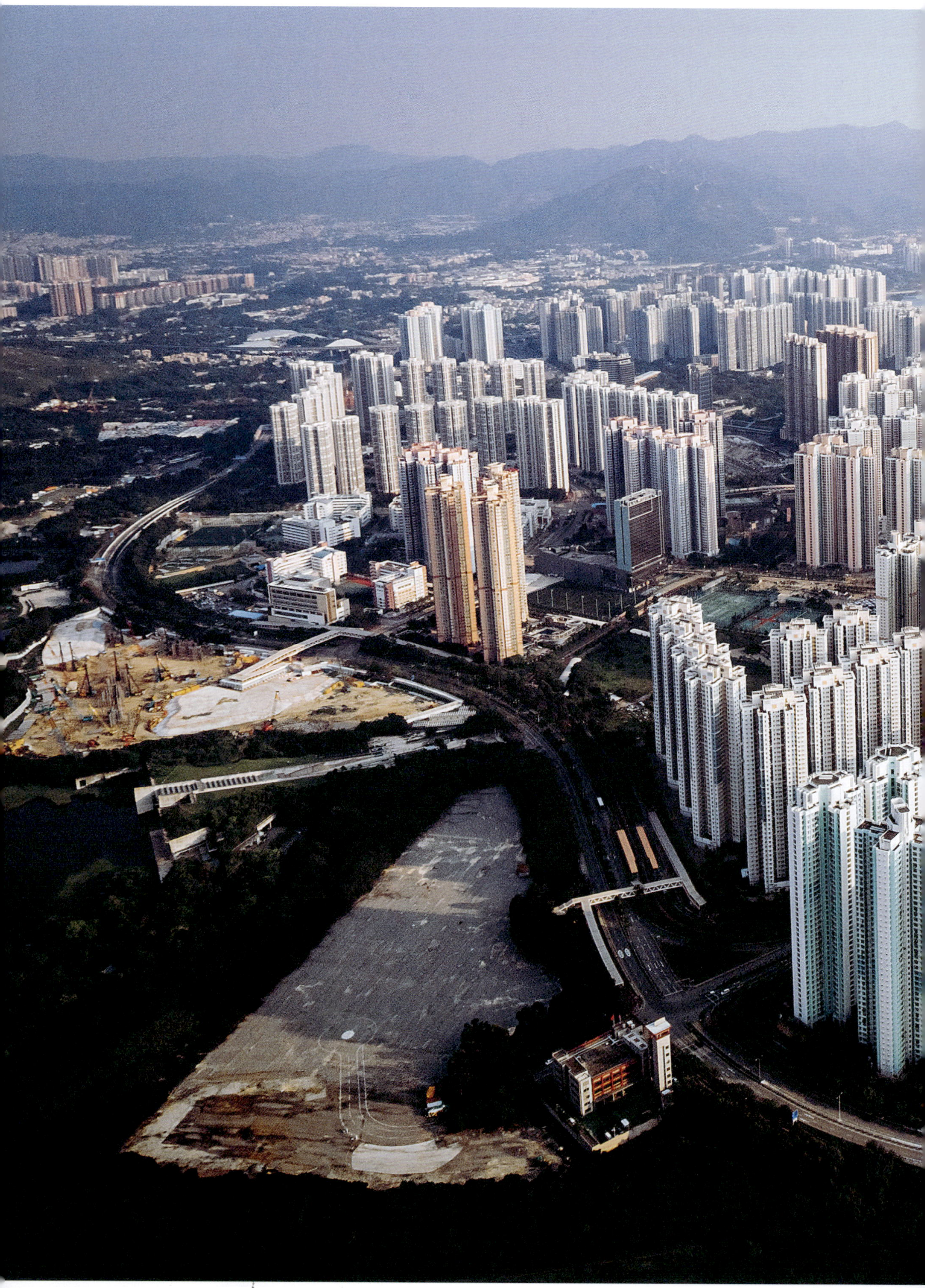

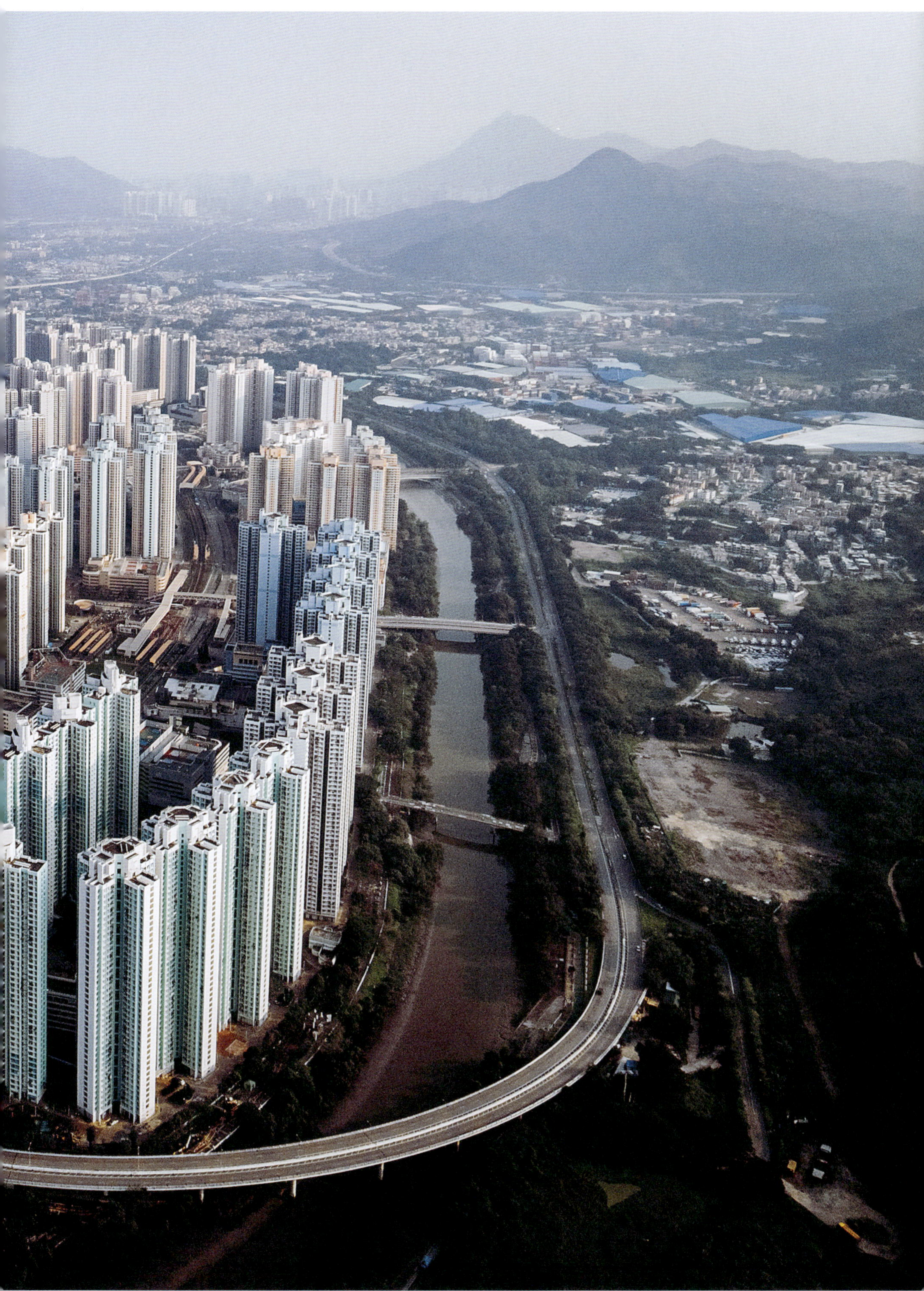

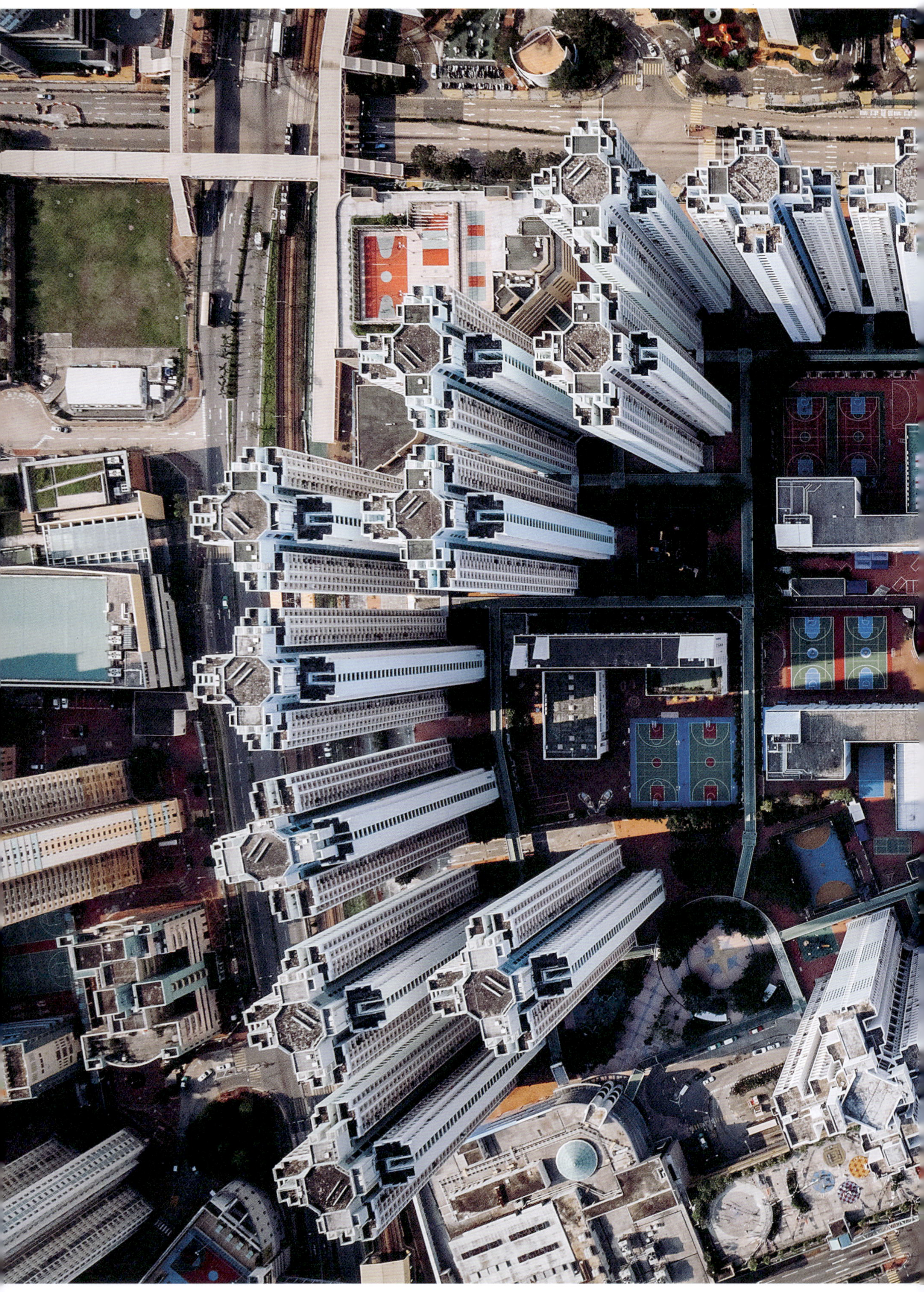

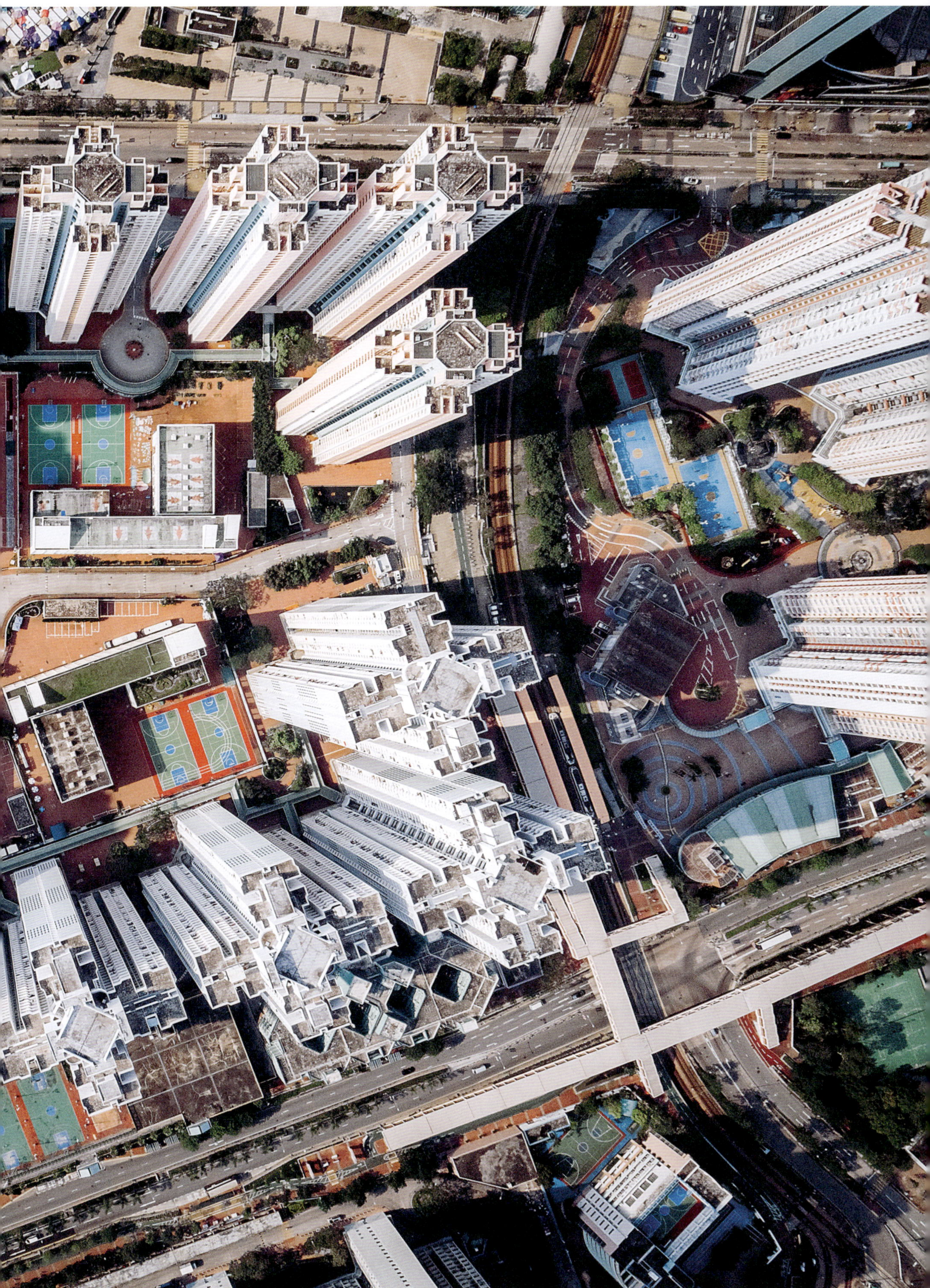

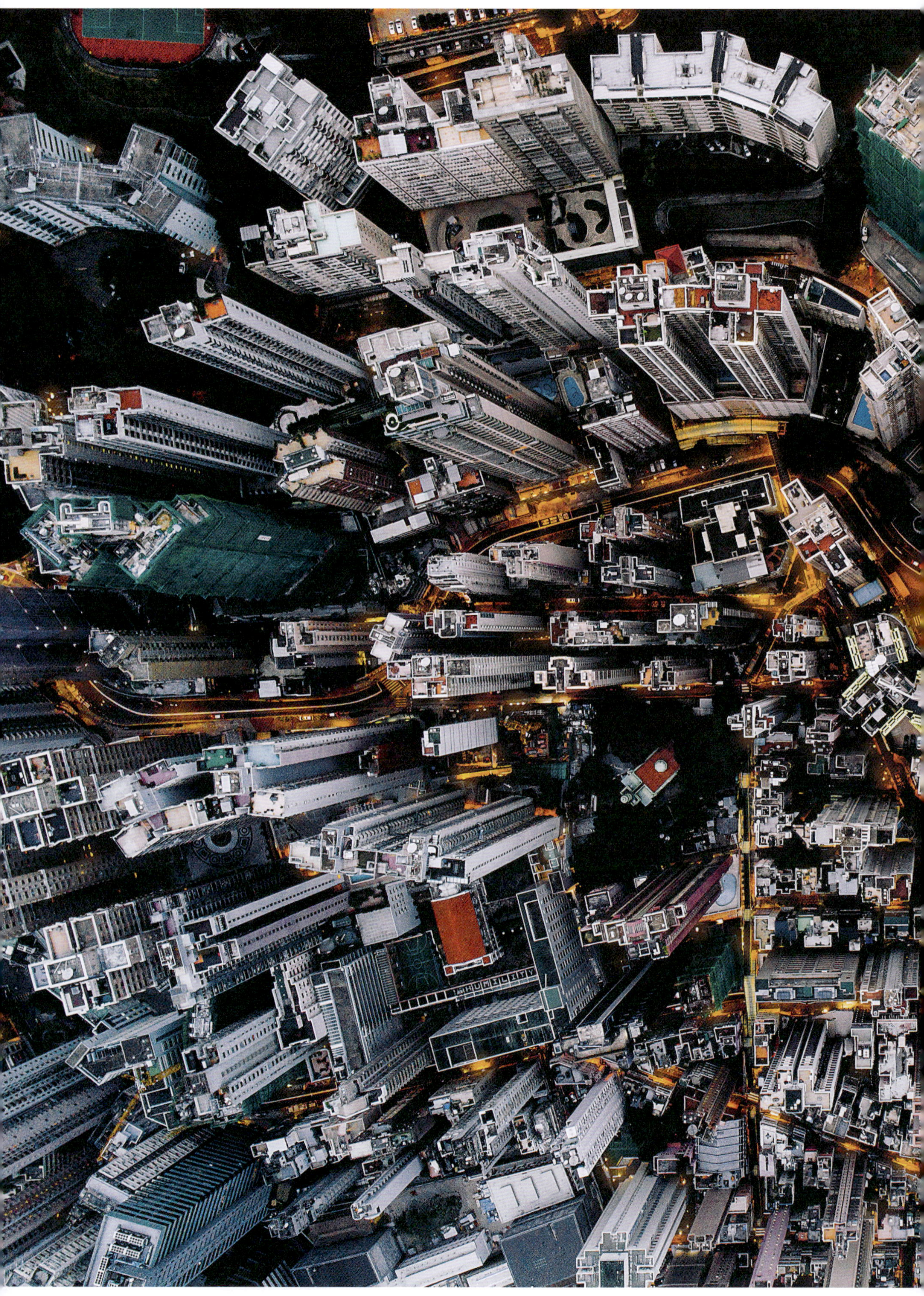

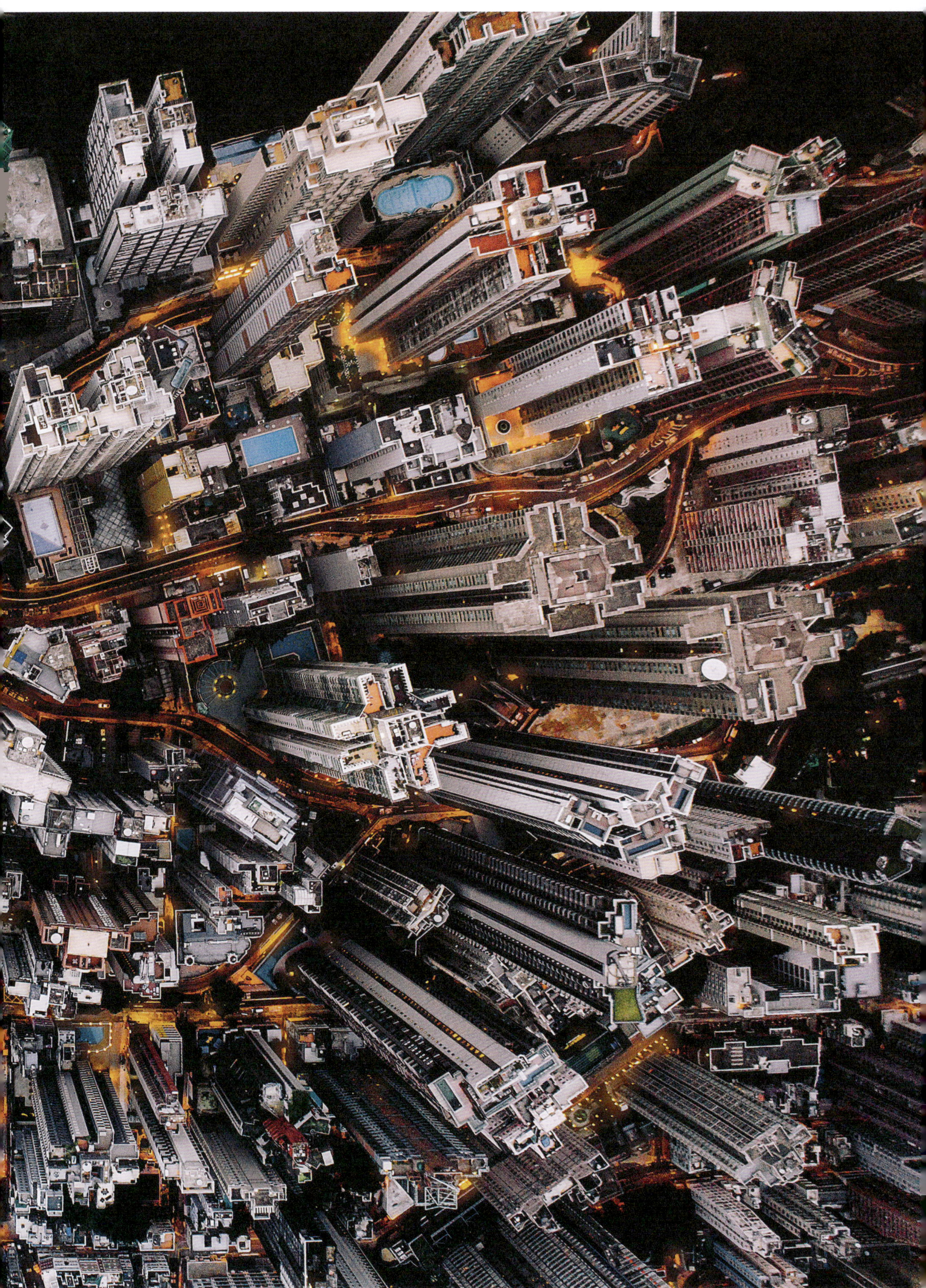

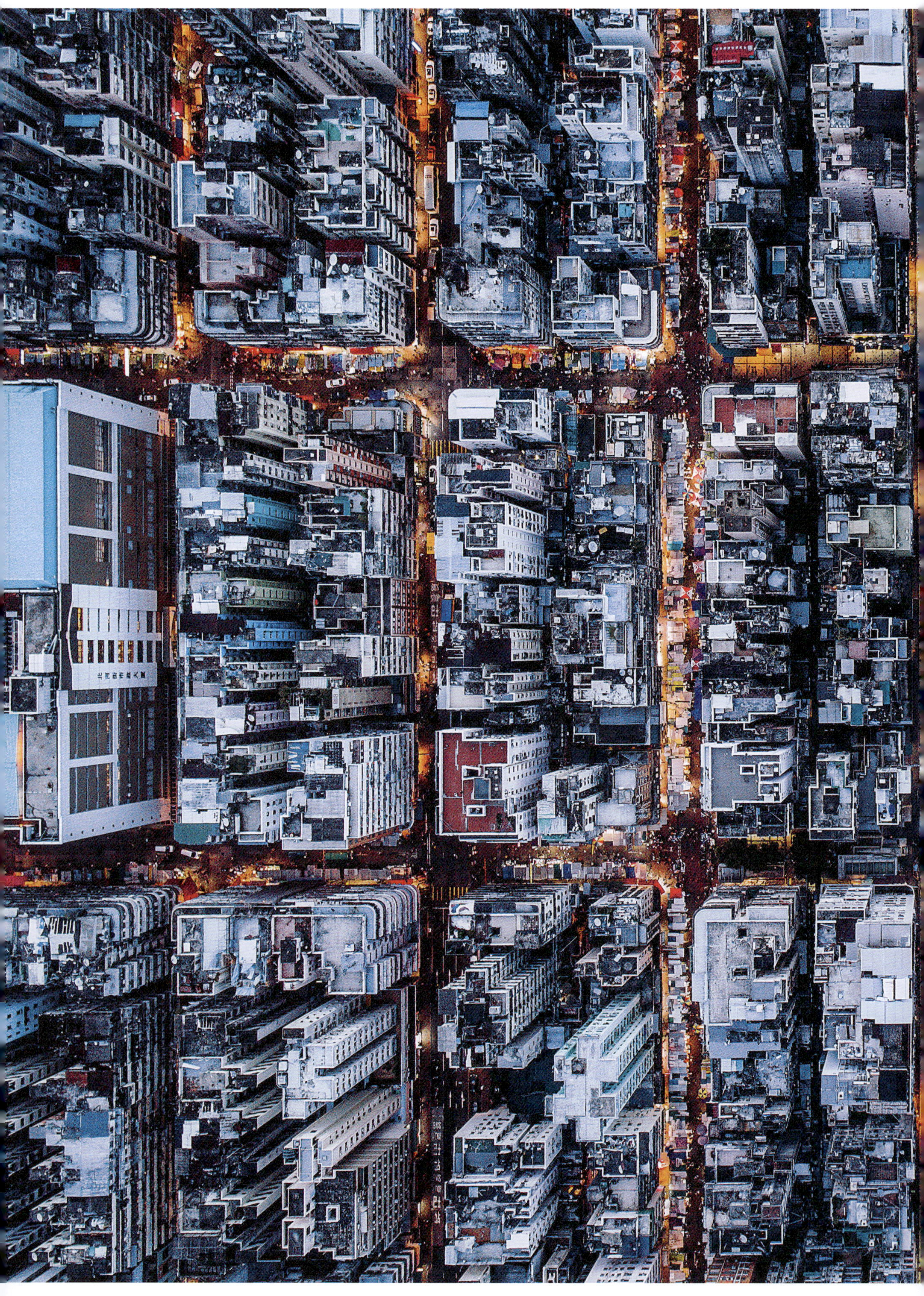

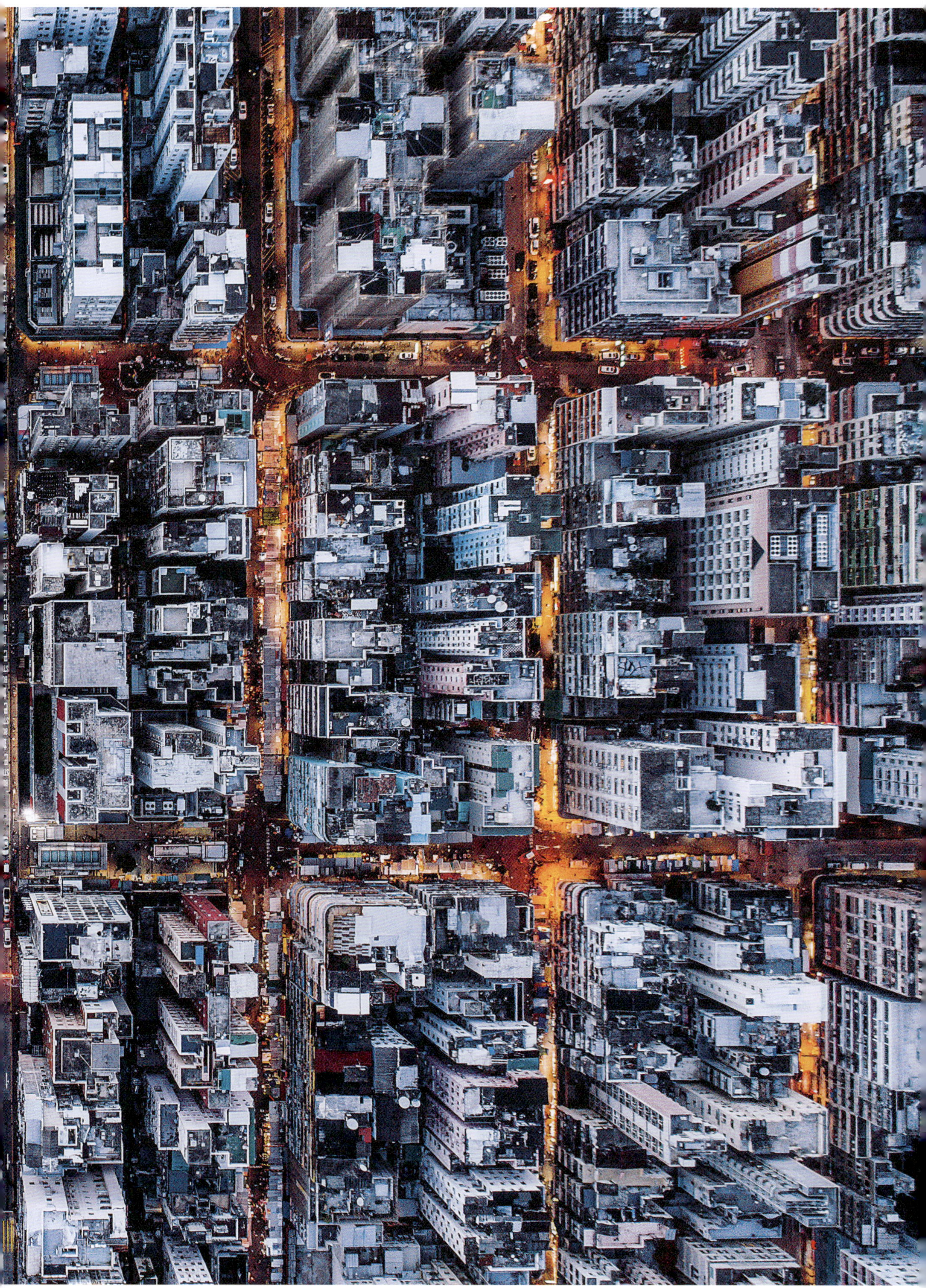

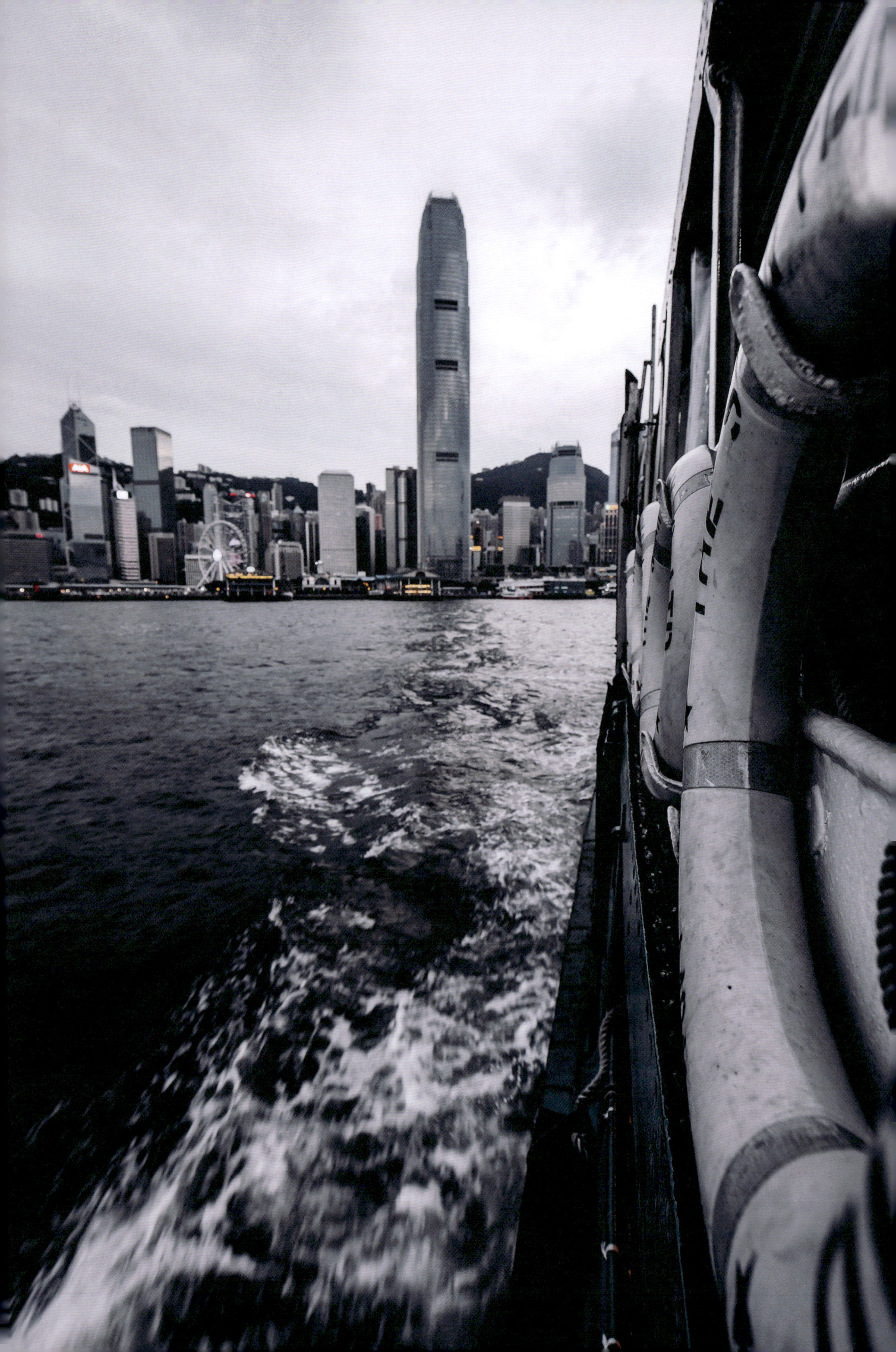

BEING ON THE STAR FERRY.
IT'S SUCH A CONTRAST FROM THE CITY BY BEING
TEMPORARILY REMOVED FROM IT. THERE IS
TRANQUILITY THERE.

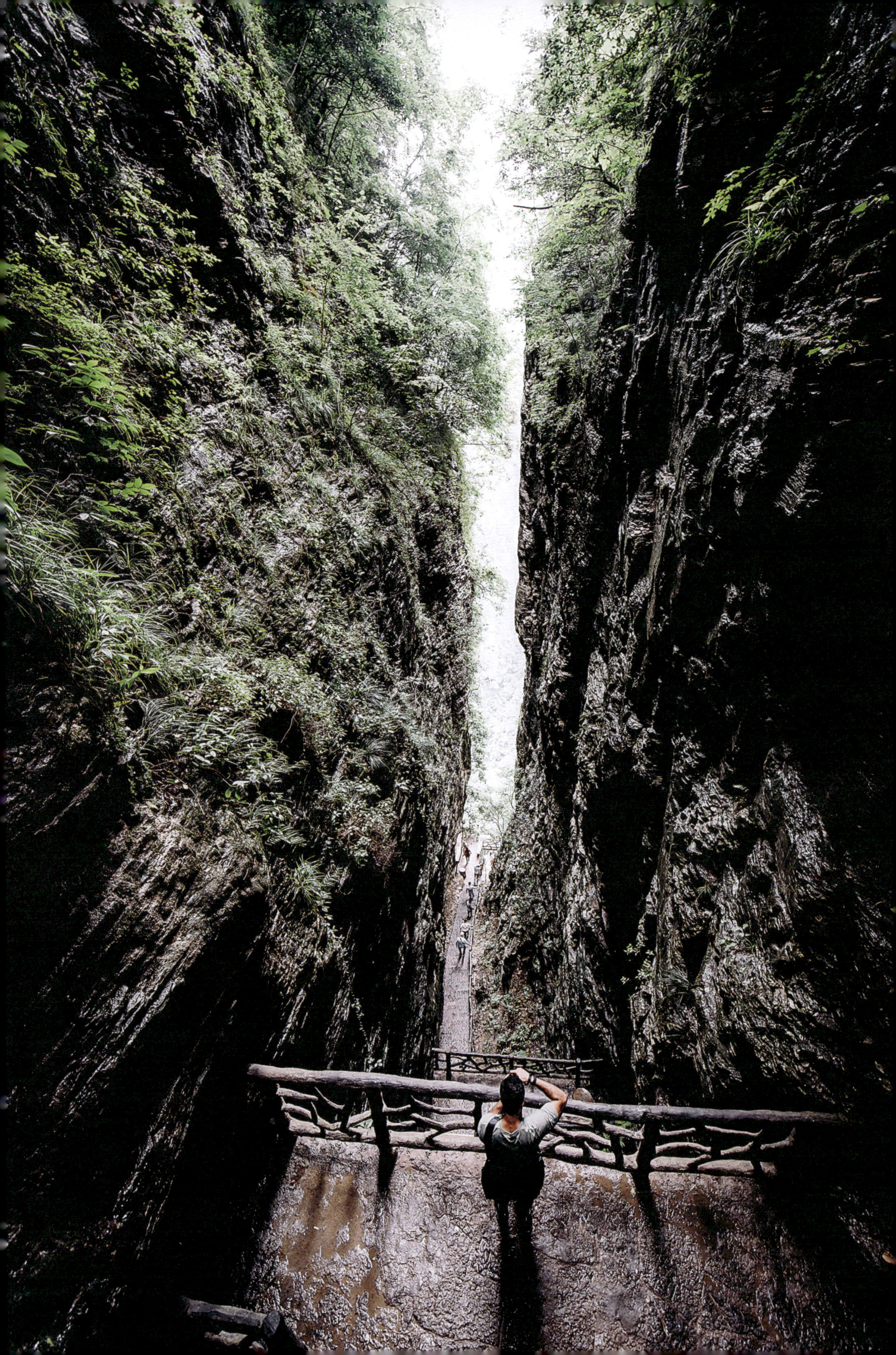

mainland
china

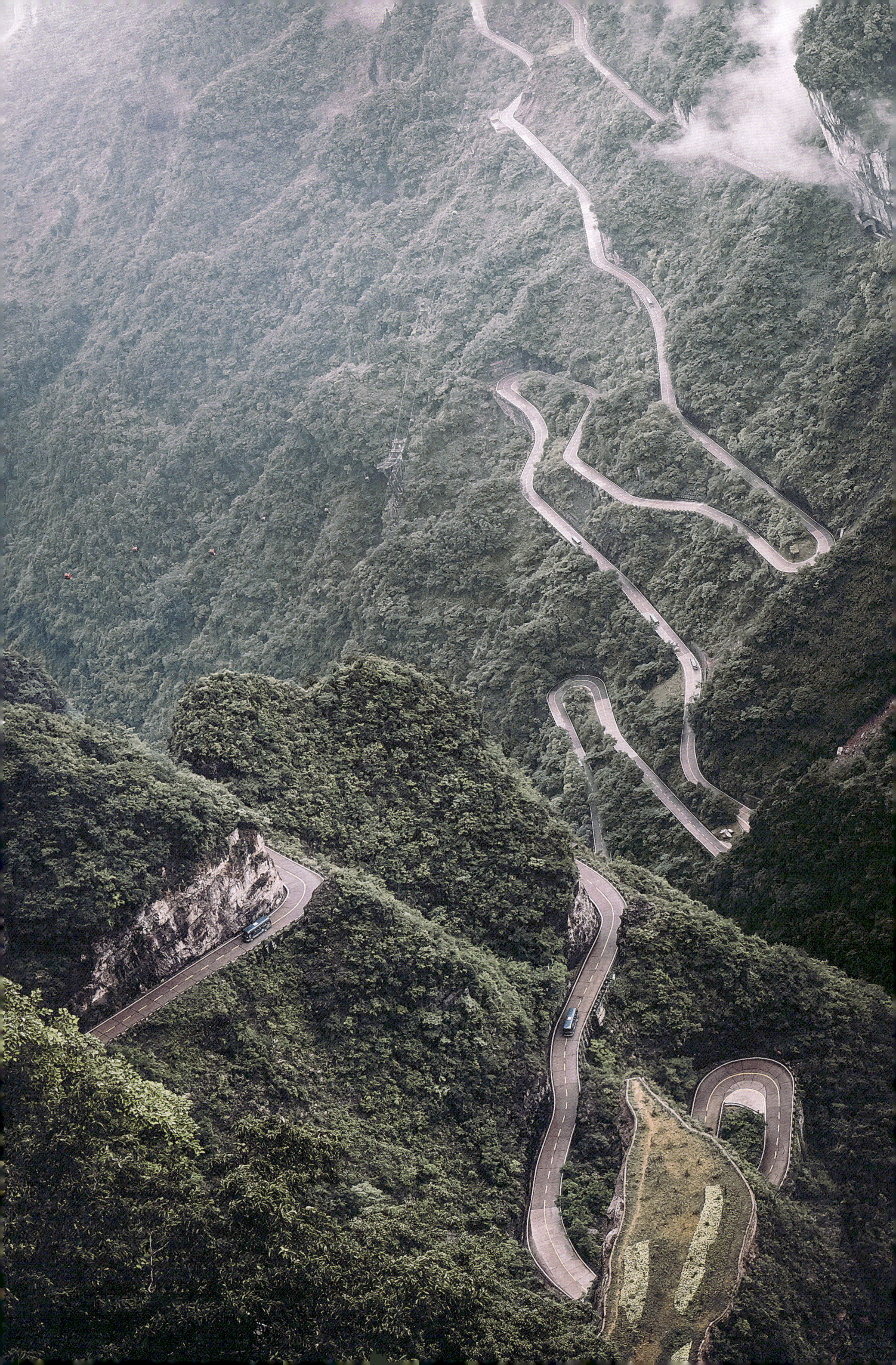

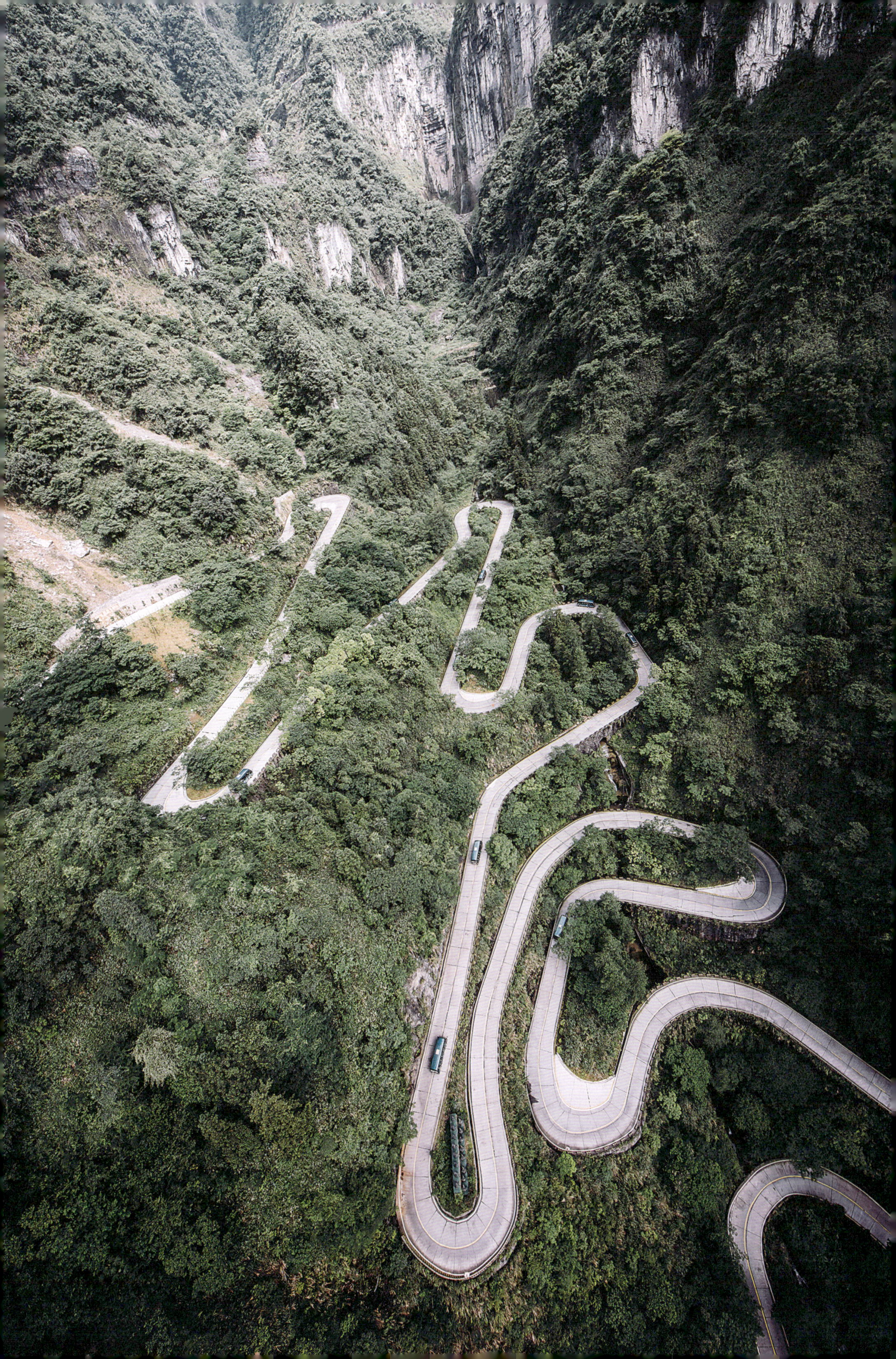

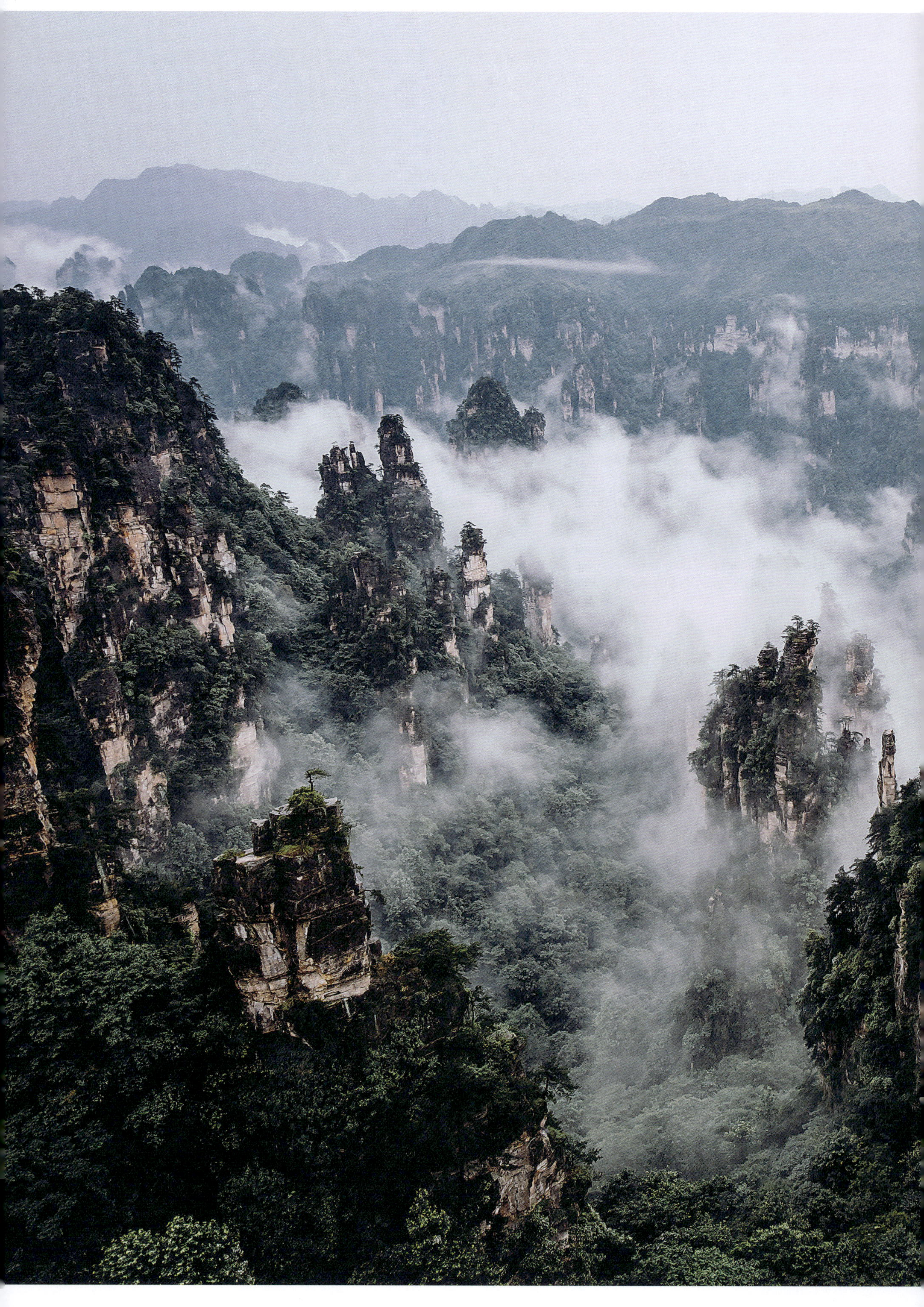

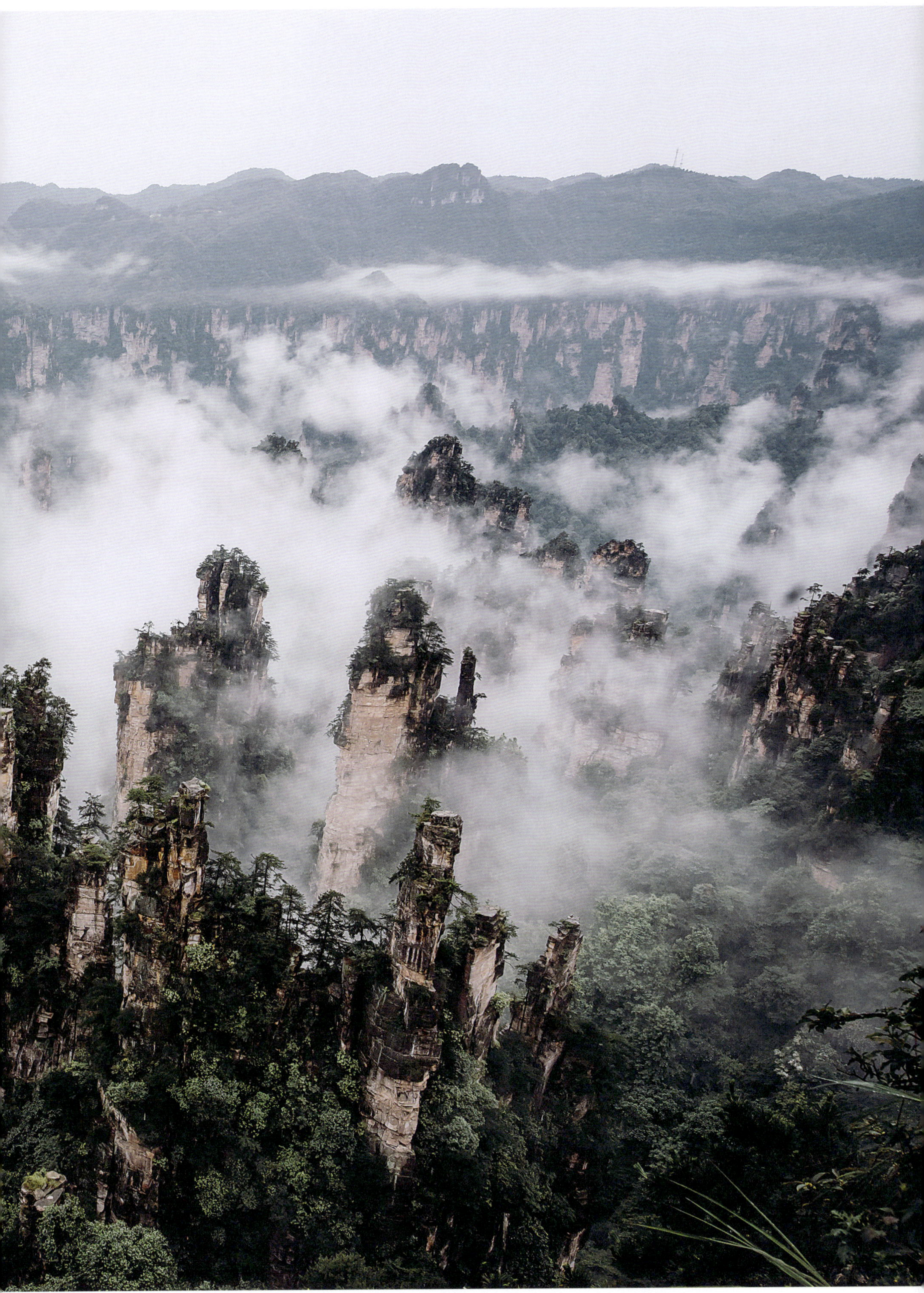

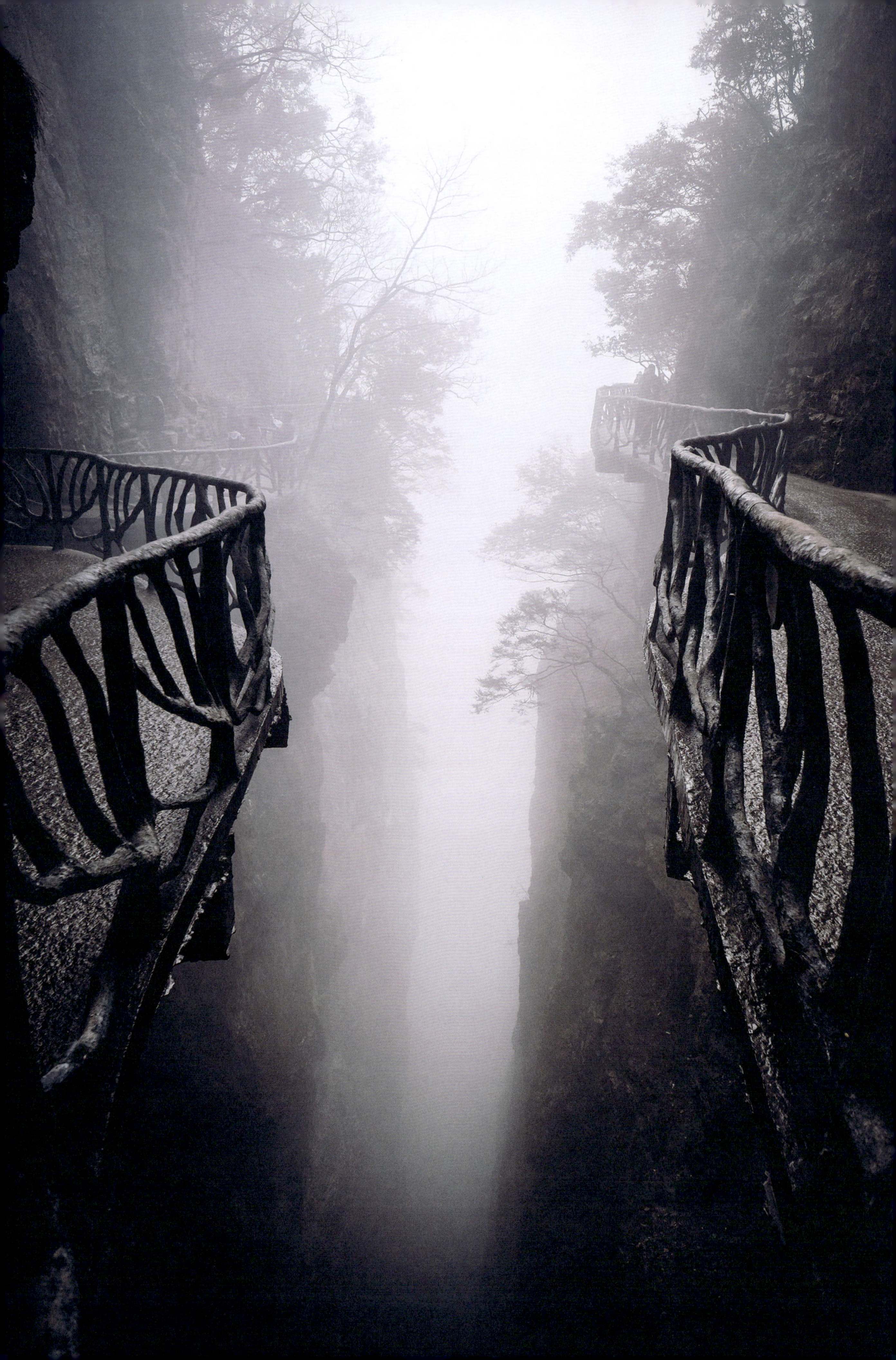

A COMPLETE CONTRAST TO CHINA'S RAPID URBANIZATION, ECONOMIC GROWTH AND RAMPANT INDUSTRIALIZATION IS ZHANGJIAJIE – A UNIQUE AND **EXTREME NATURAL BEAUTY**.

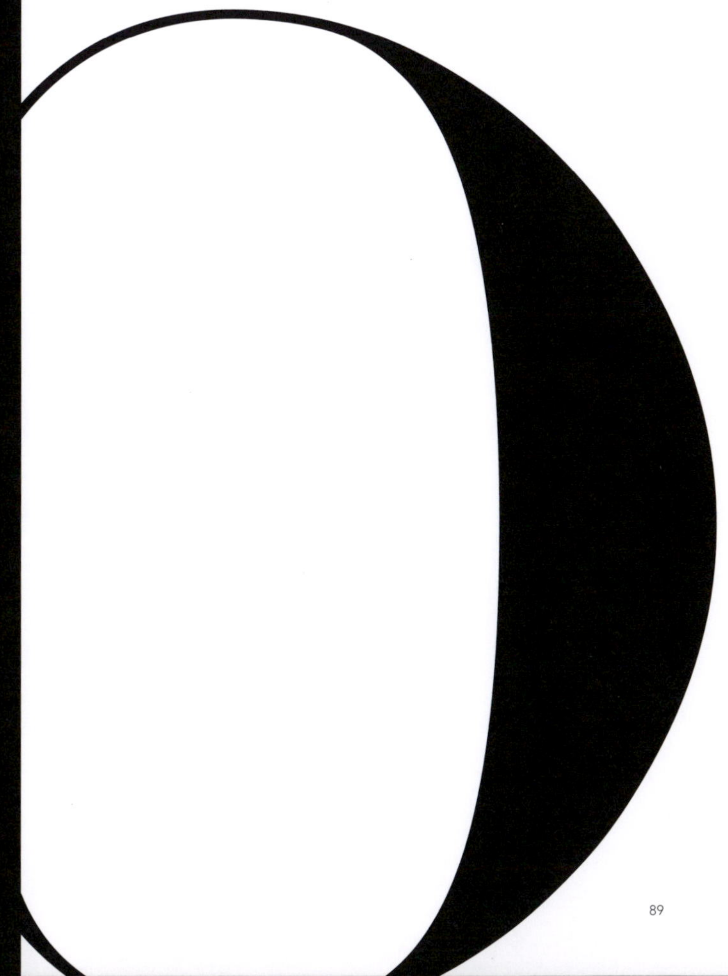

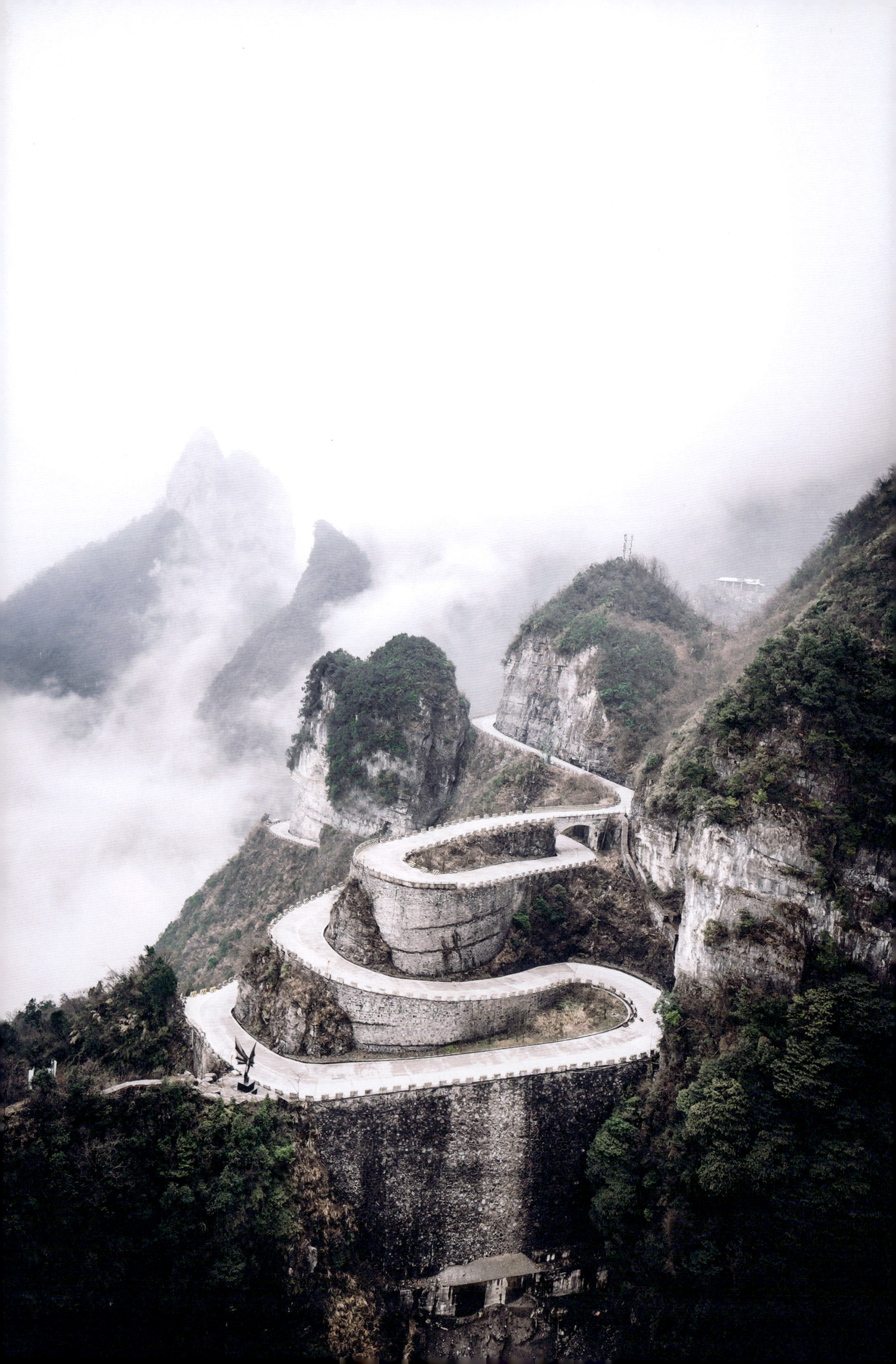

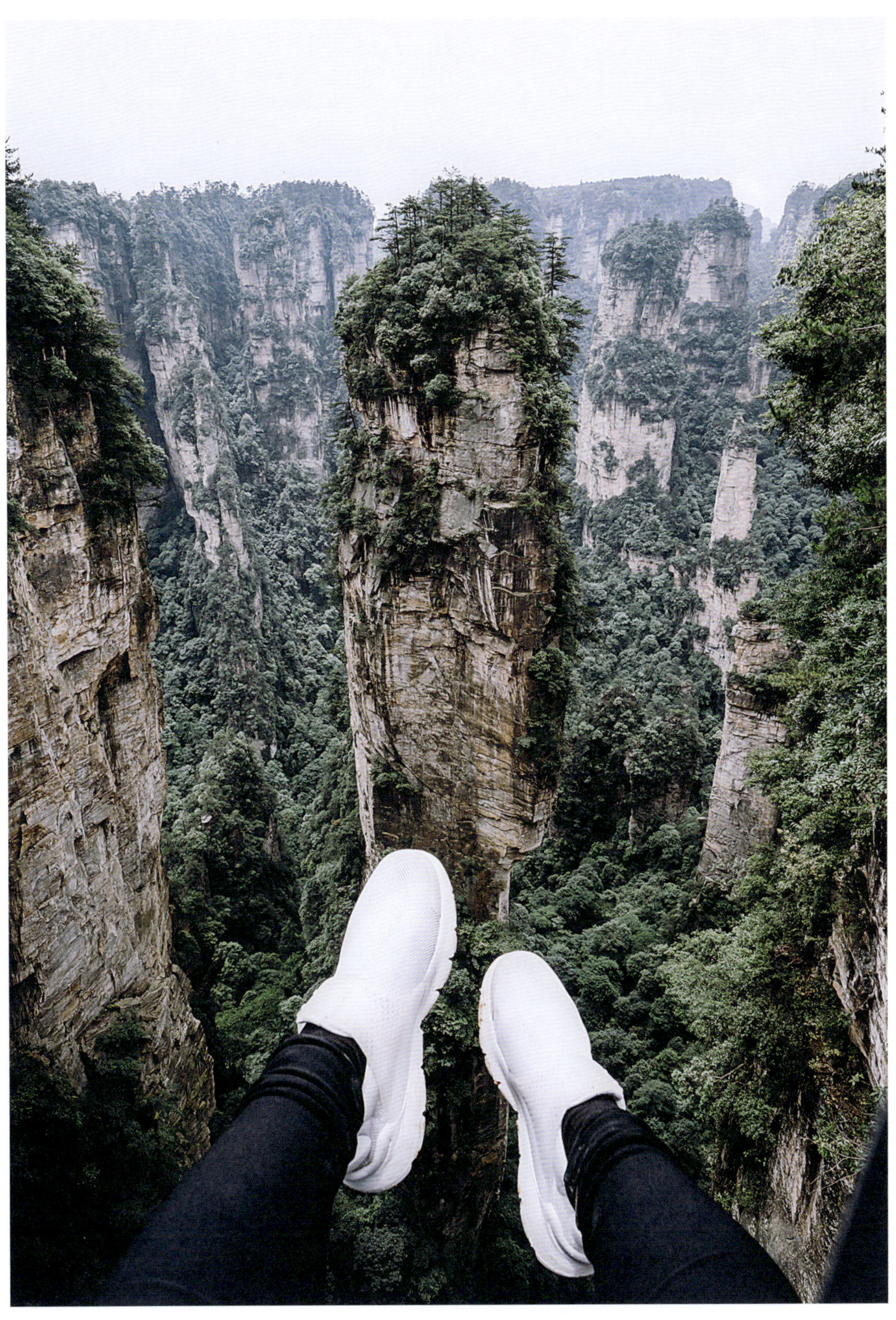

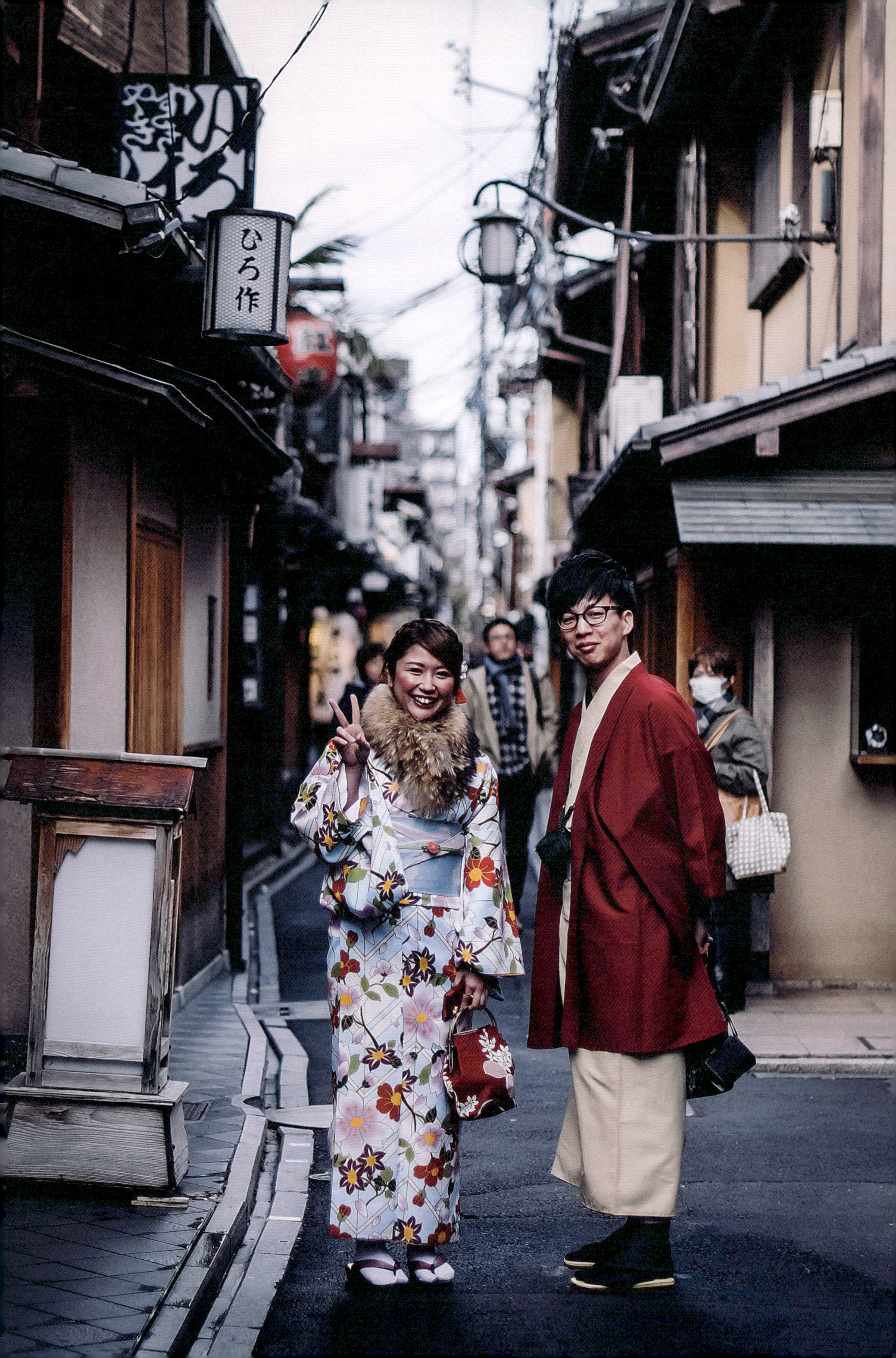

ひら作

japan

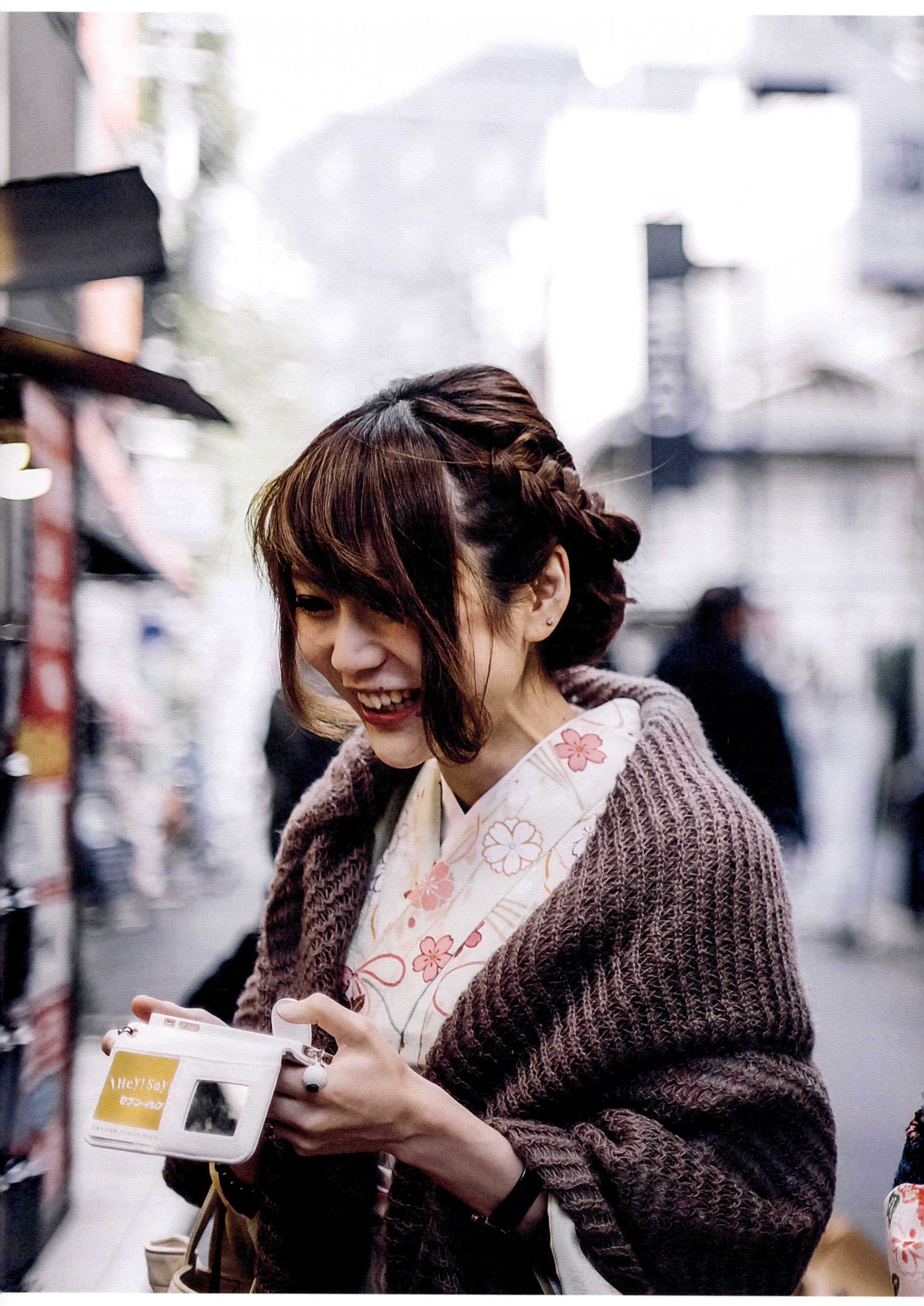
Hey! Say!

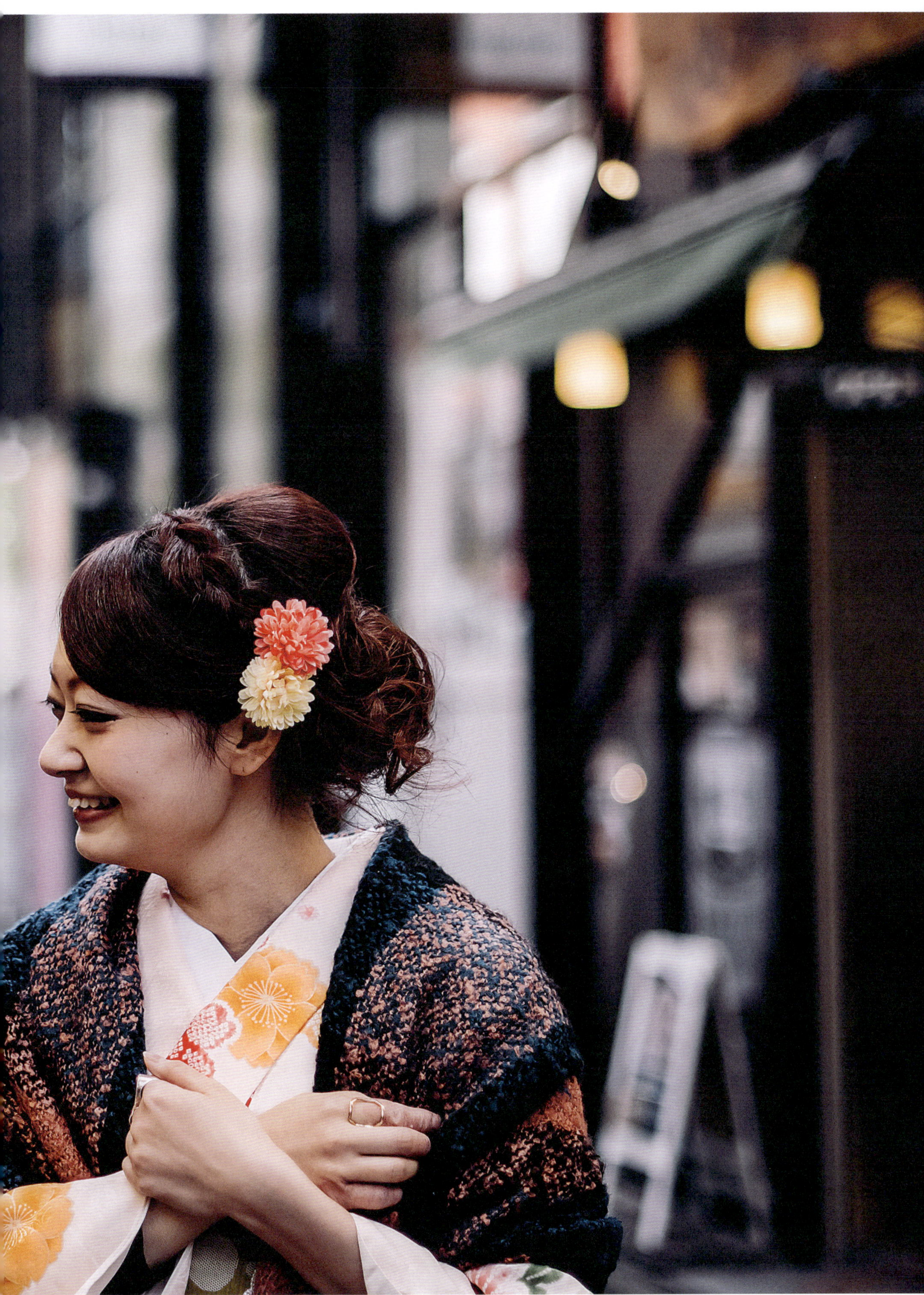

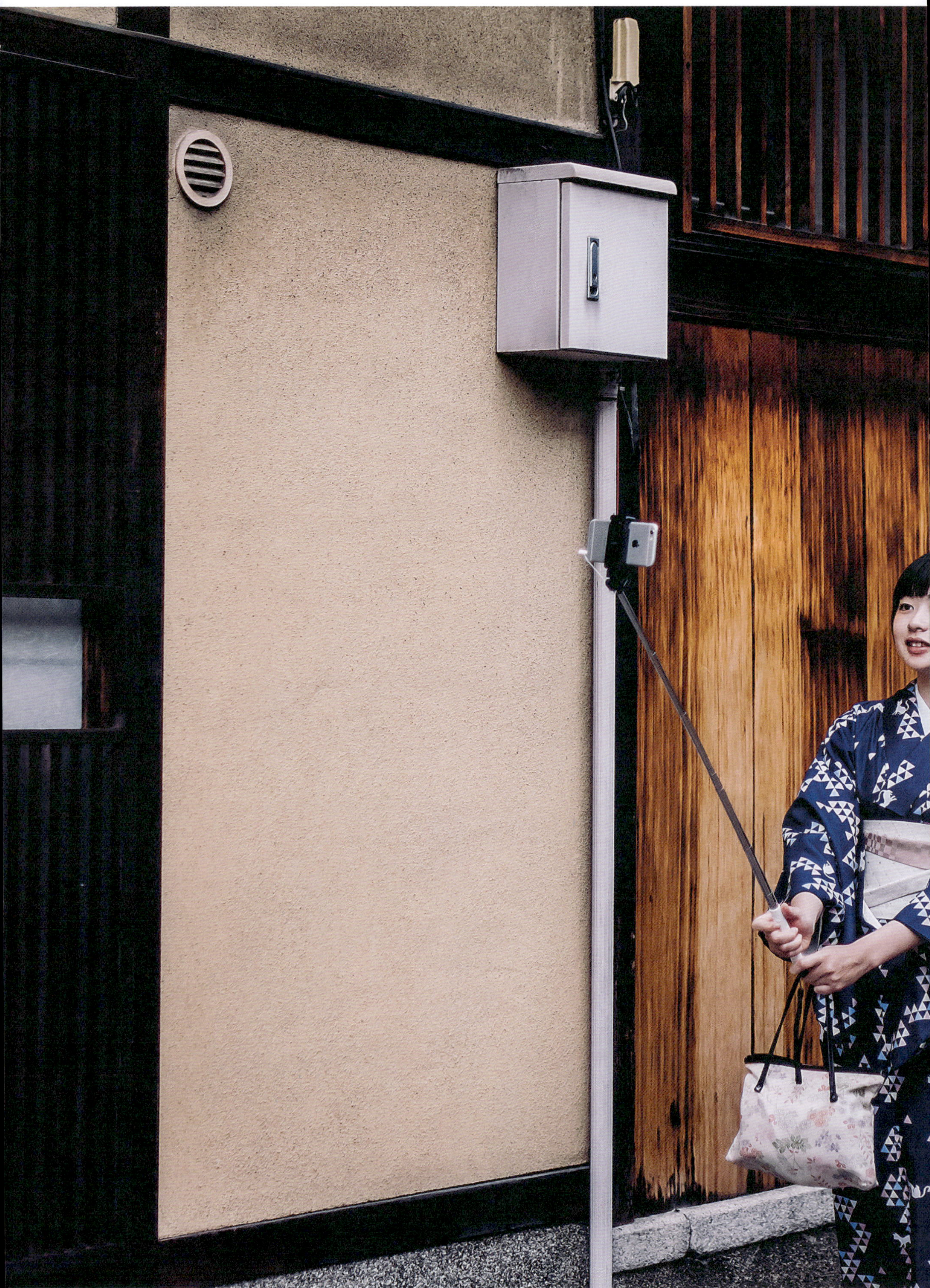

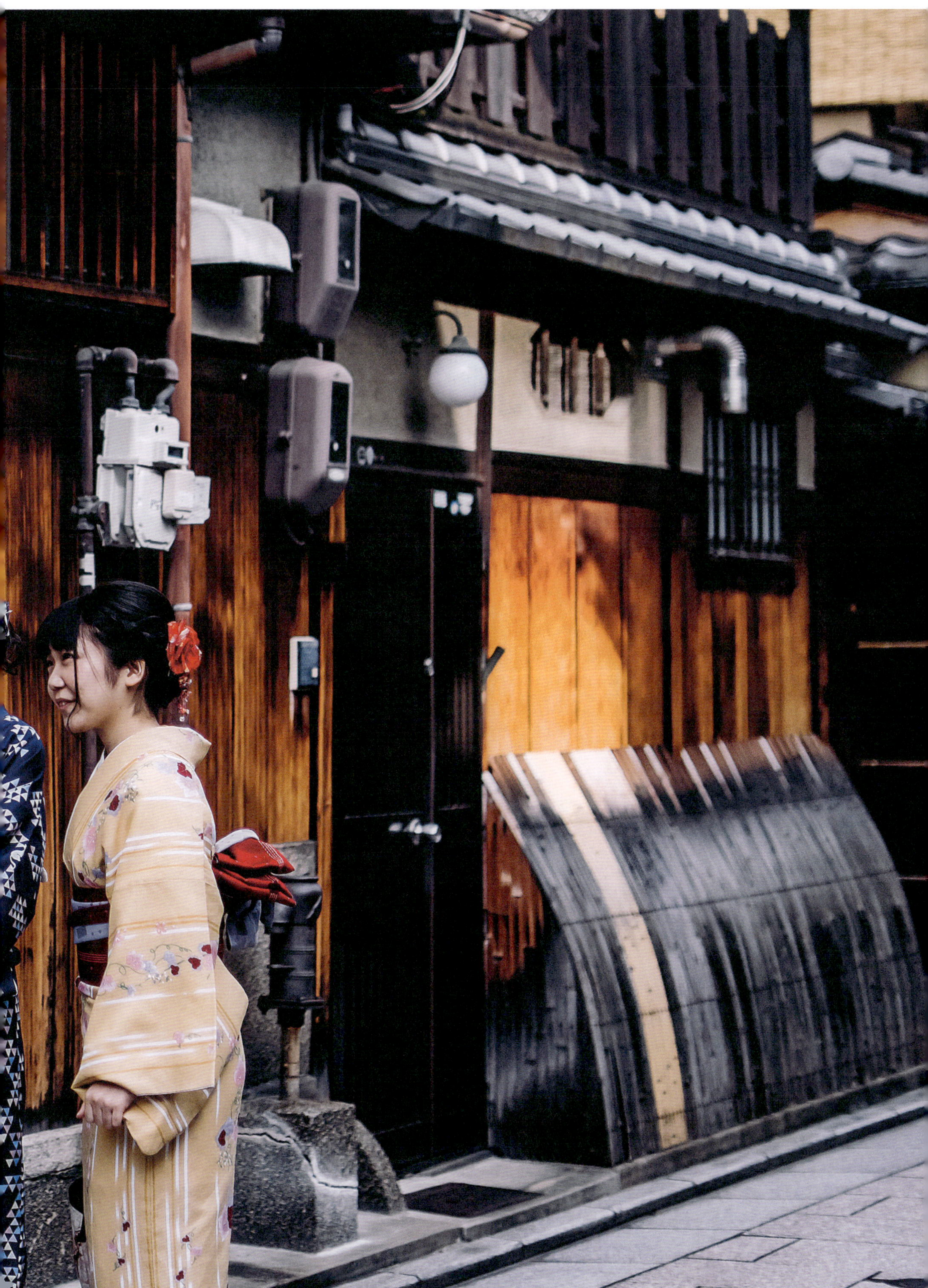

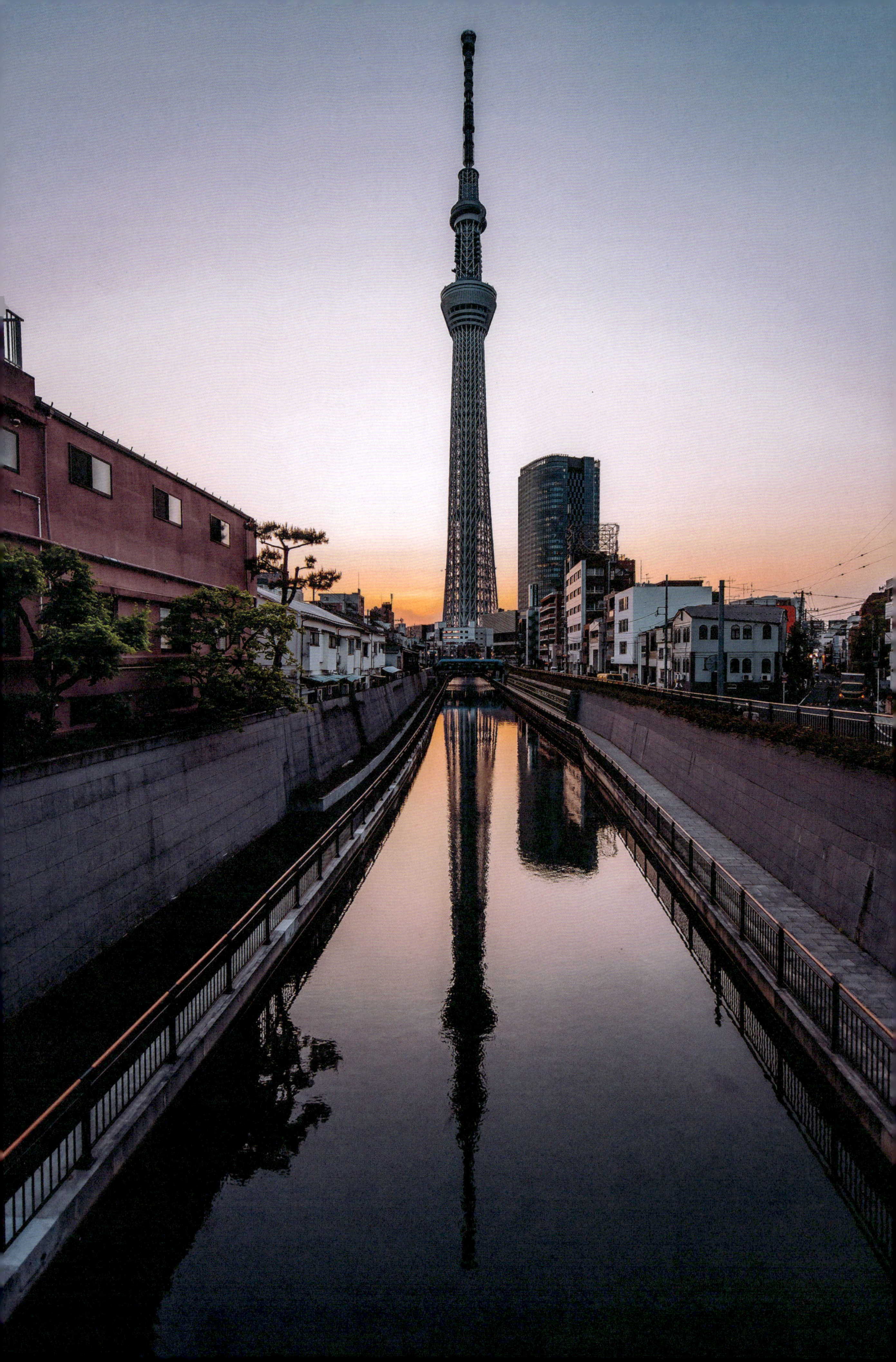

THROUGH SHOWING THE BEAUTY OF PLACES TO A WIDER AUDIENCE, WE BOLSTER ITS **BEST QUALITIES**, AND HOPEFULLY WE CAN PROLIFERATE THESE QUALITIES BY INCORPORATING THEM INTO FUTURE CITY BUILDING.

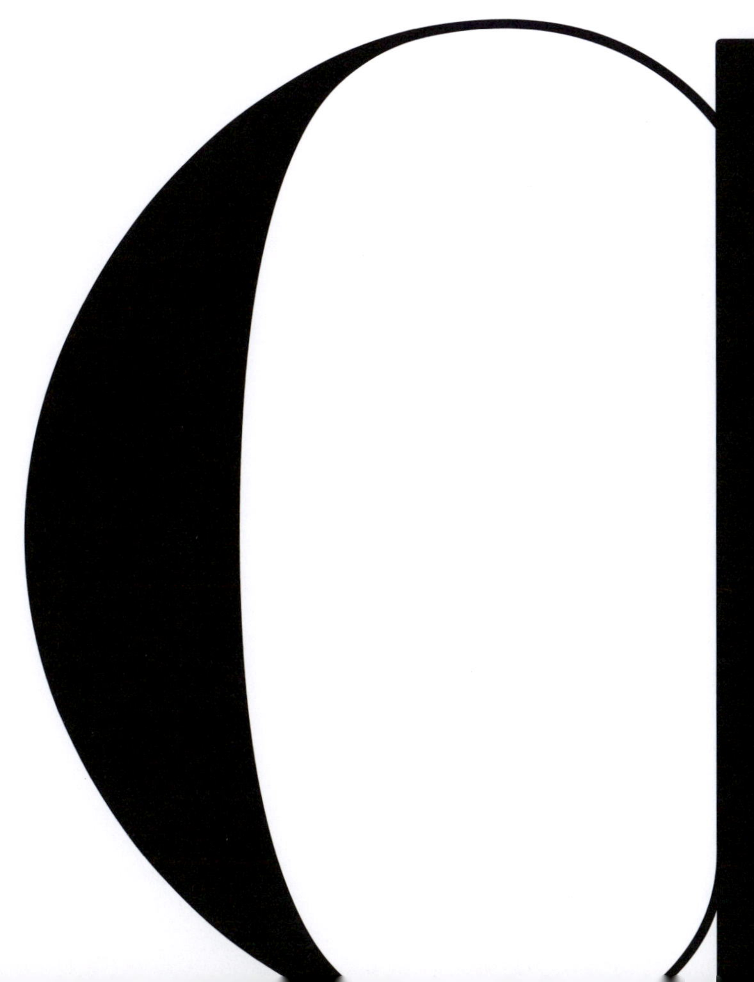

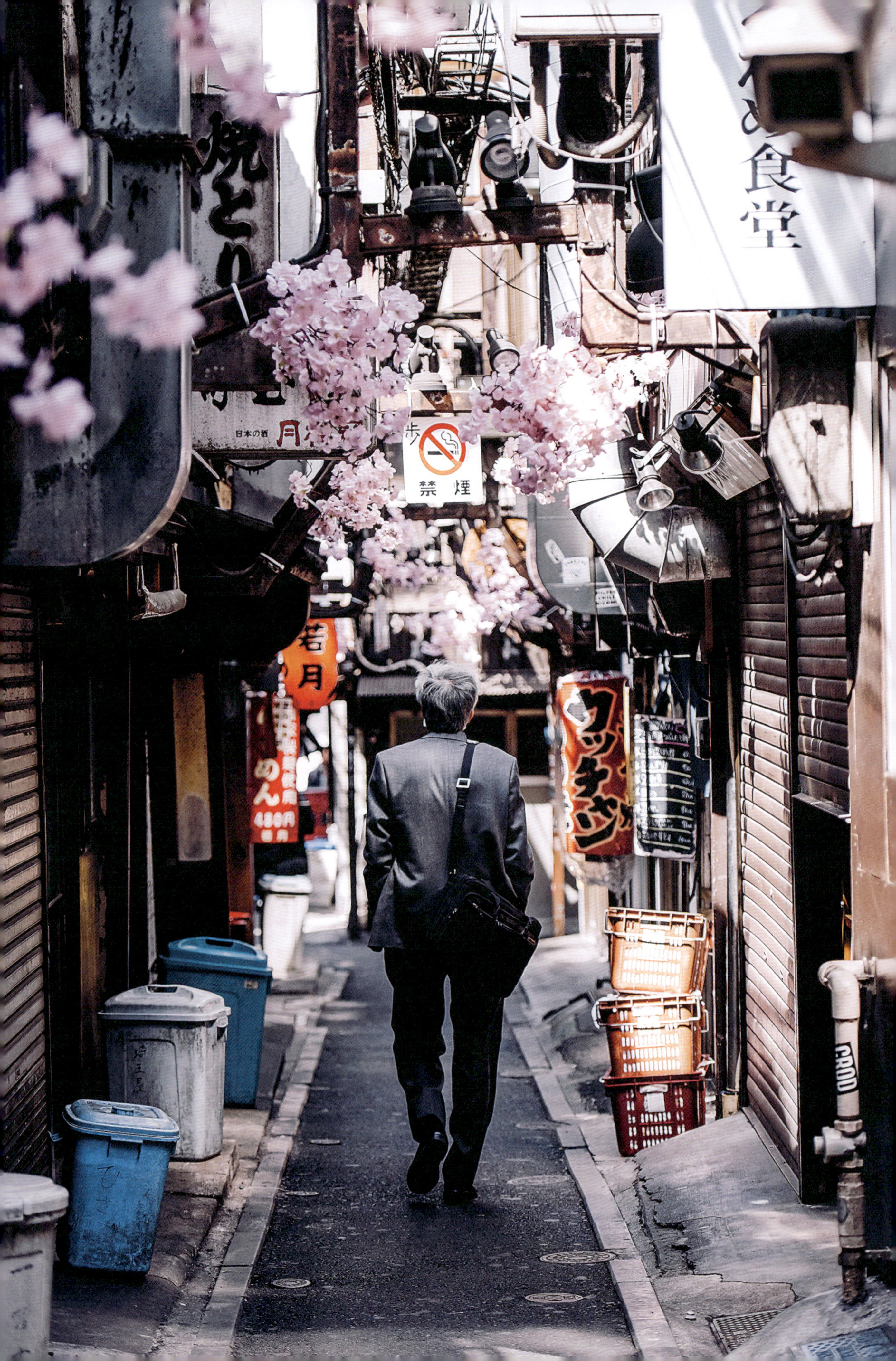

焼とり
と食堂
日本の酒 月
岩月
めん
480円
ウッチャン
禁煙
歩

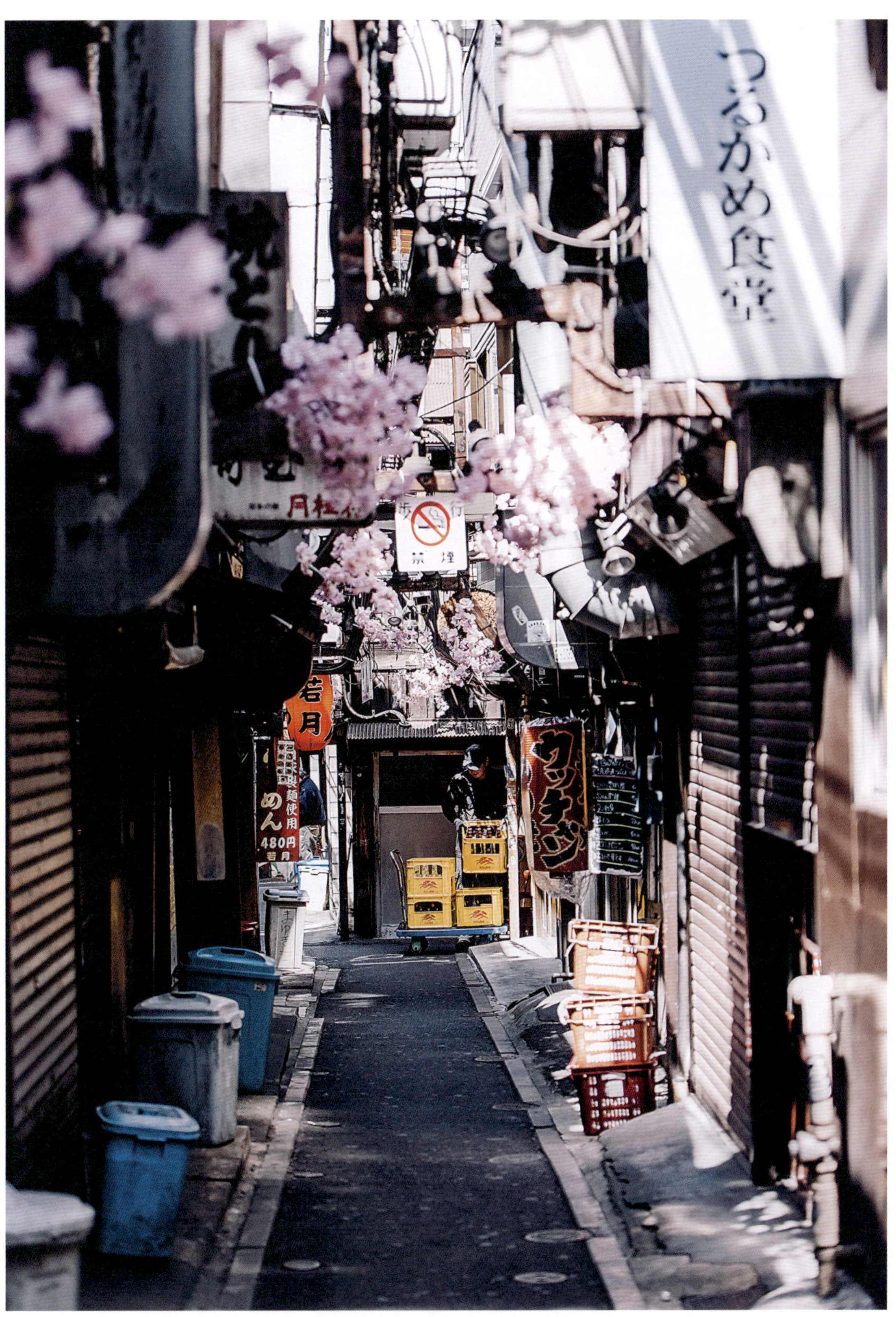

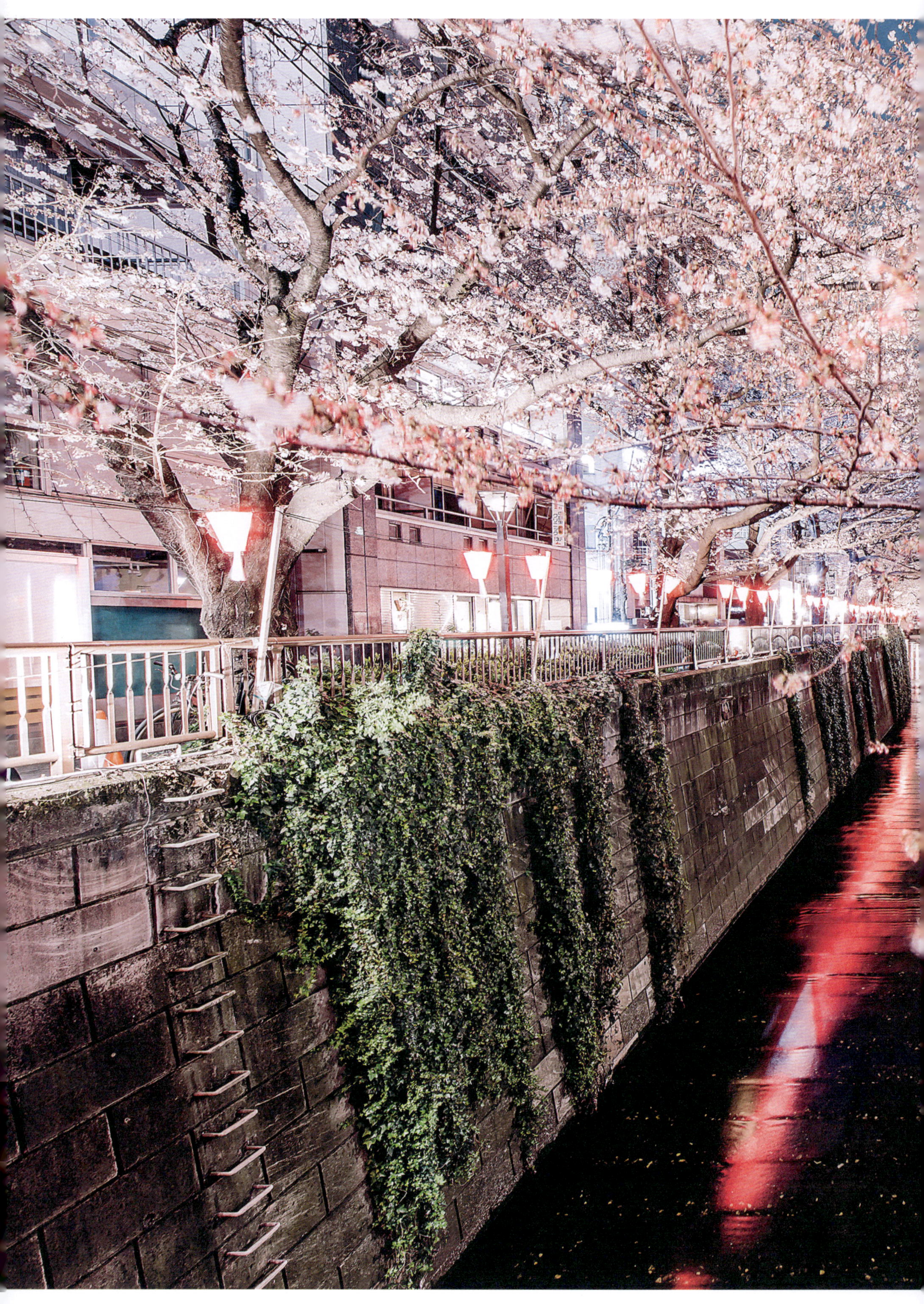

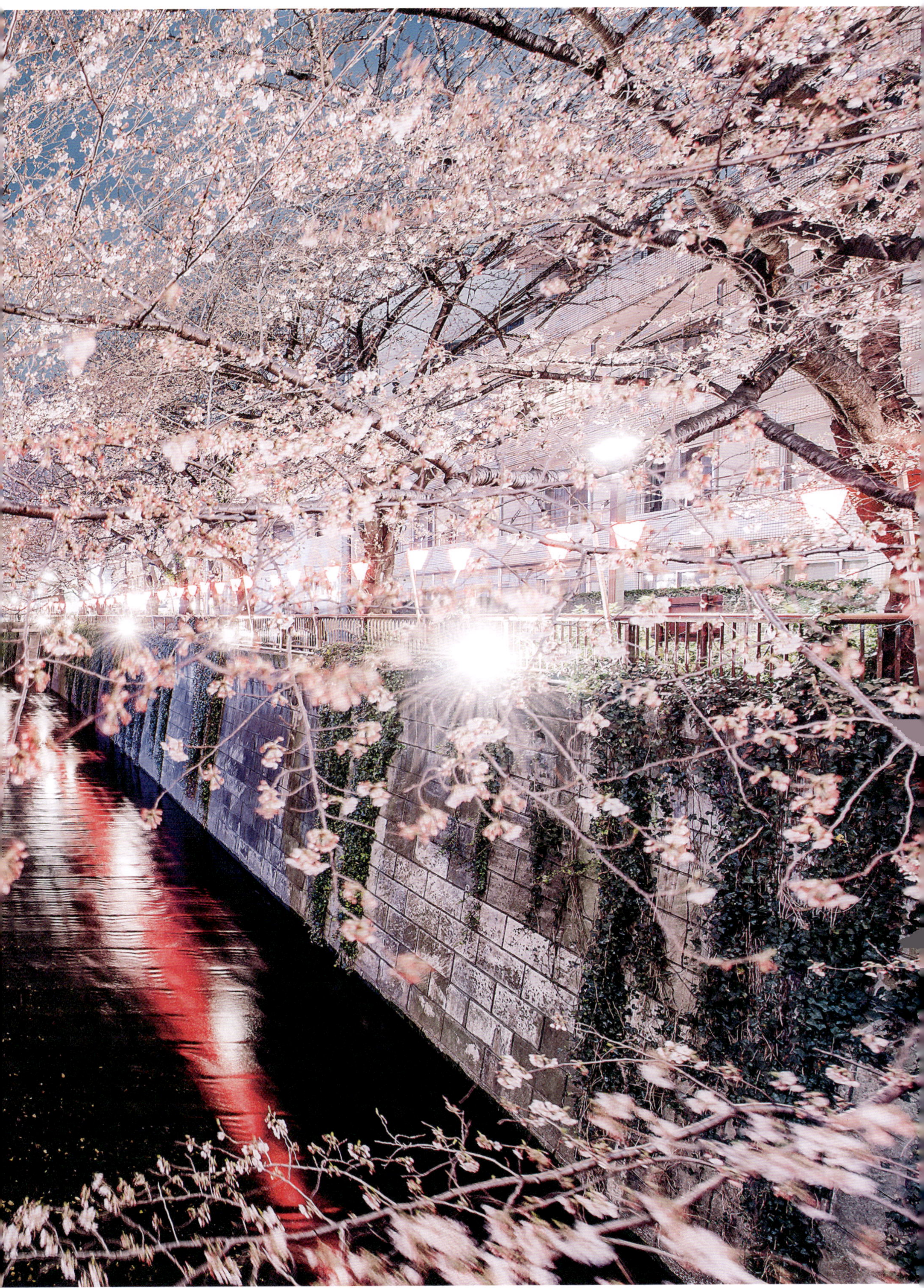

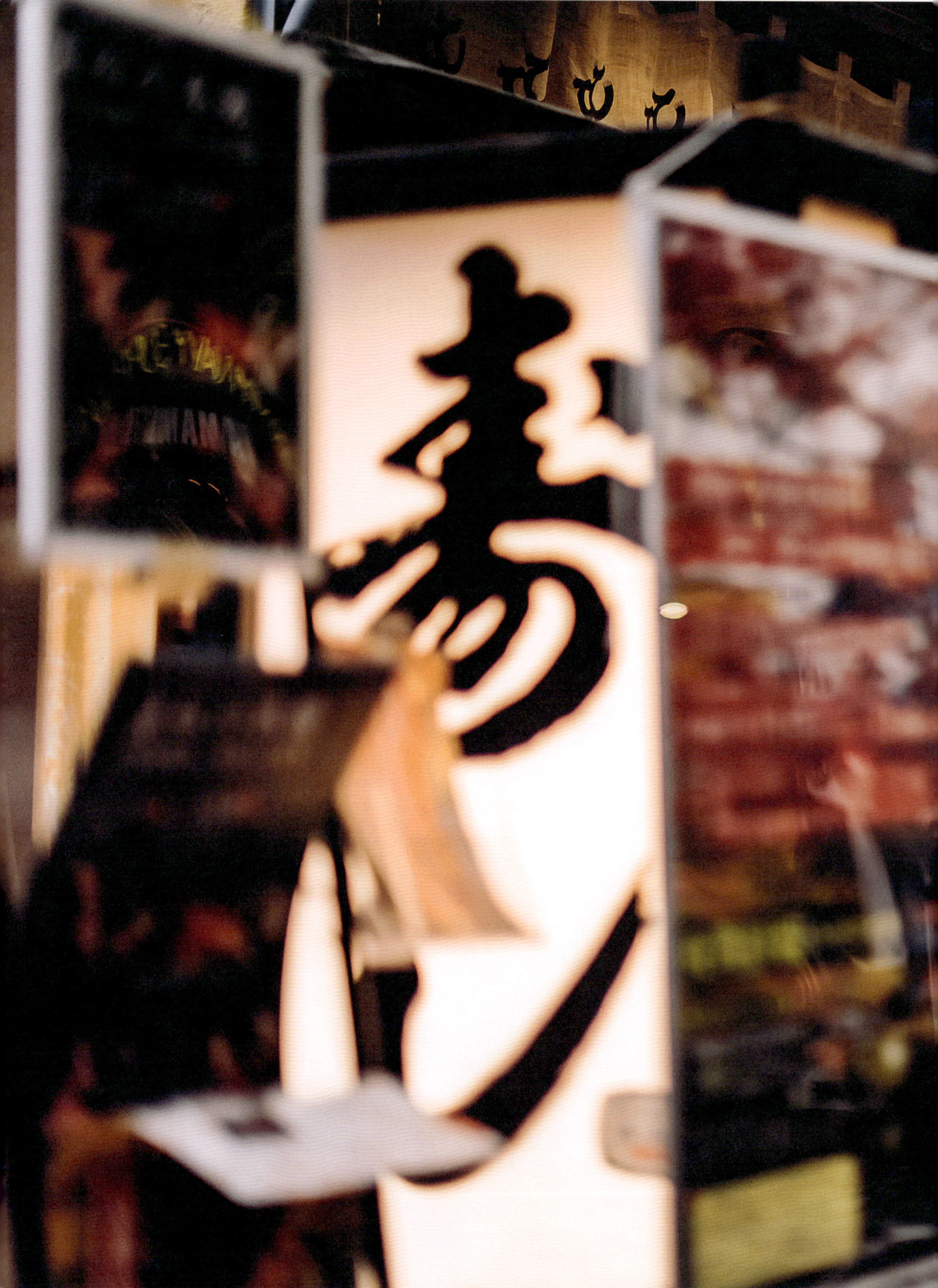

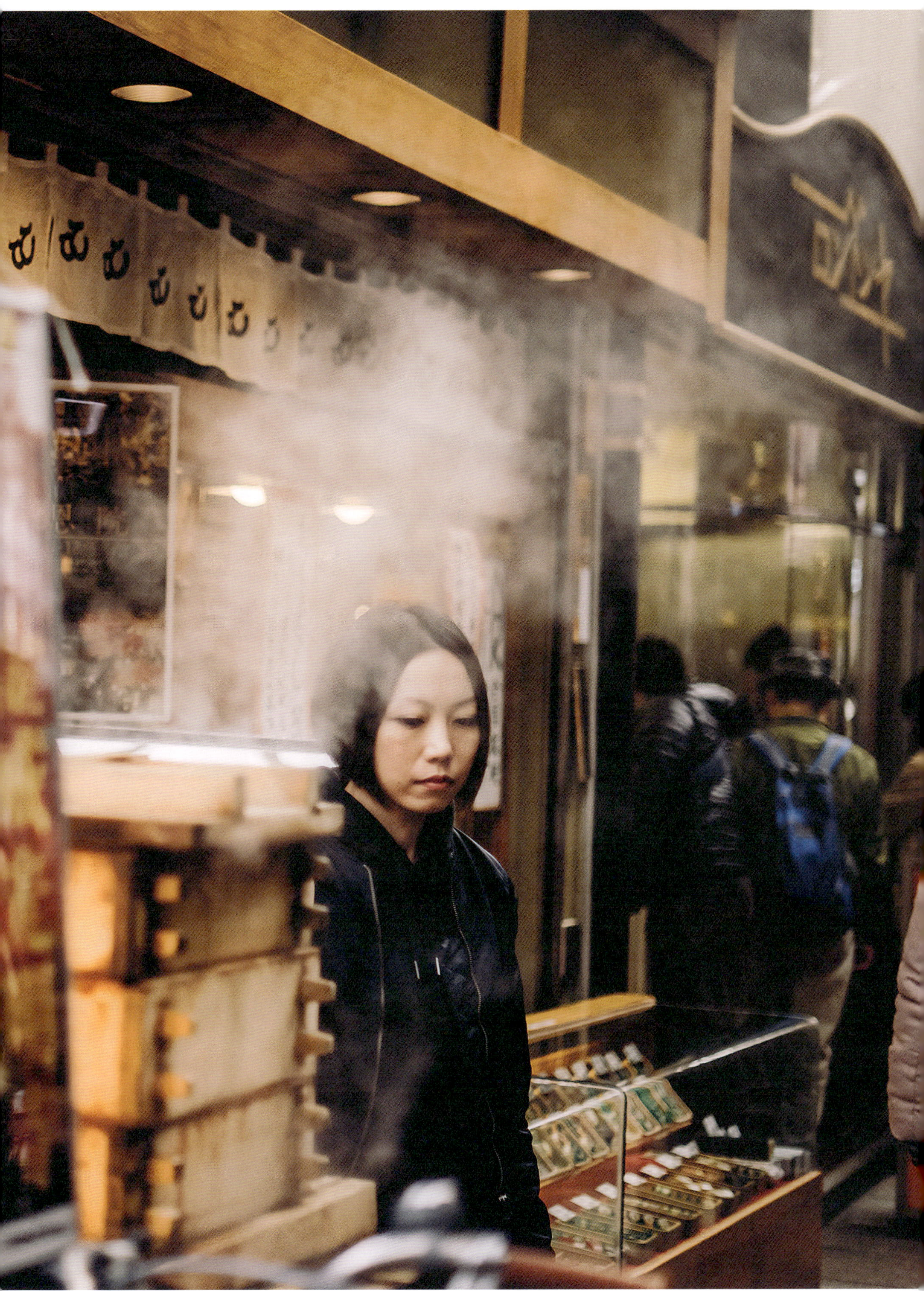

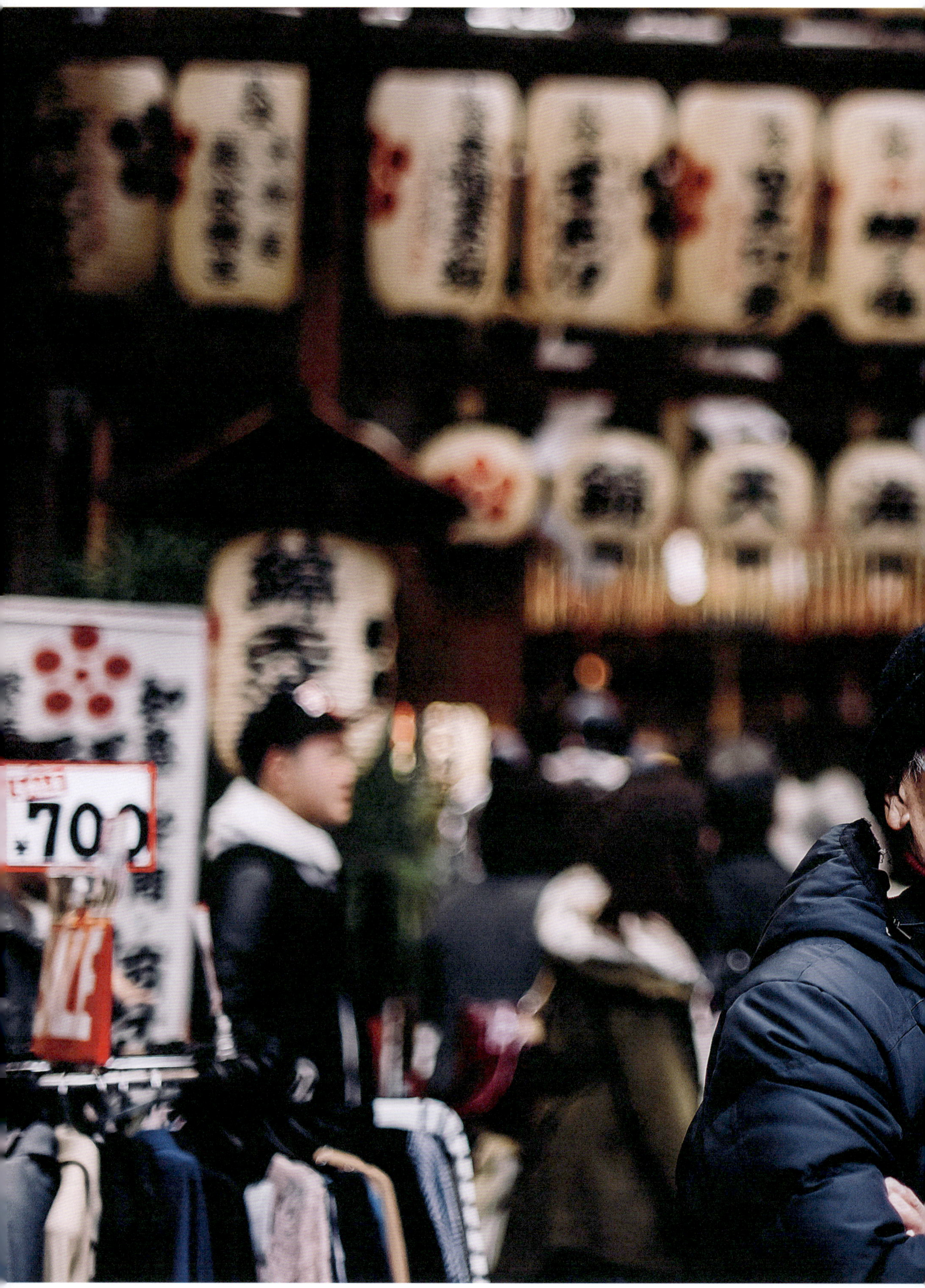

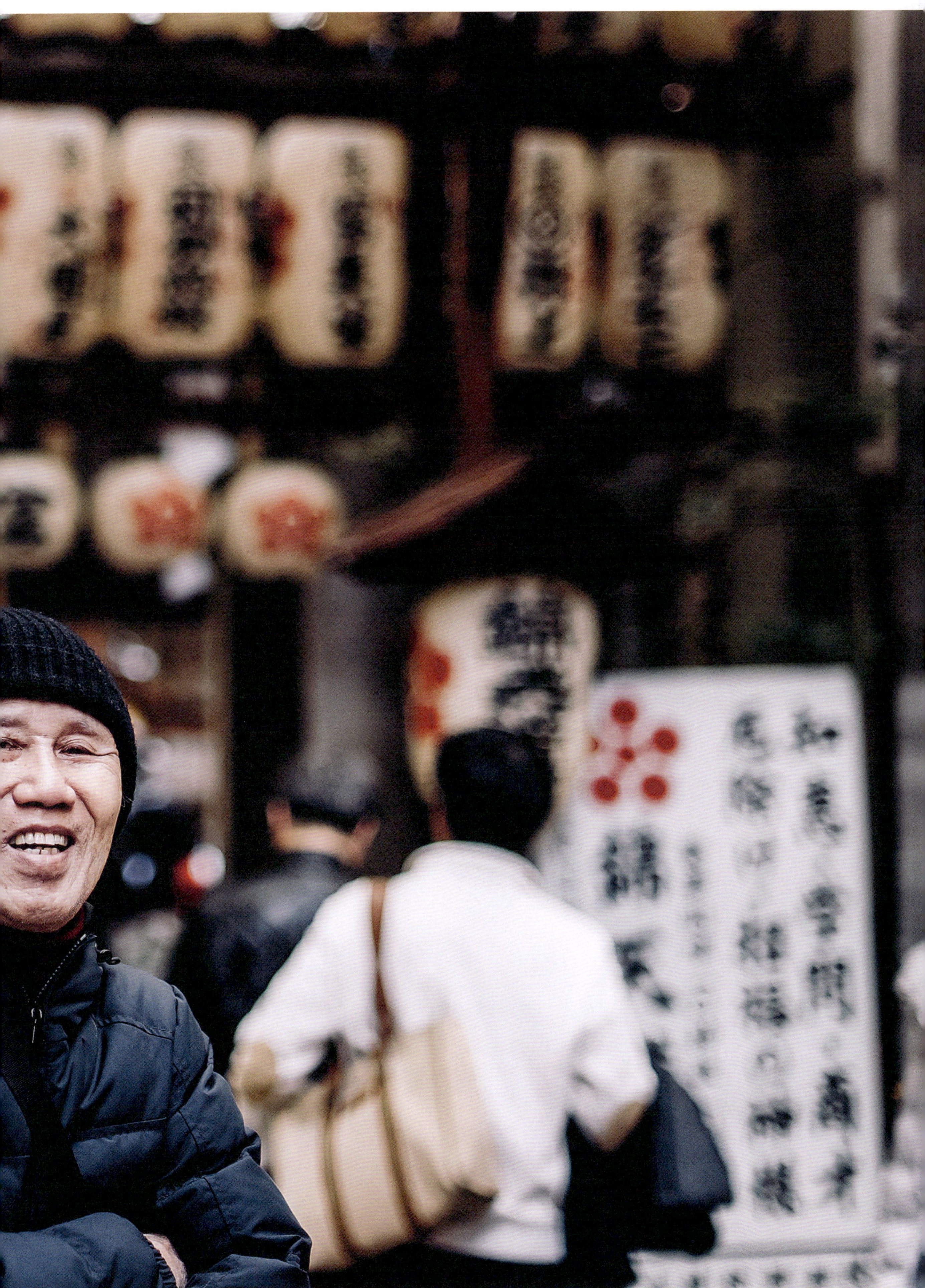

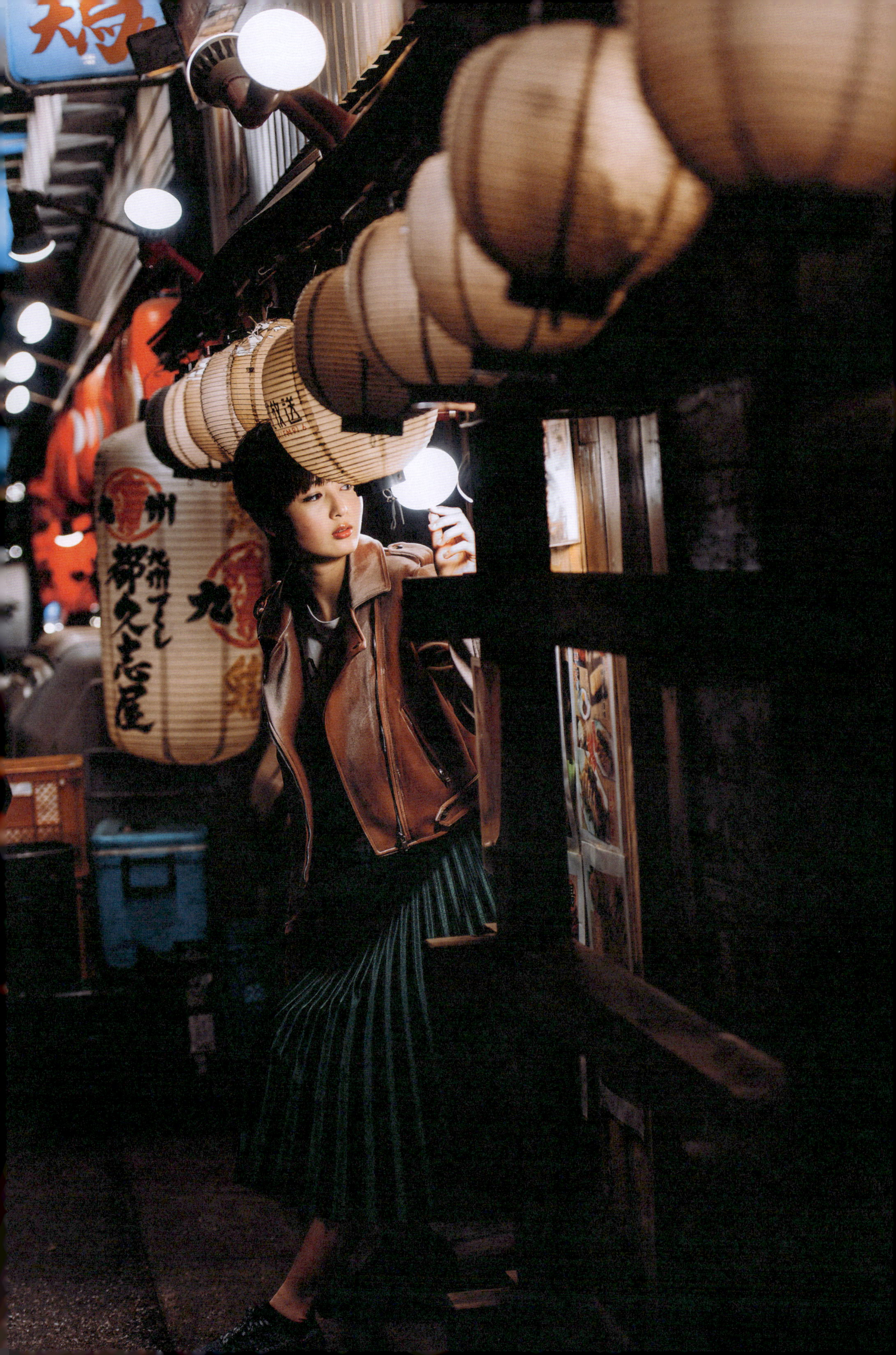
信州
信州てしこ
都久志屋
丸
物送

THE CITY AND ITS PEOPLE ARE DEPENDENT ON ONE ANOTHER AND THEREFORE THE TWO ARE **INSEPARABLE** IN THE PHOTOS I TAKE.

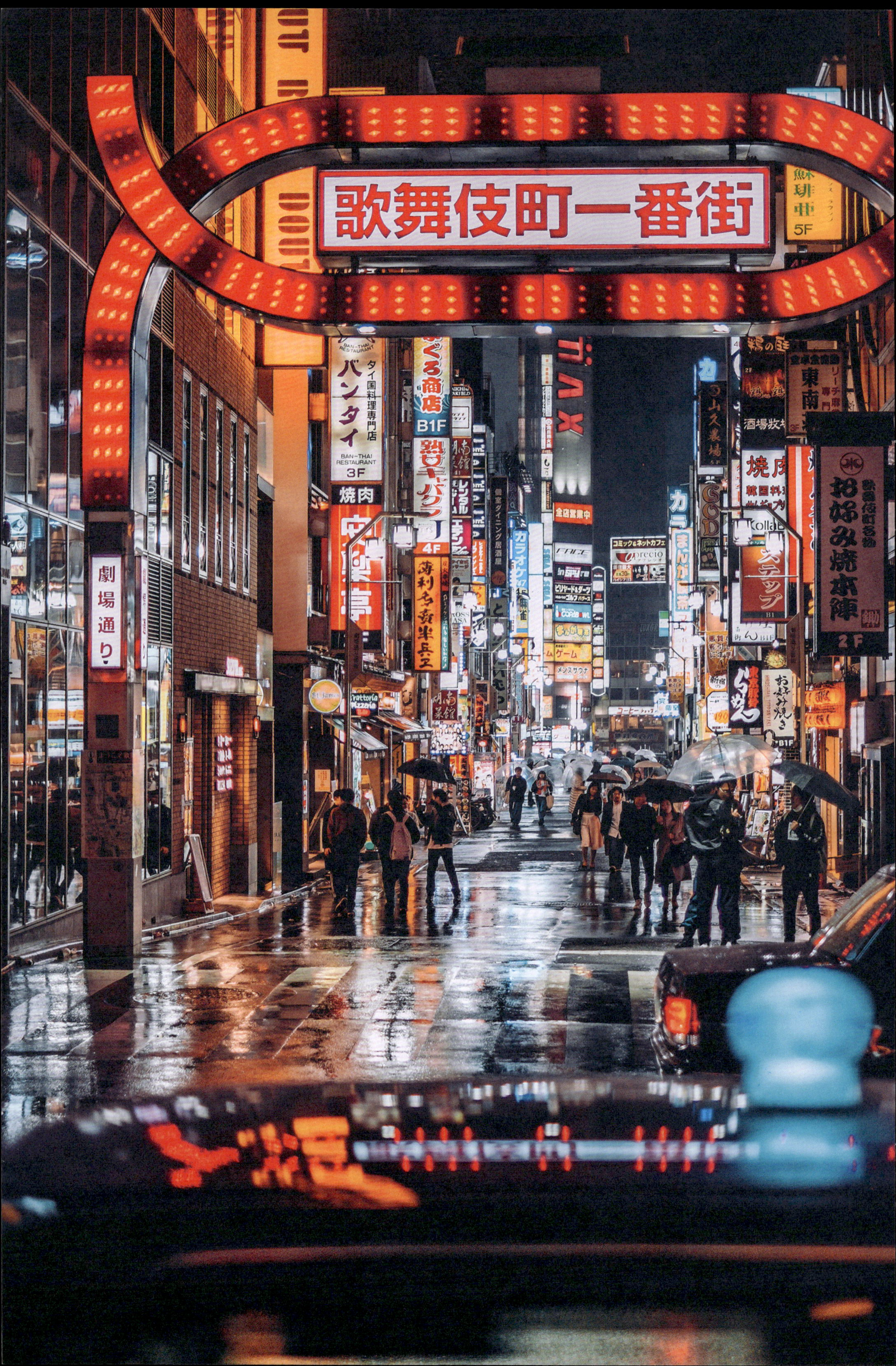

歌舞伎町一番街
珈琲
5F
劇場通り
タイ国料理専門店
バンタイ
BAN-THAI
RESTAURANT
3F
焼肉
ぐろ商店
B1F
山久農場
酒場牧場
焼肉
Kollee
コミック&ネットカフェ
precio
ステップ
B1
歌舞伎町名物
お好み焼本陣
2F
東南
お好み焼き
らめん
新宿
ムゲーム
メンズサウナ
カラオケ
microtel
Trattoria Pizzeria

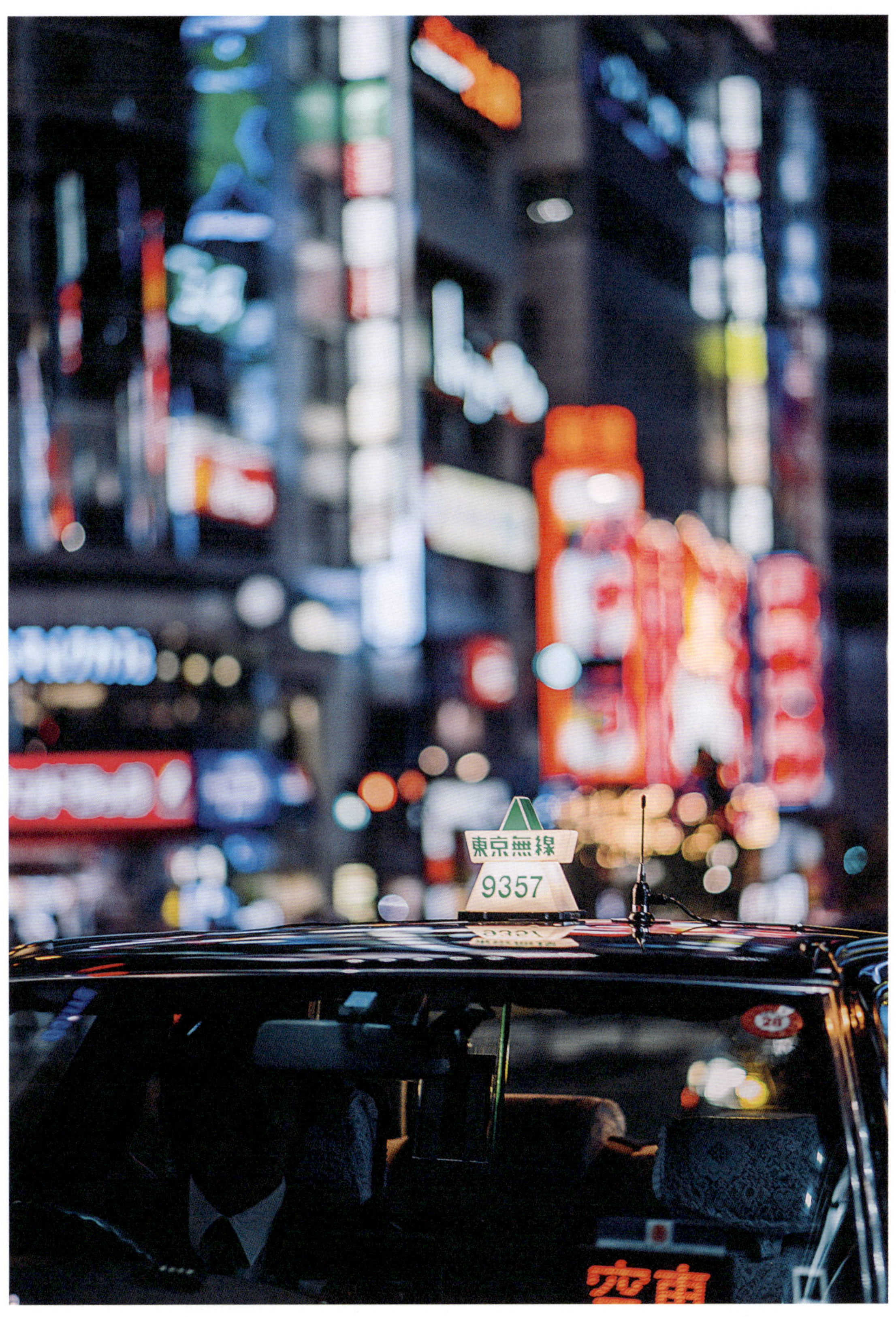

東京無線
9357
空車

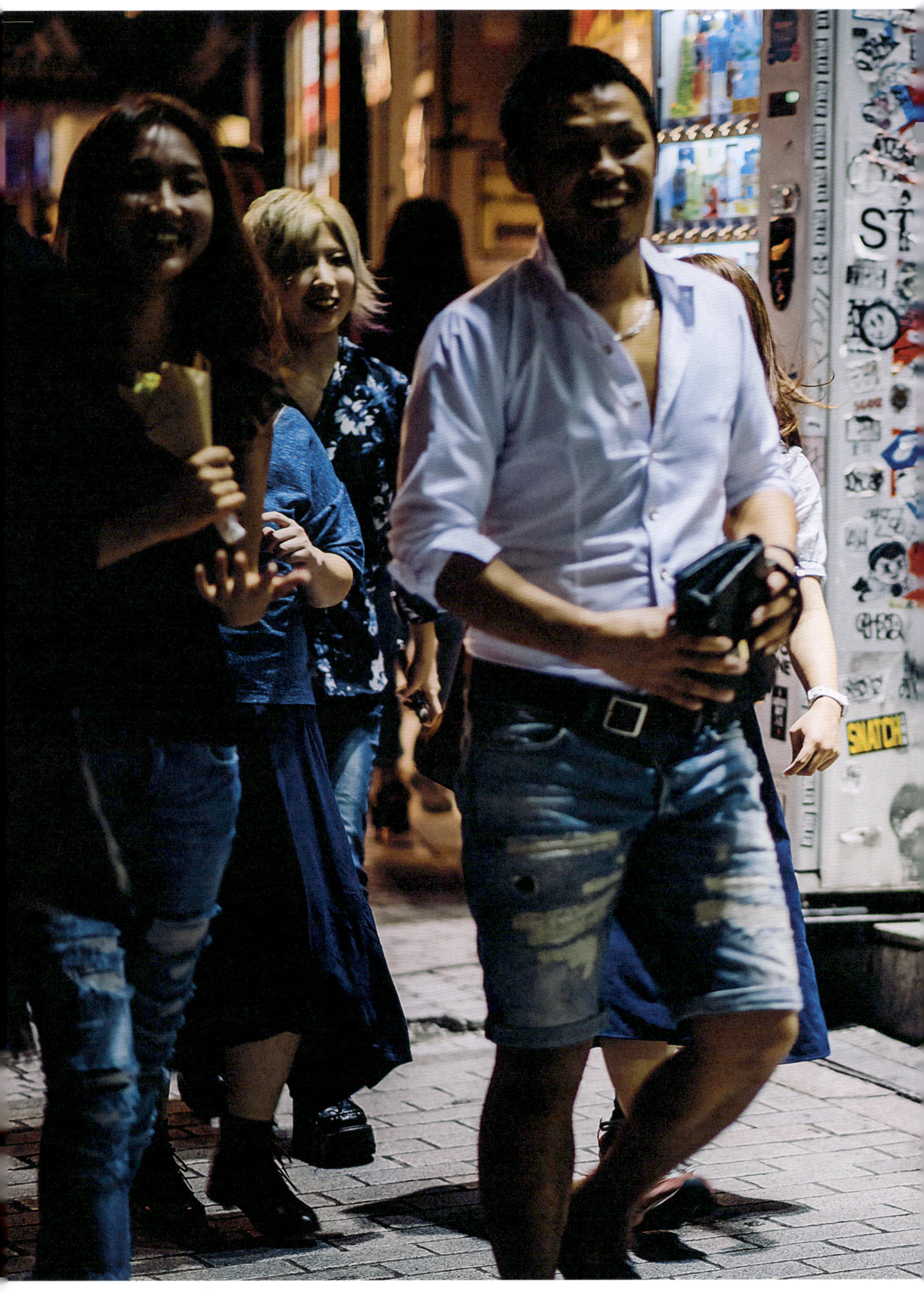

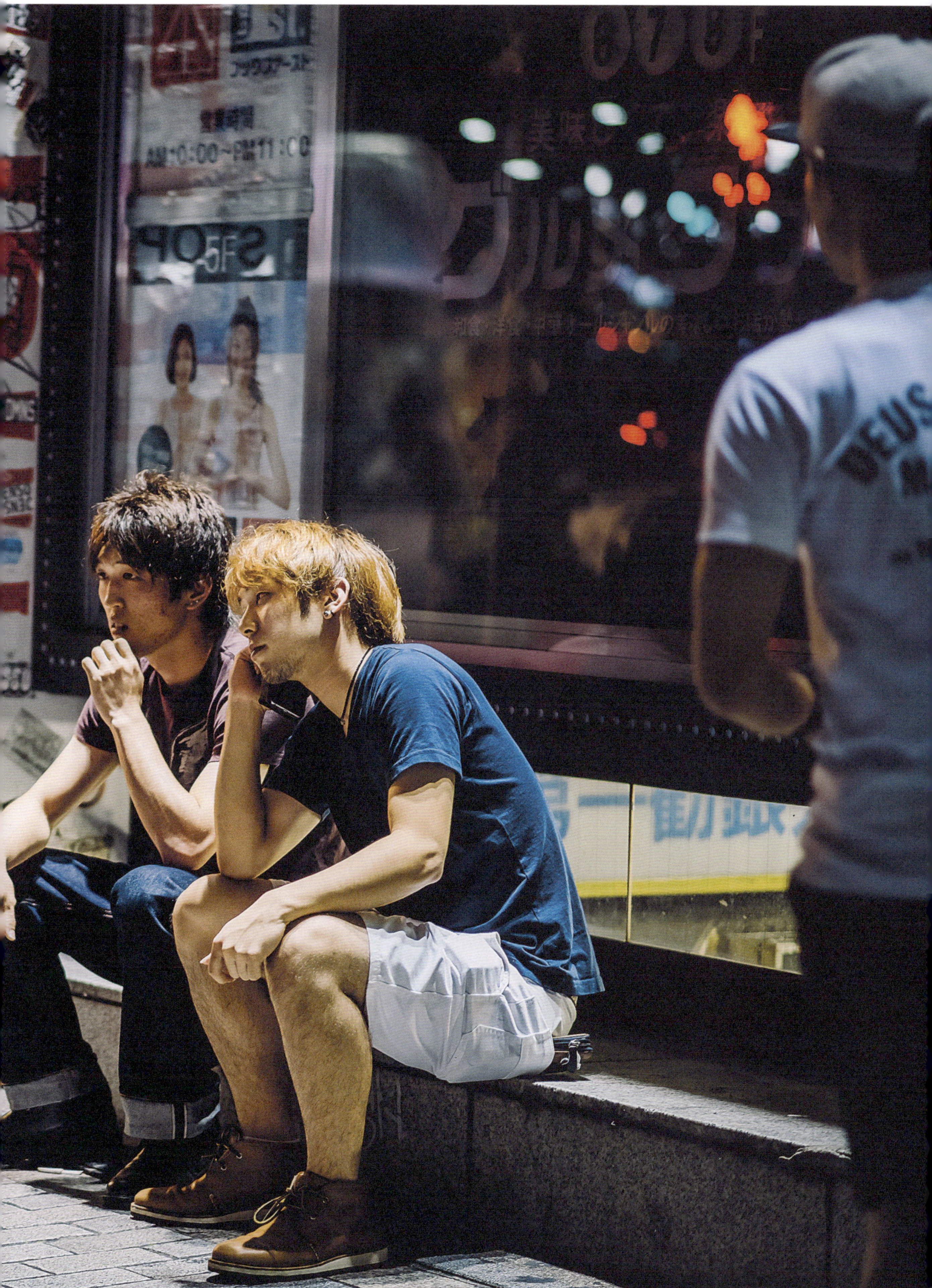

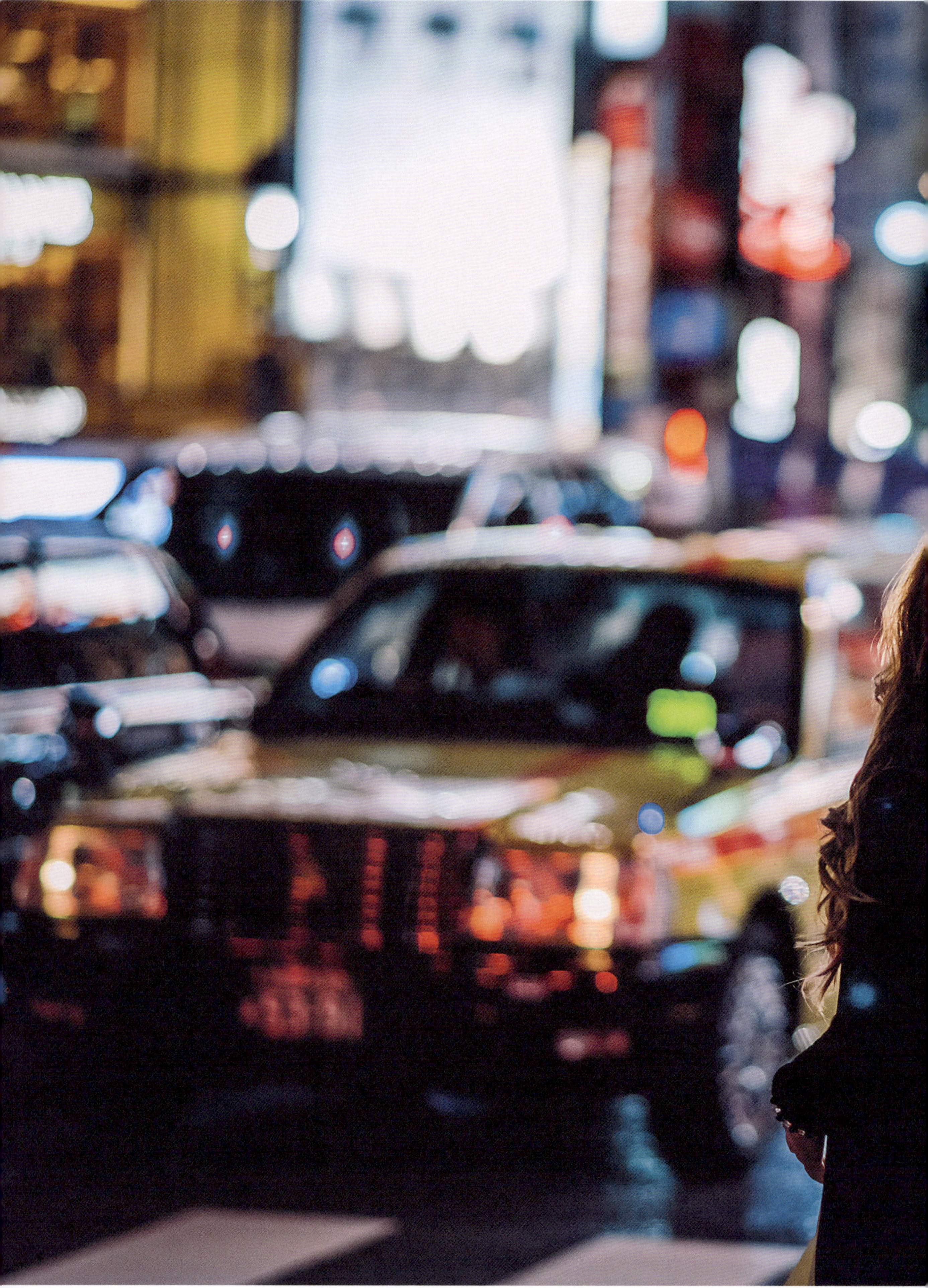

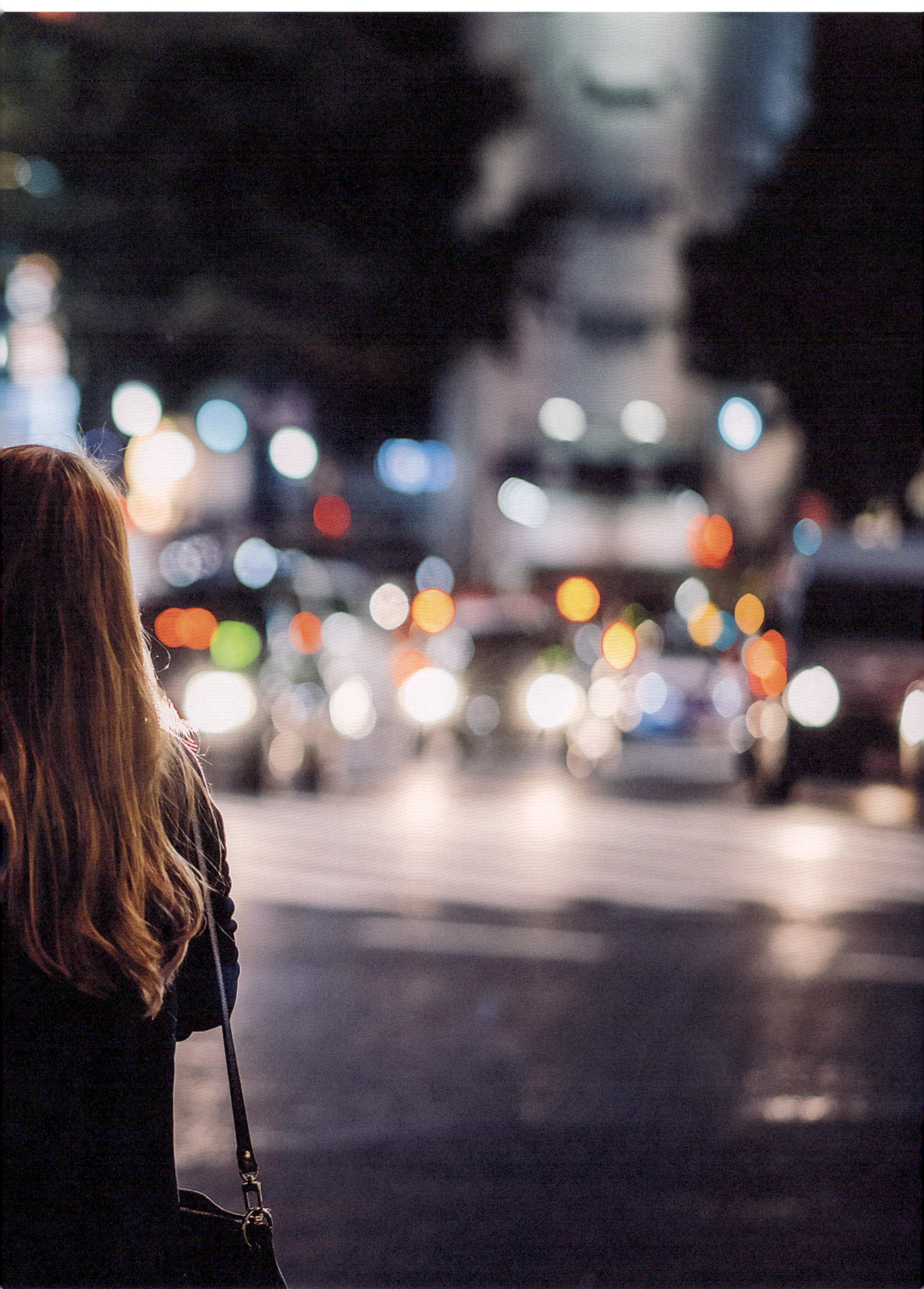

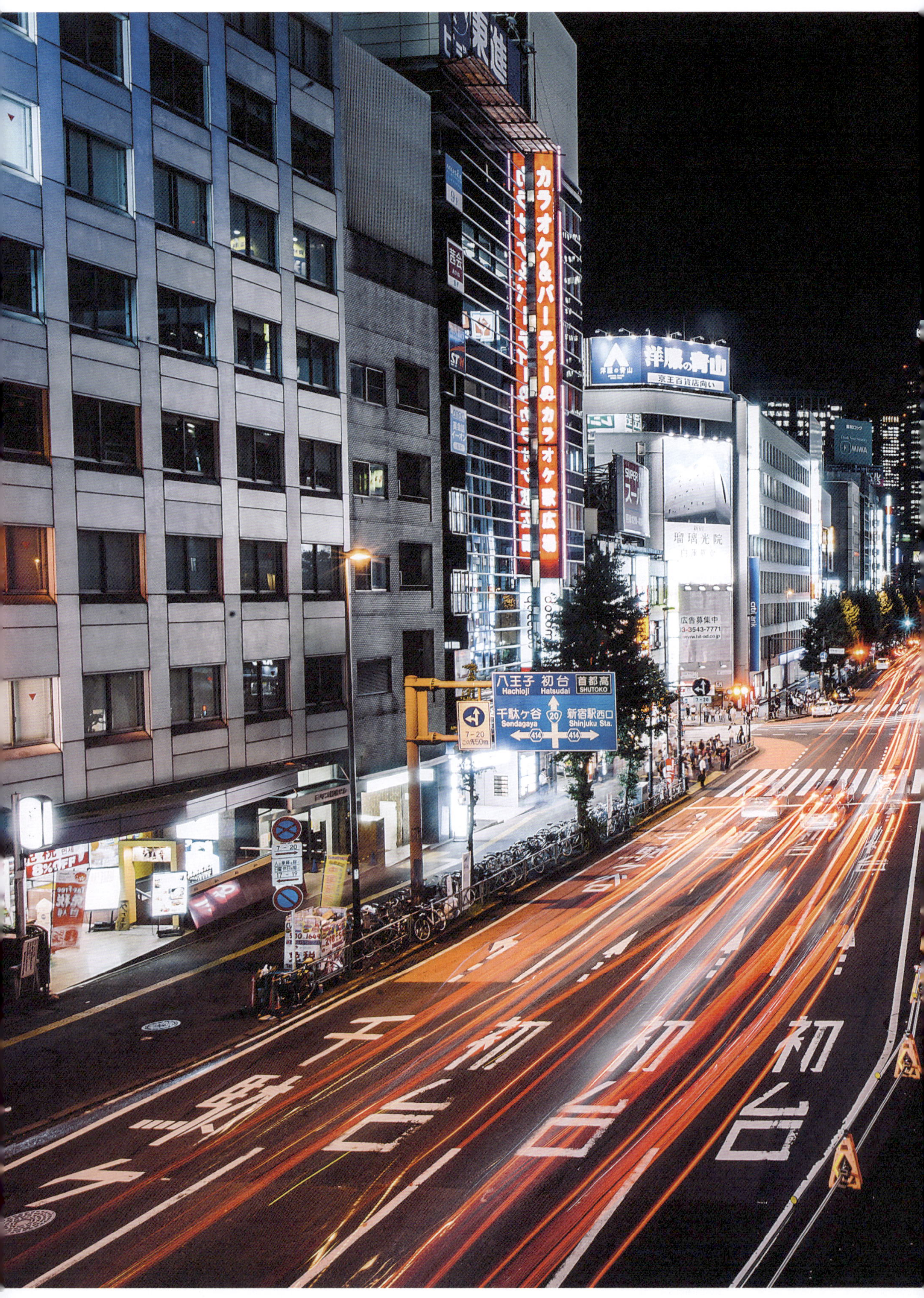

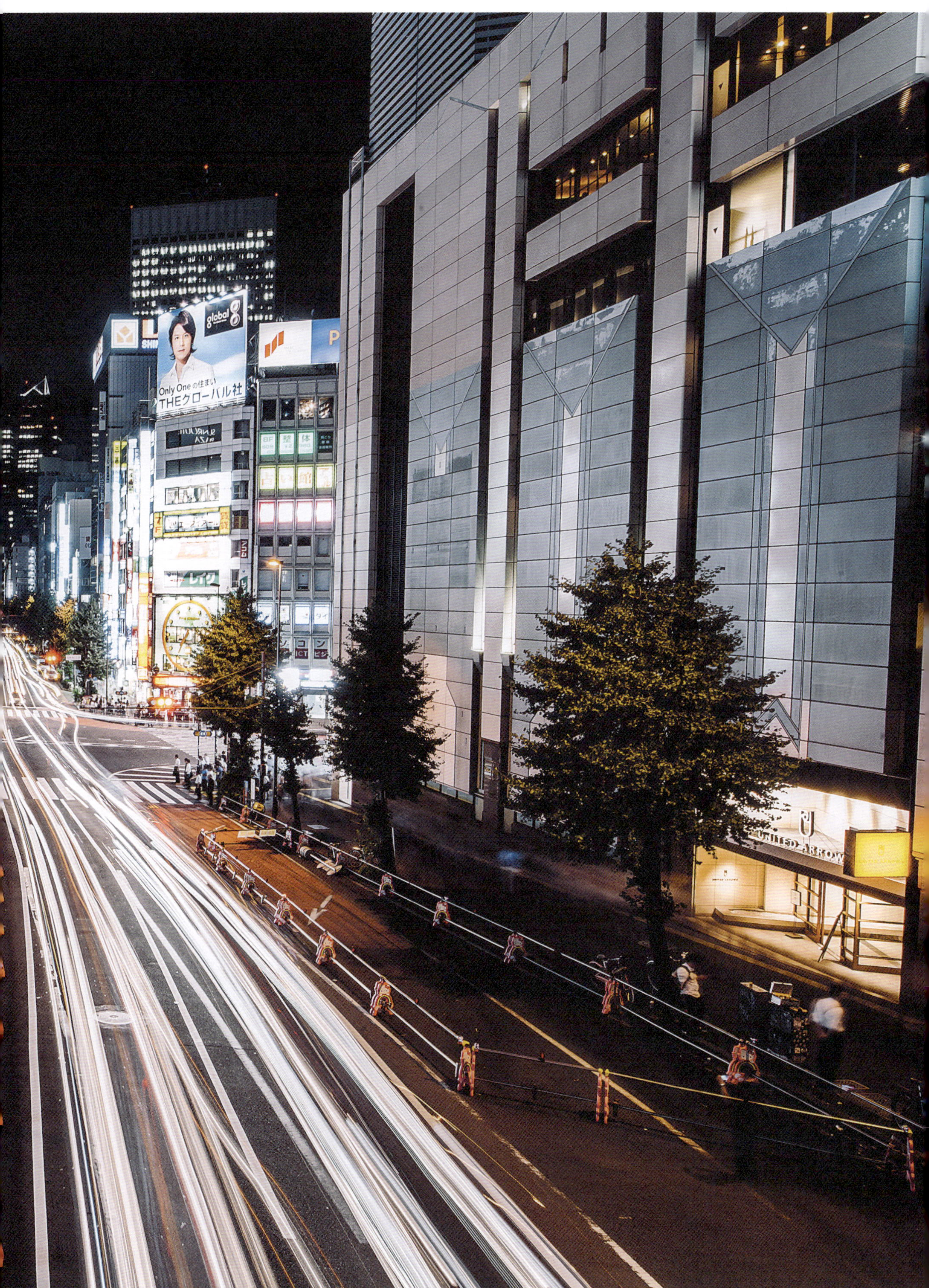

global
Only One の住まい
THEクローハル社
UNITED ARROWS
P

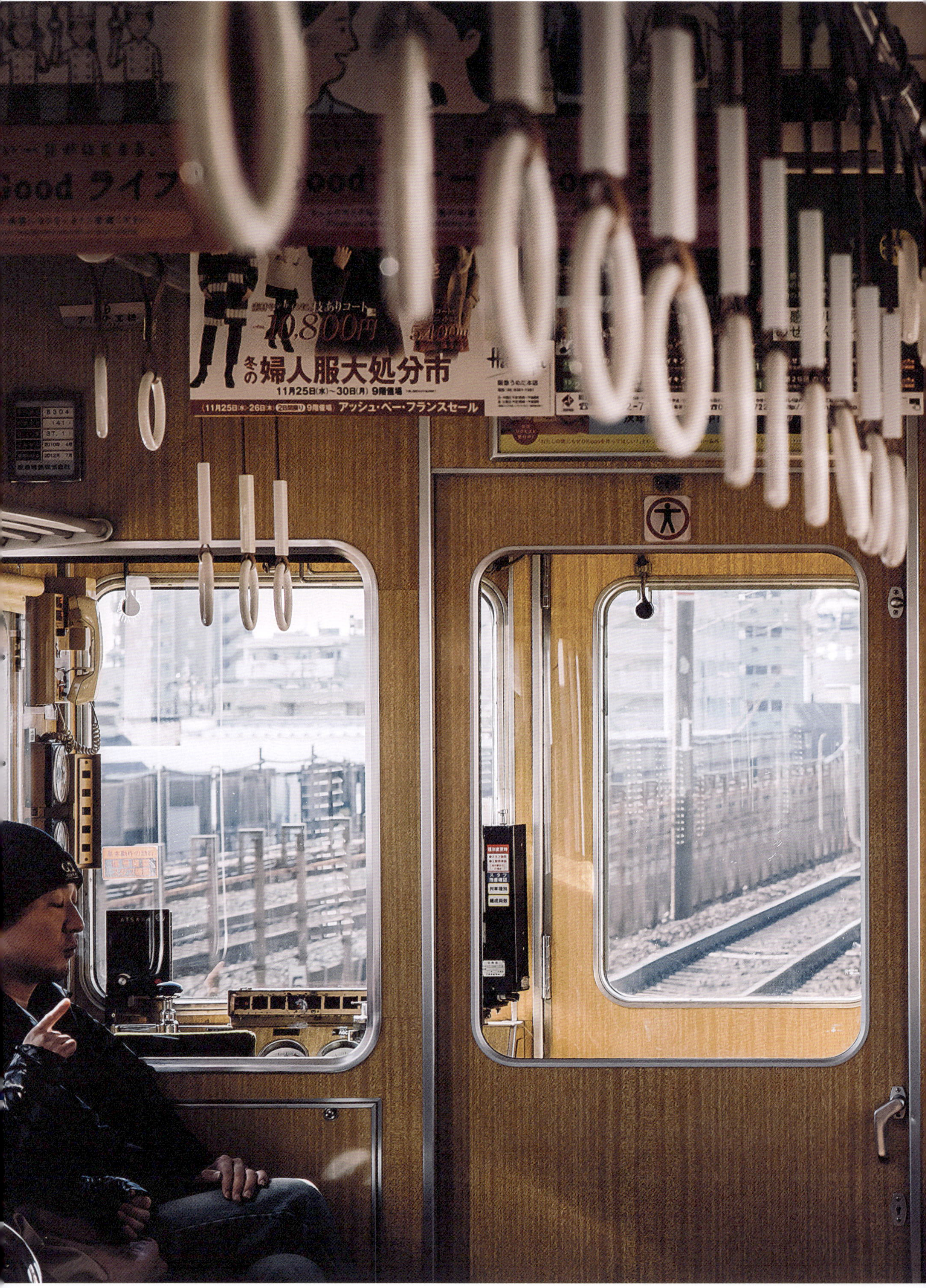
技ありコート
10,800円
5,400円
冬
の 婦人服大処分市
11月25日(水)〜30日(月) 9階催場
〈11月25日(水)・26日(木) 2日間限り 9階催場〉 アッシュ・ベー・フランスセール
Good ライフ

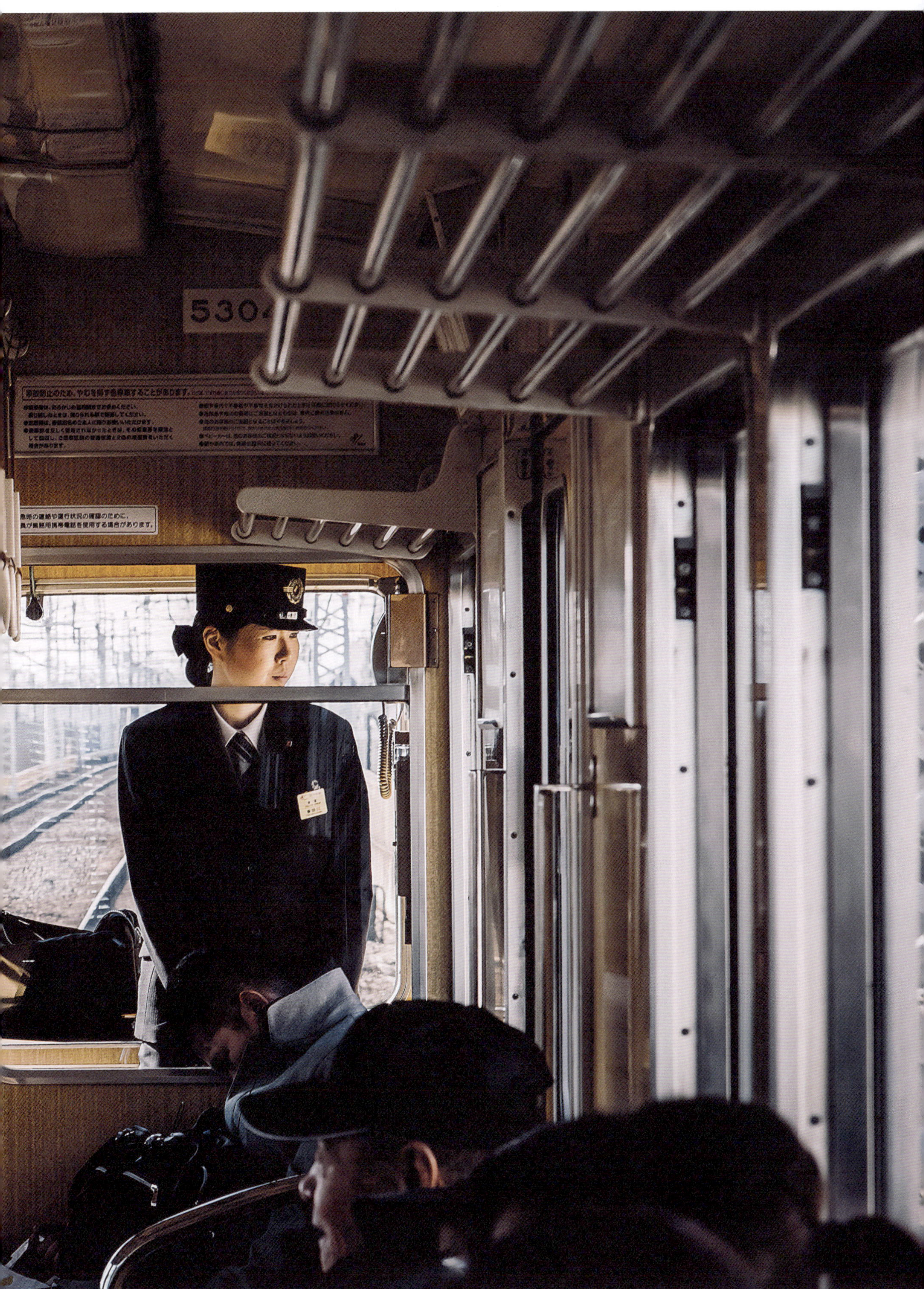

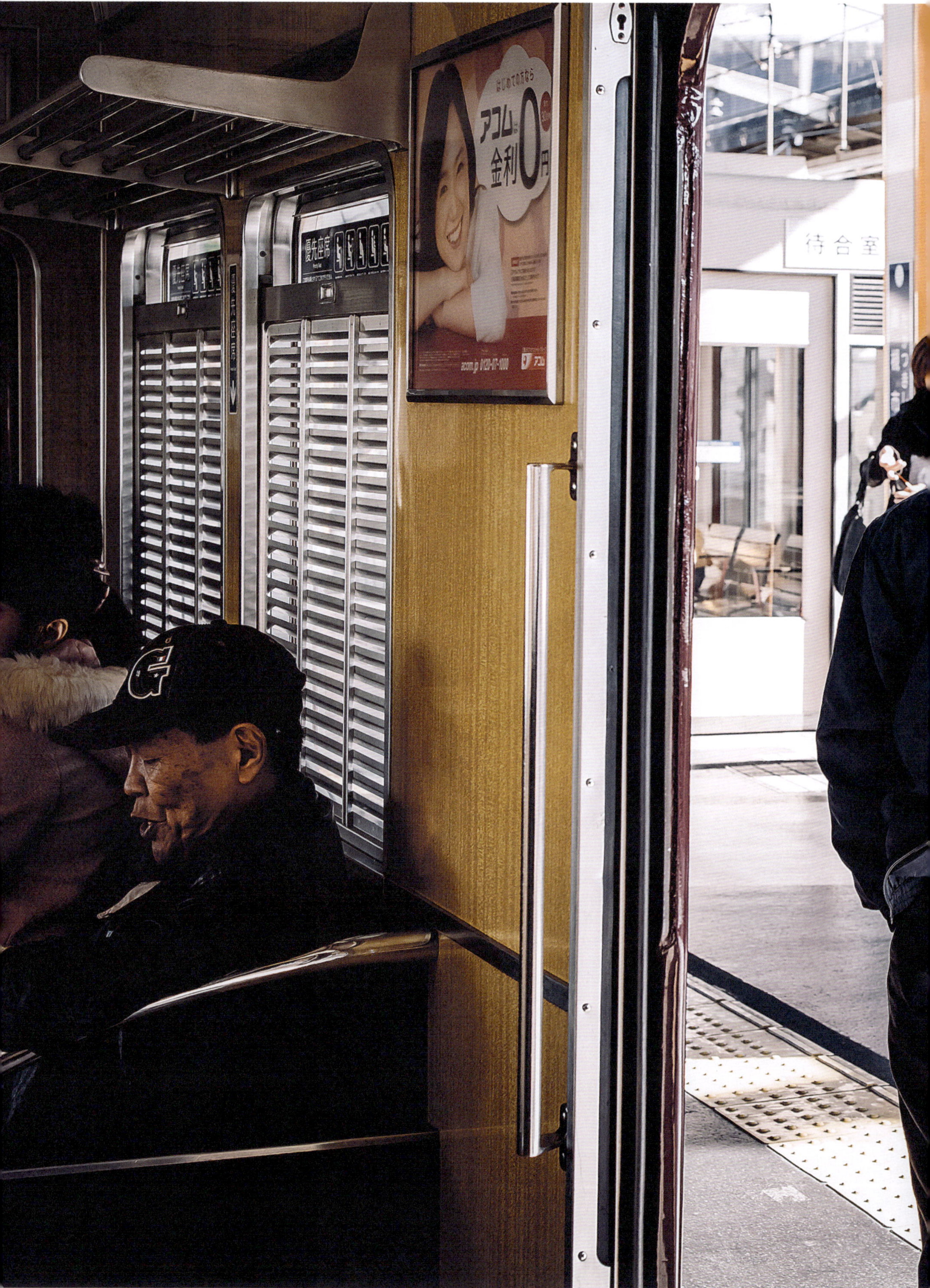
はじめての方なら
アコム
金利 0円
acom.jp 0120-07-1000
優先座席
待合室

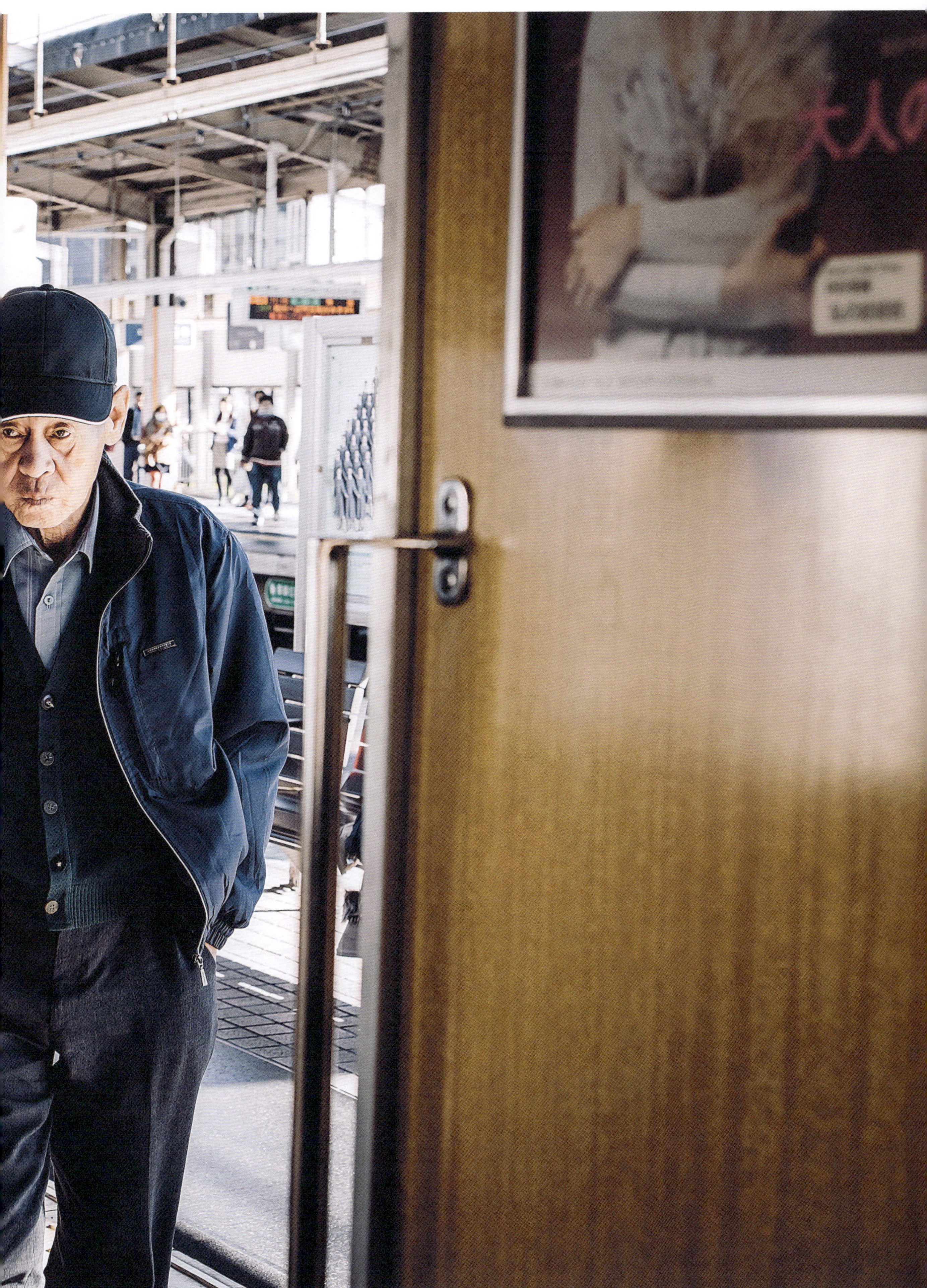

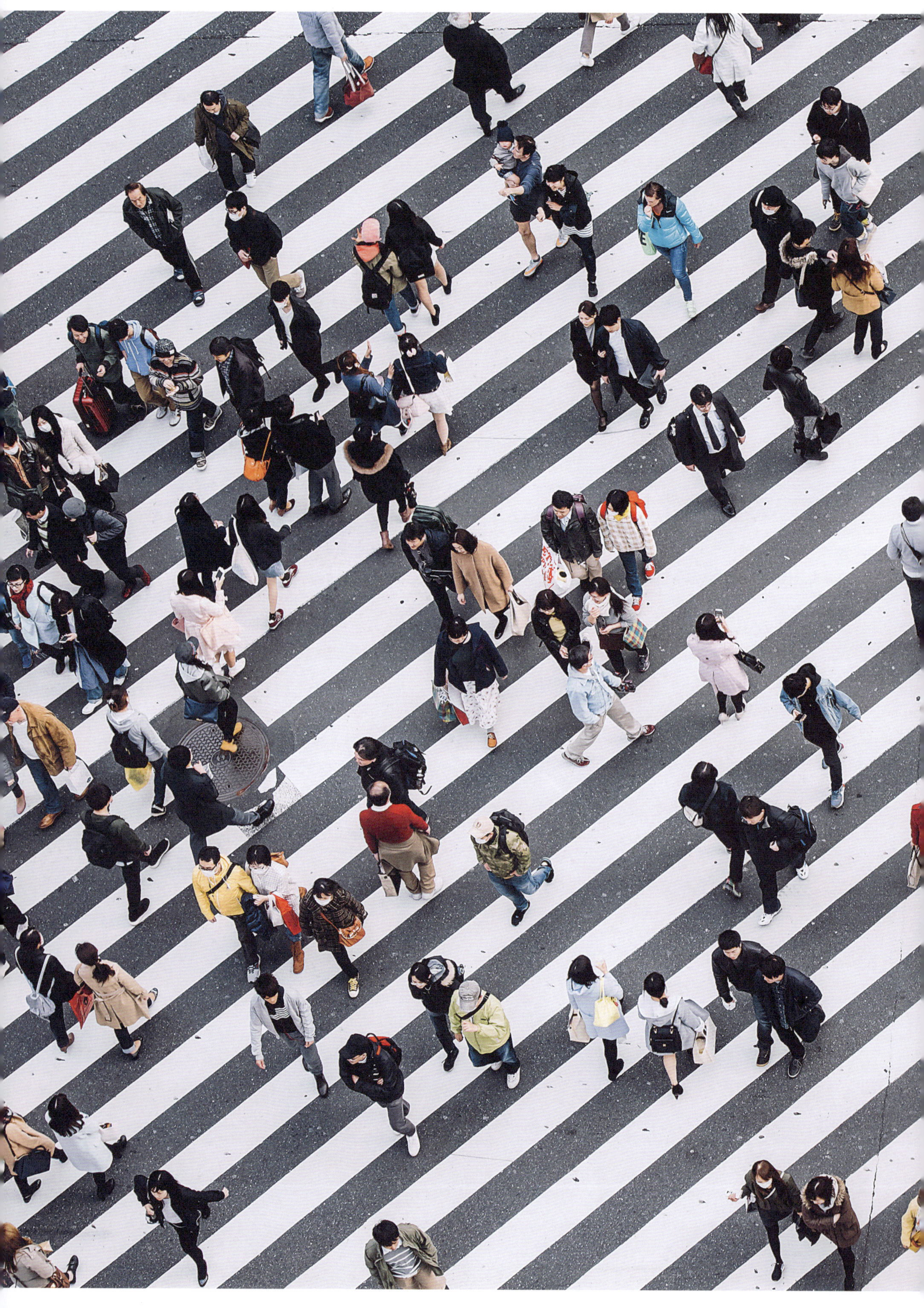

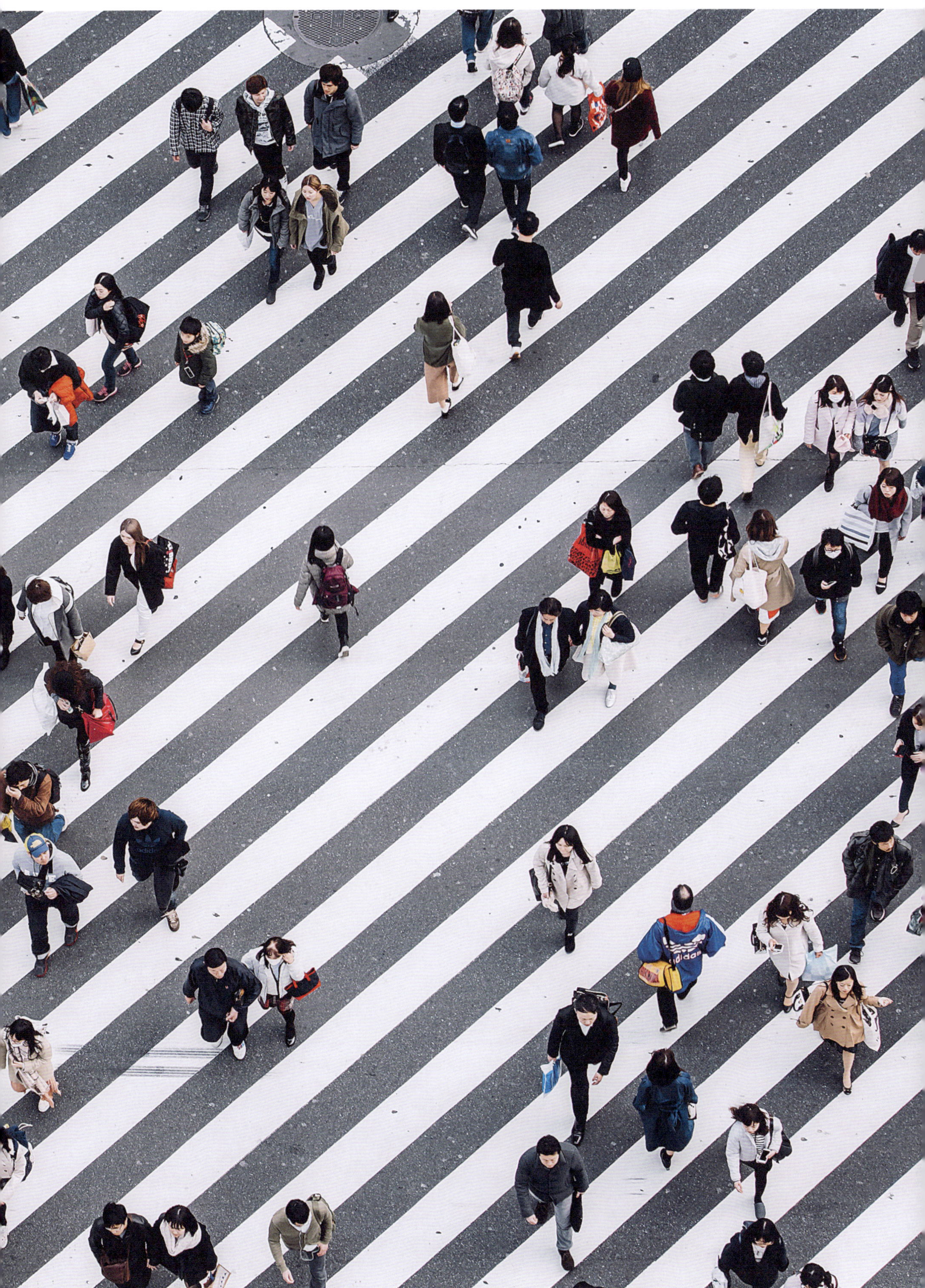

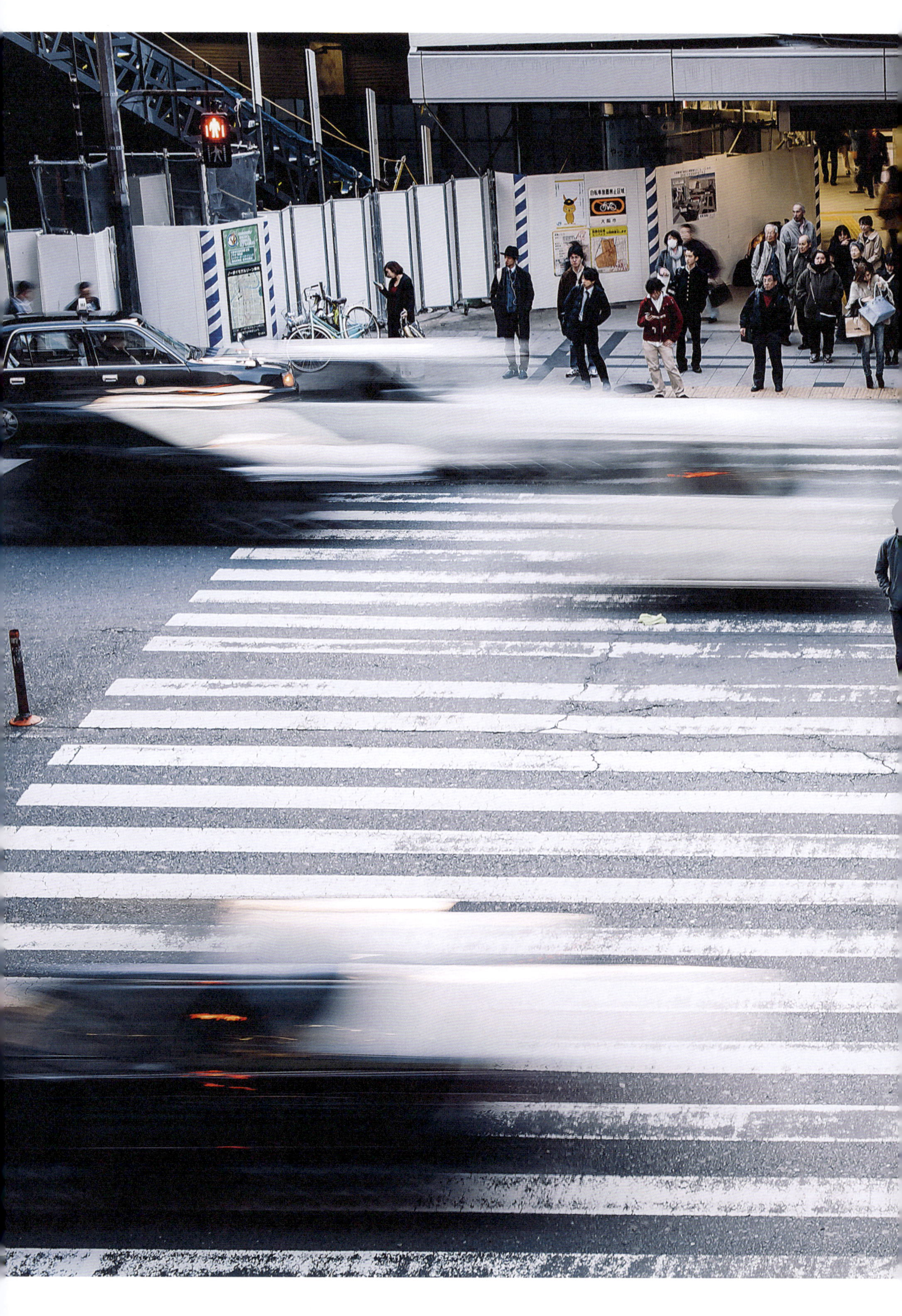

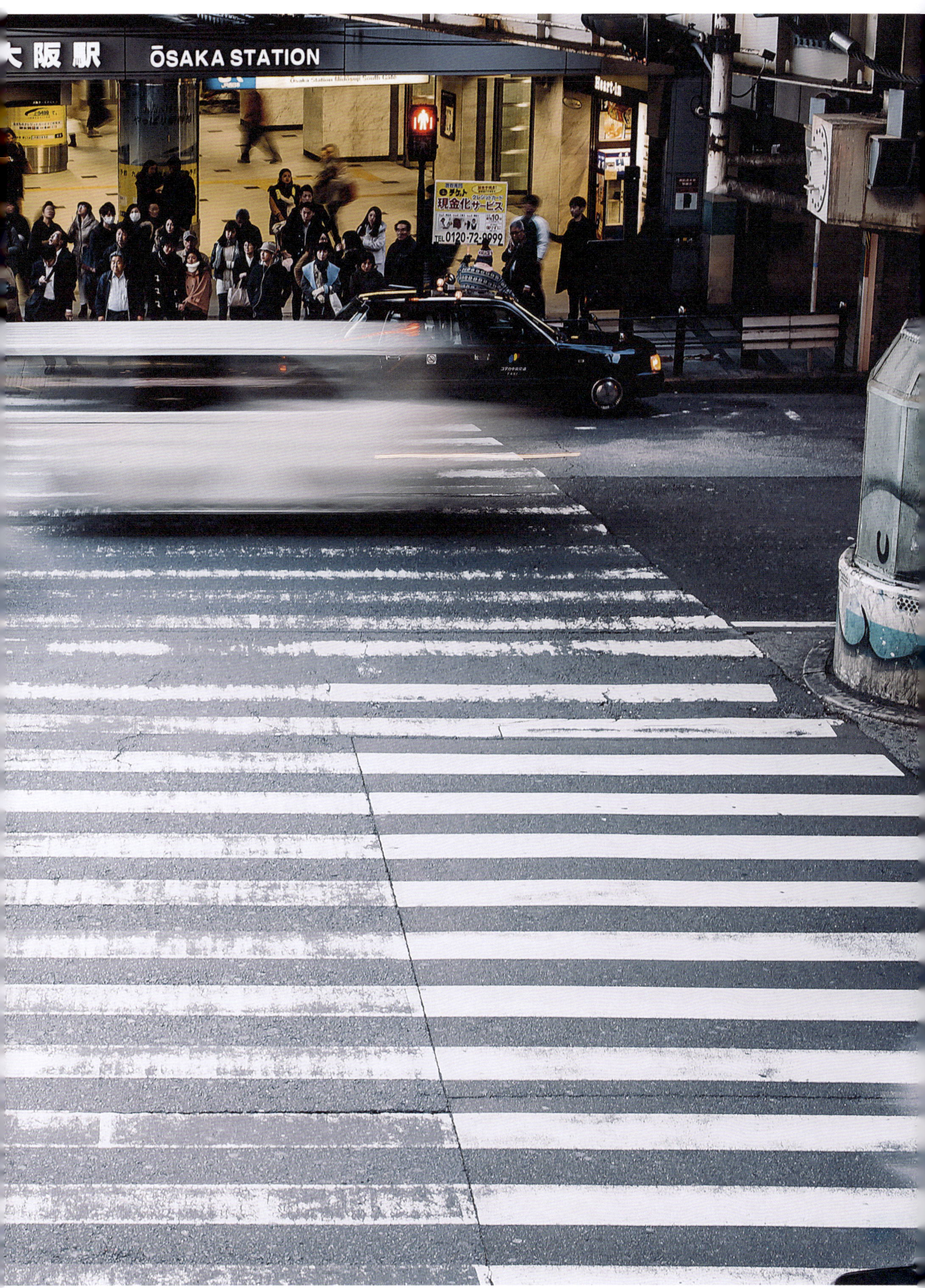

大阪駅　ŌSAKA STATION
現金化サービス
TEL 0120-72-9992
Heart-in

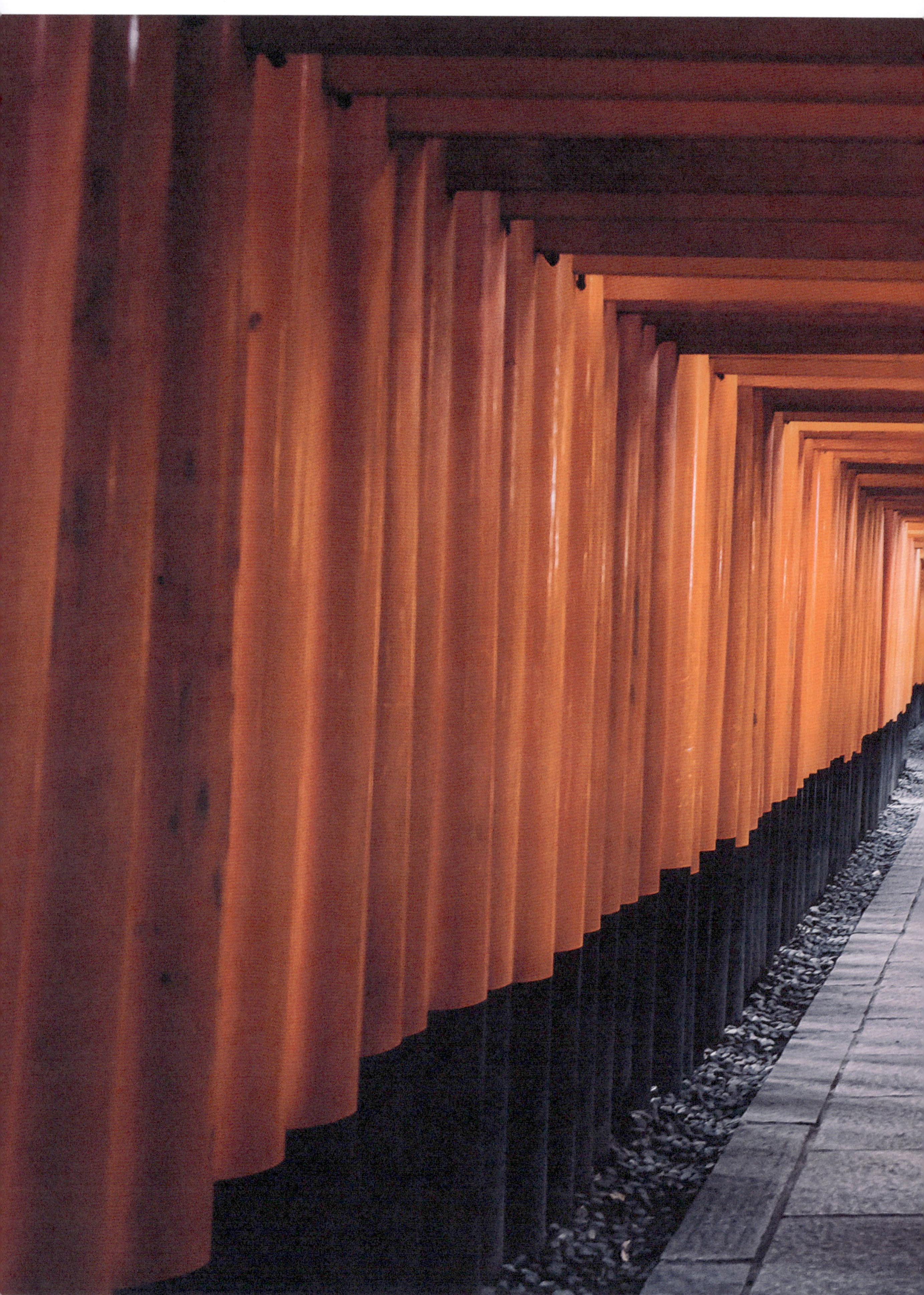

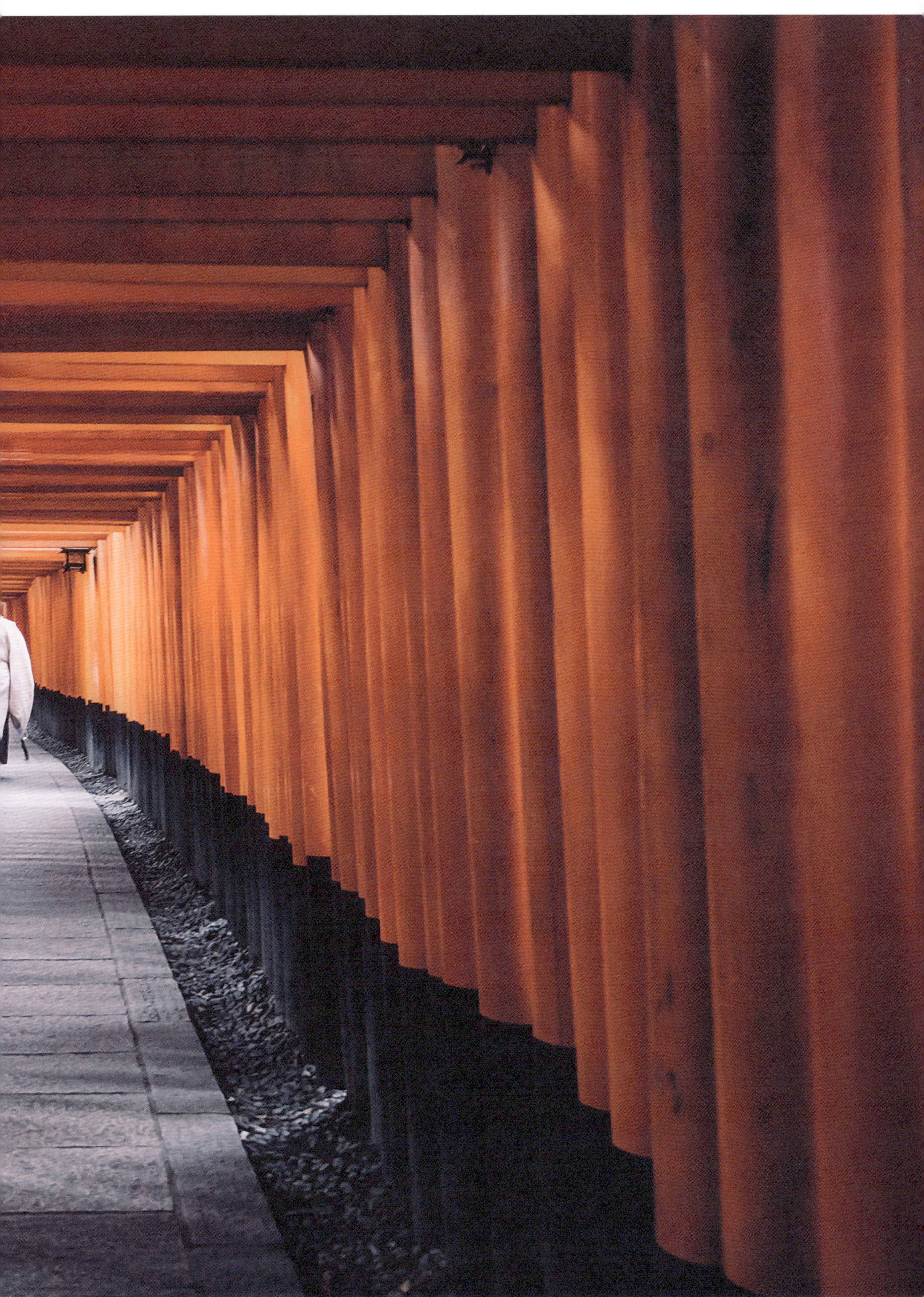

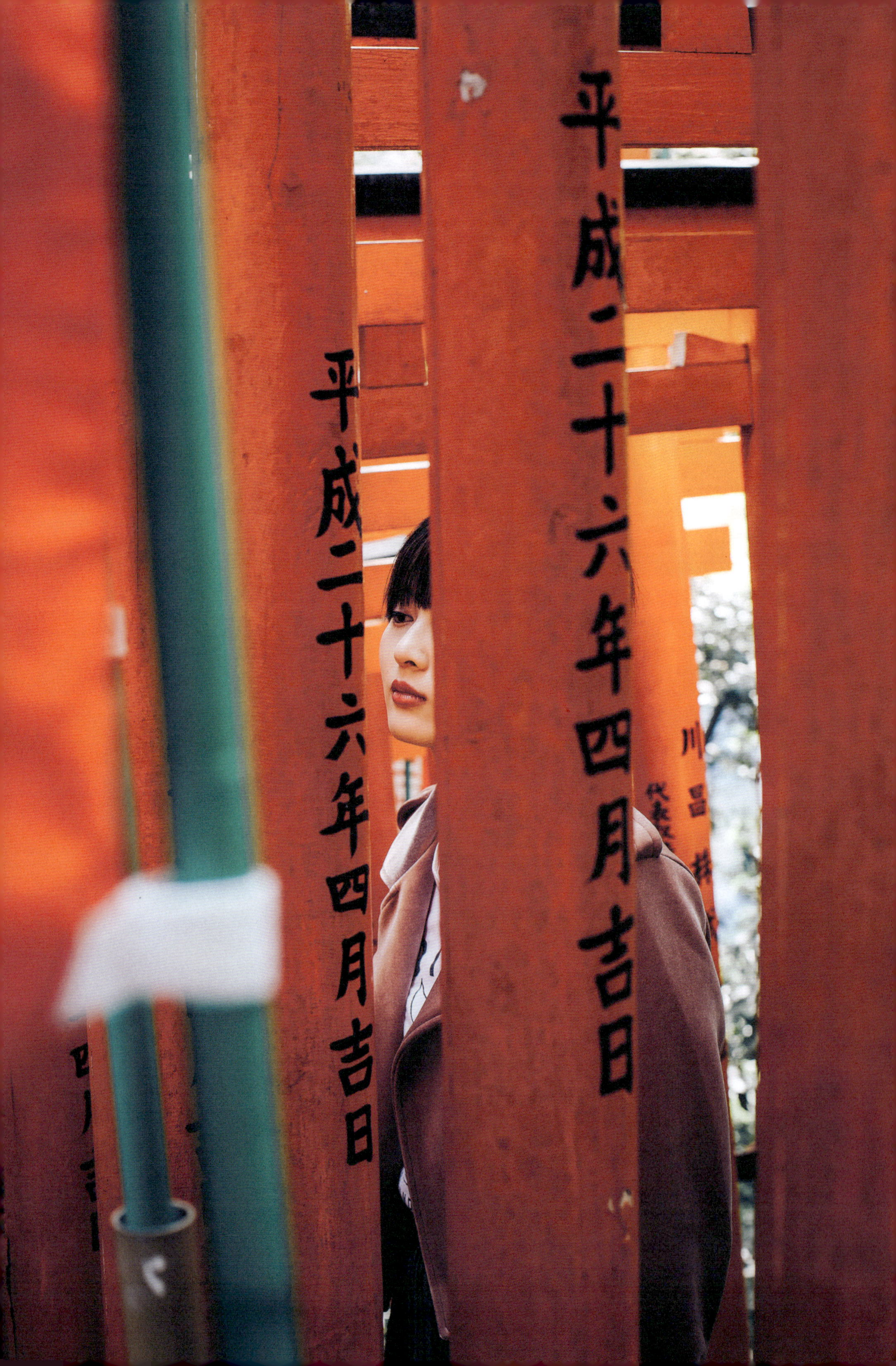

平成二十六年四月吉日
平成二十六年四月吉日
四月吉日
川昌株
代表取締

IN PORTRAITS, THE DYNAMIC BETWEEN THE SUBJECT
AND HOW THEY INTERACT WITH THE ENVIRONMENT ARE
RECURRING THEMES.

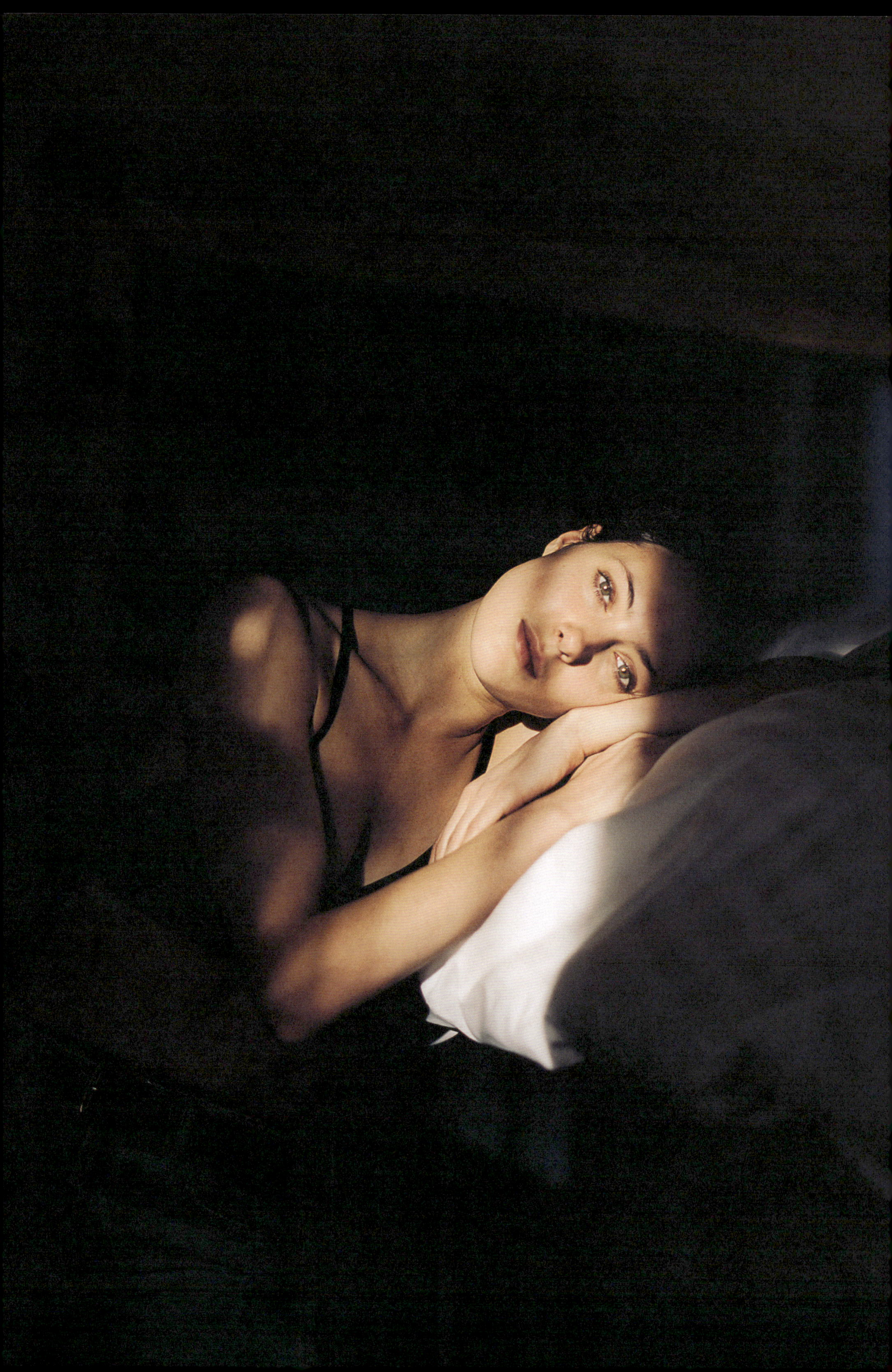

beyond asia

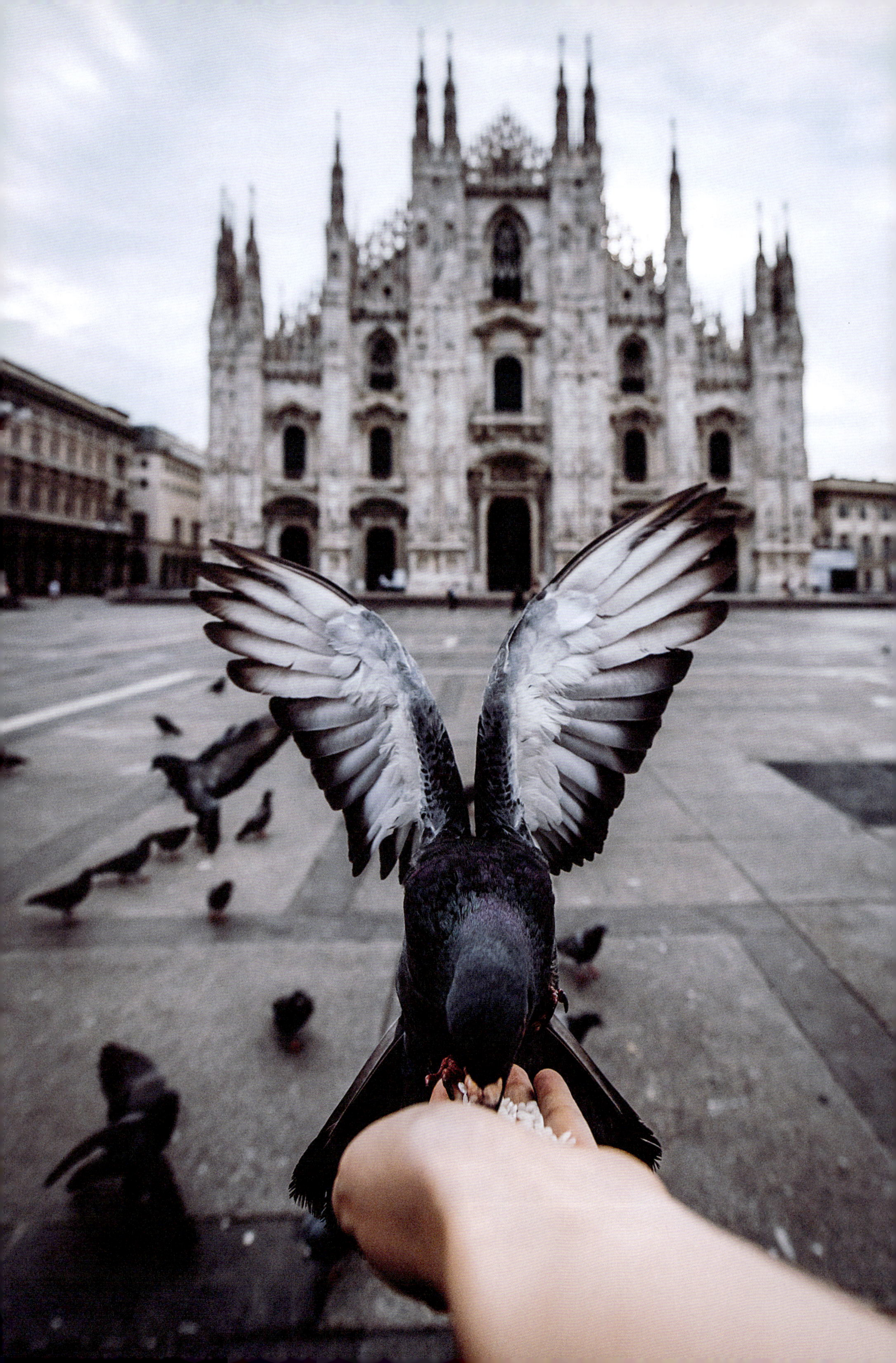

EAST AND WEST

Throughout my architectural career, I have tried to take every opportunity to travel and live in other places. Doing so not only helps to broaden my horizons as a designer, but also makes me look back at the place I call home with a fresh perspective.

Hong Kong is by no means a 'historical' place when compared to cities like Rome or Moscow. In such cities, I experienced an environment so deeply weathered by history it was as though every structure, every corner and every stone had a plethora of stories to tell. A place with a history simply cannot be replicated. Being so used to the trend of Western cultural simulacrum in the midst of modernization in parts of Asia, visiting (and revisiting) historical cities in Europe reminded me about the importance of preserving the *zeitgeist* (the spirit of an age) and the *genius loci* (the spirit of a place) of cities.

The critique of the rapid modernization and urban renewal schemes in cities like Hong Kong is that we fail to cherish and protect the architecture that preserves character and sense of place. Neon signs, old tenement buildings and traditional shops have rapidly perished. Because of this, the character of these places is mostly preserved through memorabilia - photographs, films and occasional lone objects collected through often personal preservation efforts.

Through traveling and living in historical cities, you notice true timelessness - it is as though the only variable factor of change is people themselves.

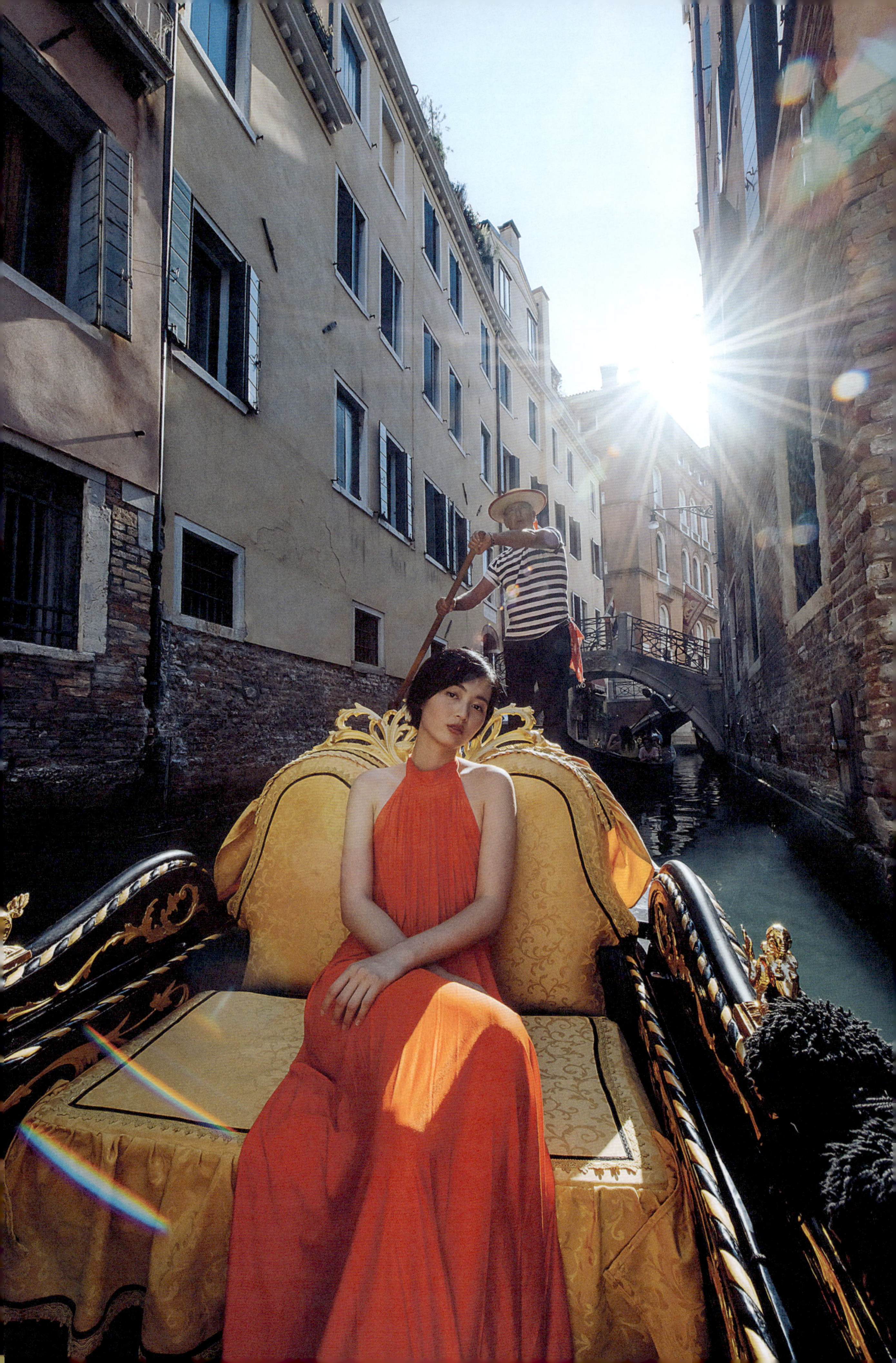

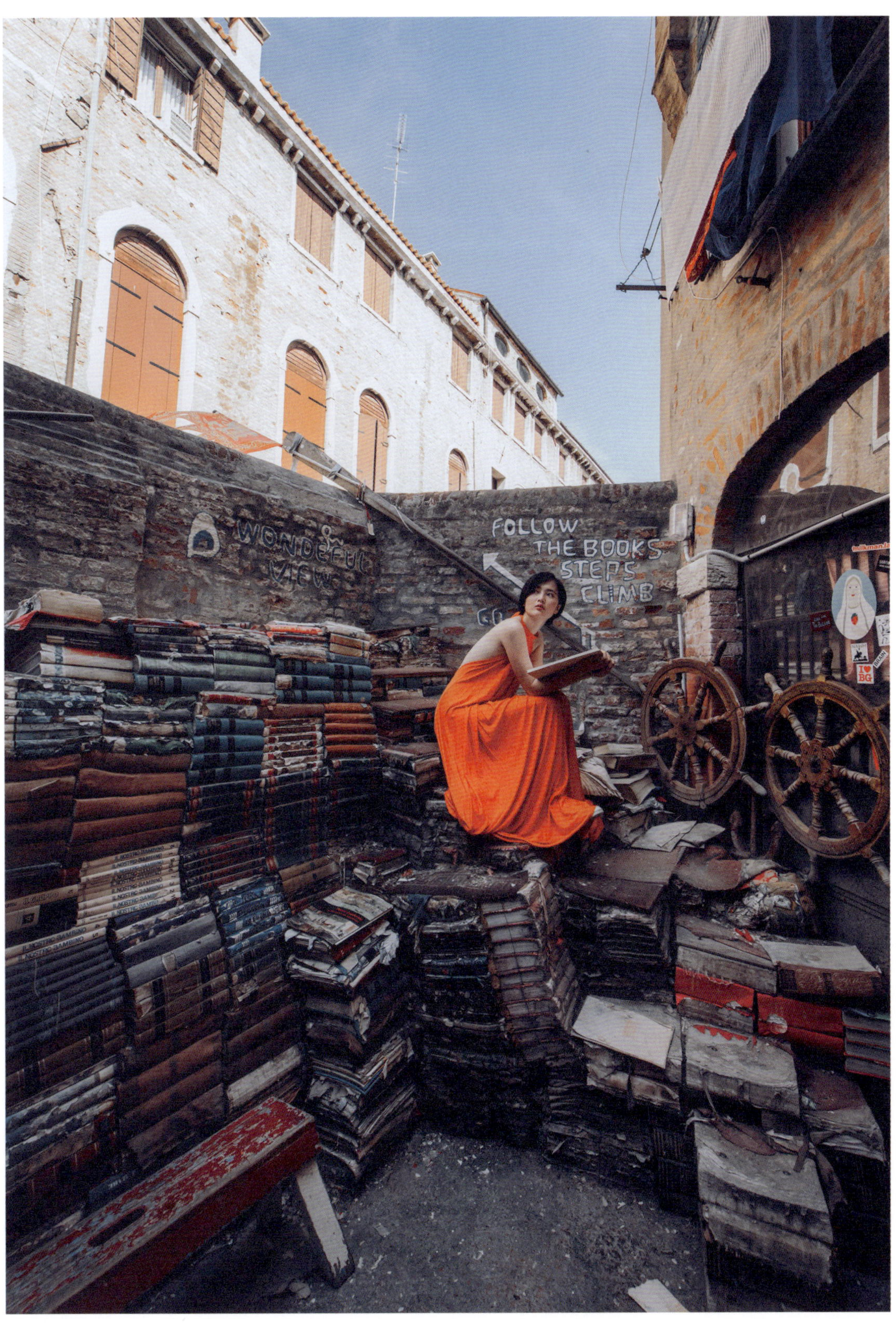

WONDERFUL VIEW
FOLLOW
THE BOOKS
STEPS
CLIMB
I ♥ BG

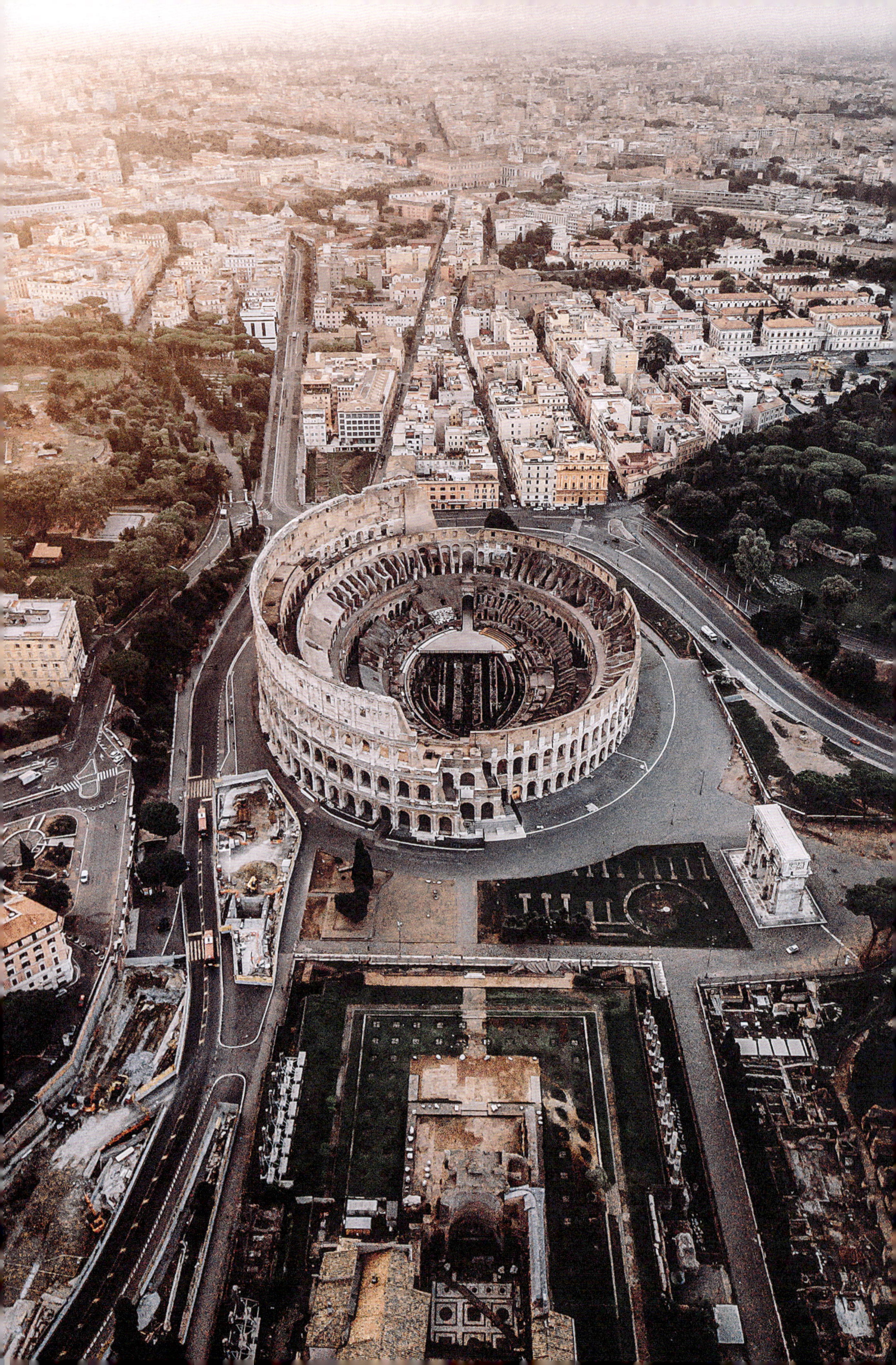

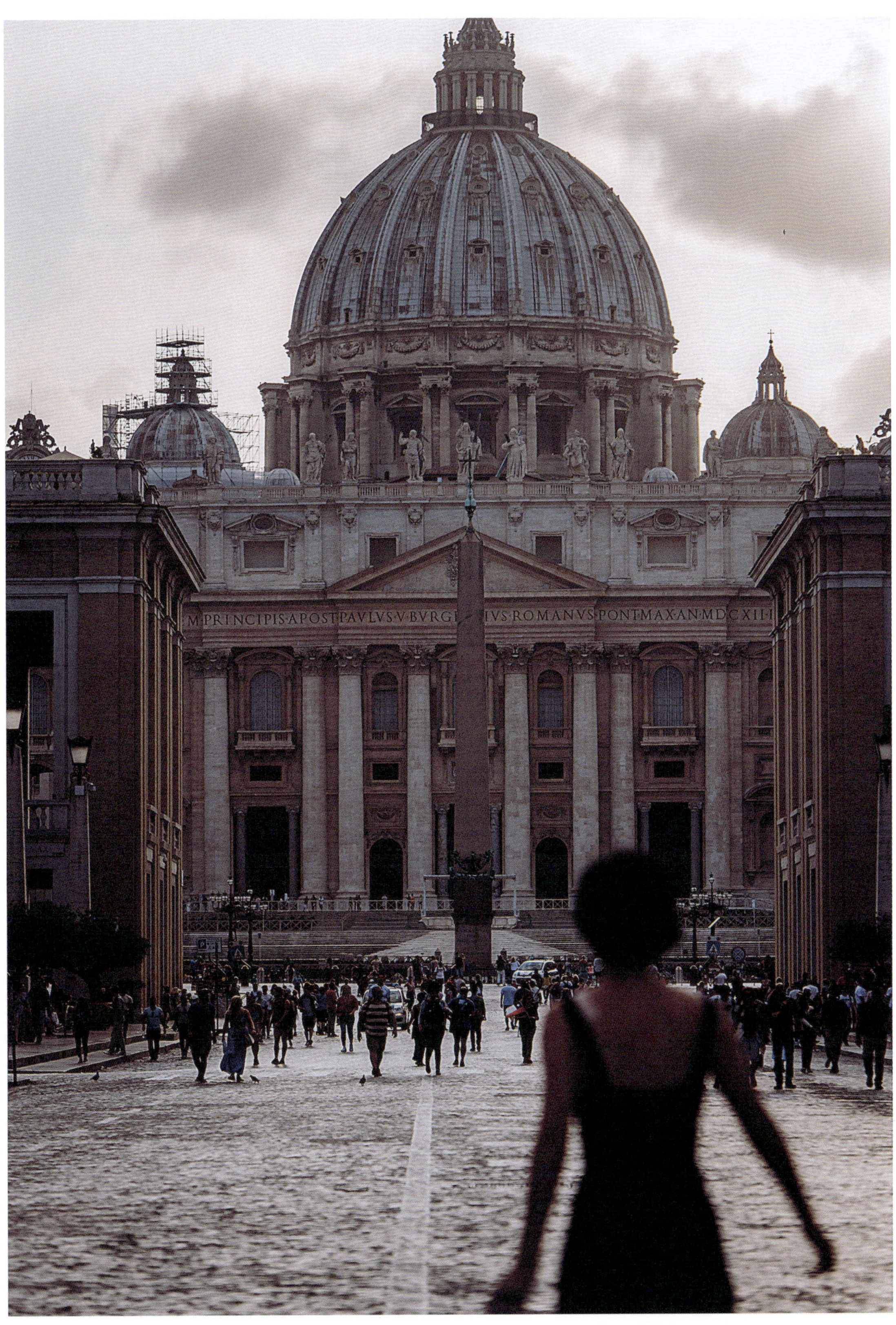
M·PRINCIPIS·APOST·PAVLVS·V·BVRGHIVS·ROMANVS·PONT·MAX·AN·MDCXII·I

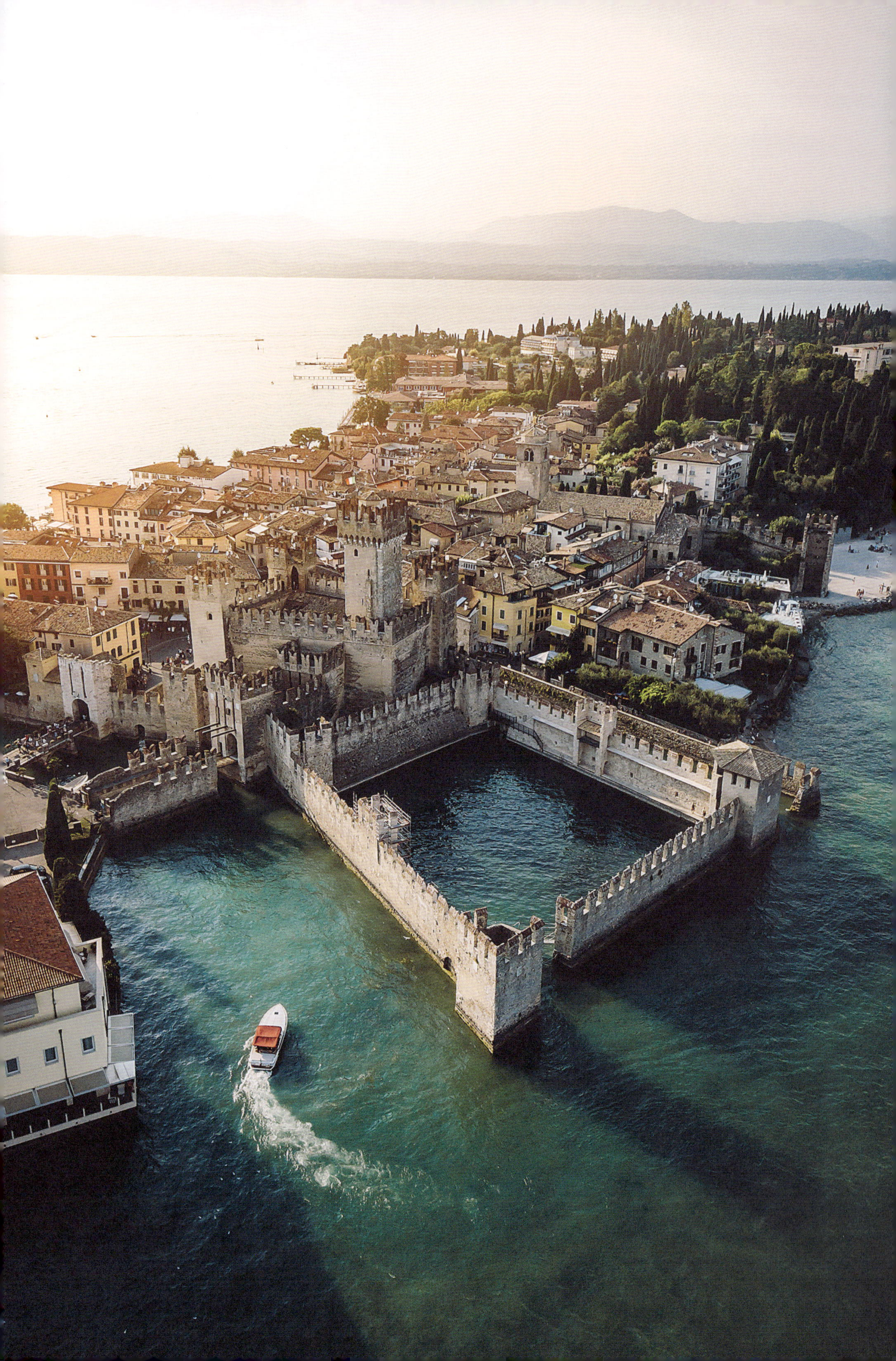

VIVIEN LIU

I EXPERIENCED AN ENVIRONMENT

SO DEEPLY WEATHERED BY HISTORY IT WAS AS THOUGH

EVERY STRUCTURE, EVERY CORNER AND EVERY STONE

HAD A PLETHORA OF STORIES TO TELL.

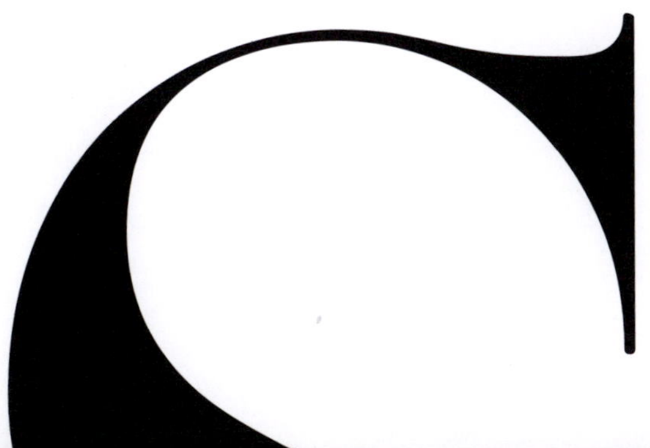

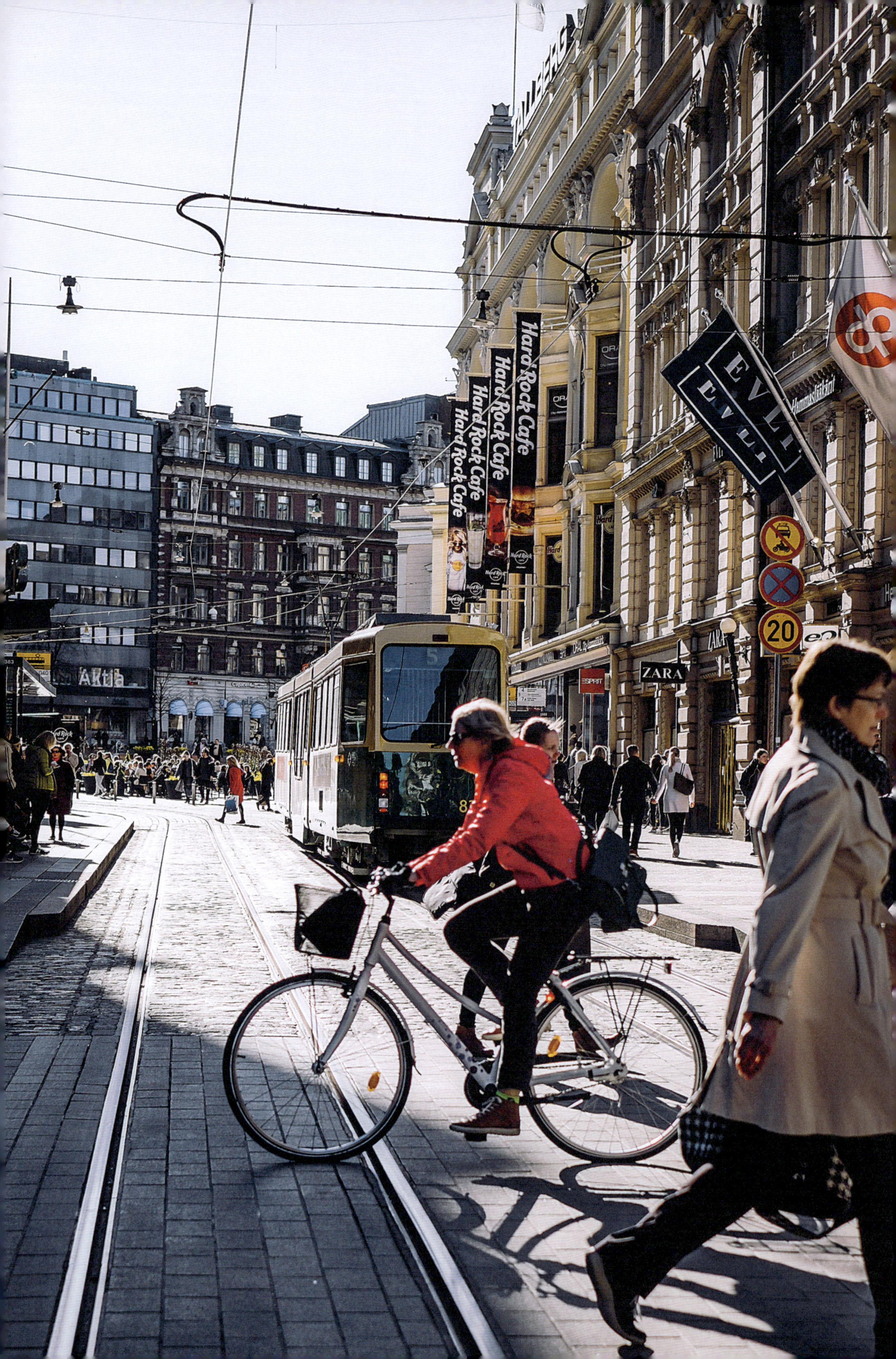

Hard Rock Cafe
Hard Rock Cafe
Hard Rock Cafe
Hard Rock Cafe
EVLI
EVLI
ZARA
ESPRIT
Aktia
Hard Rock
20

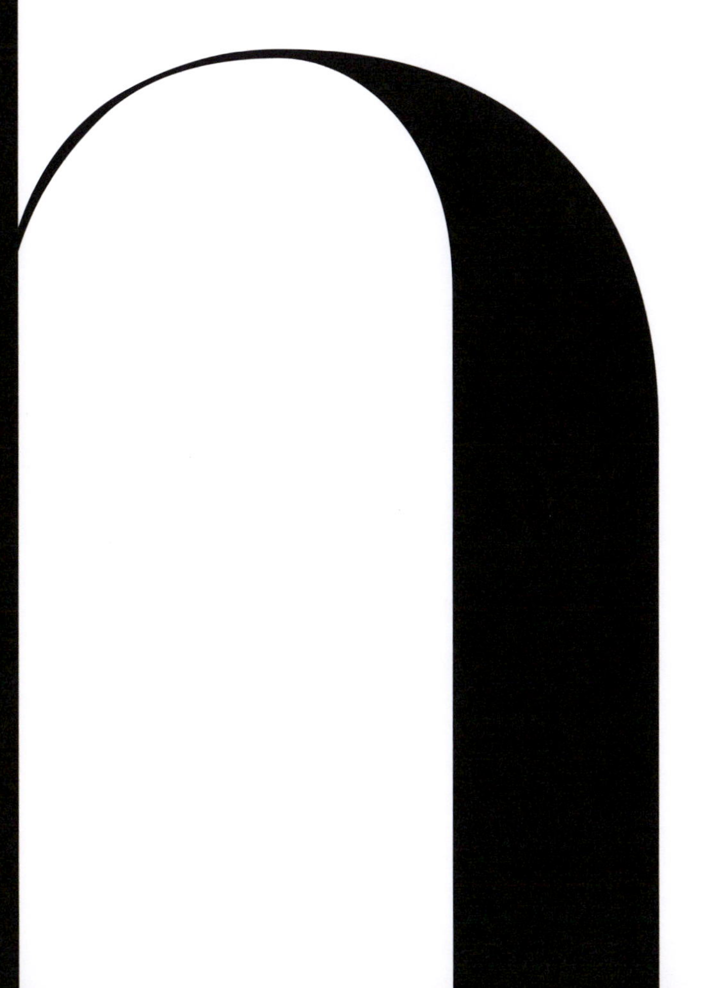

STREET PHOTOGRAPHY PORTRAYS A MORE

HUMANE SIDE OF A CITY.

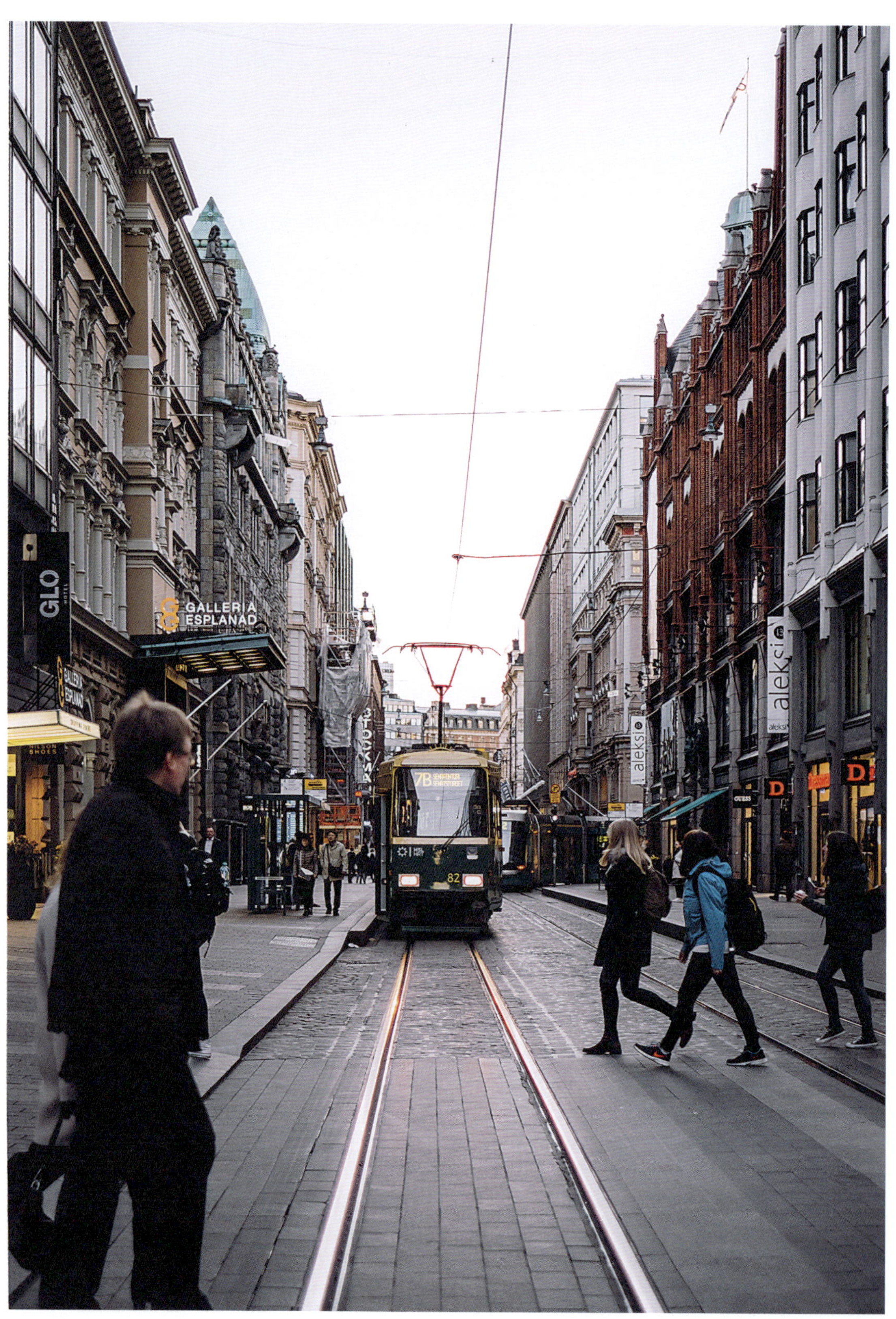

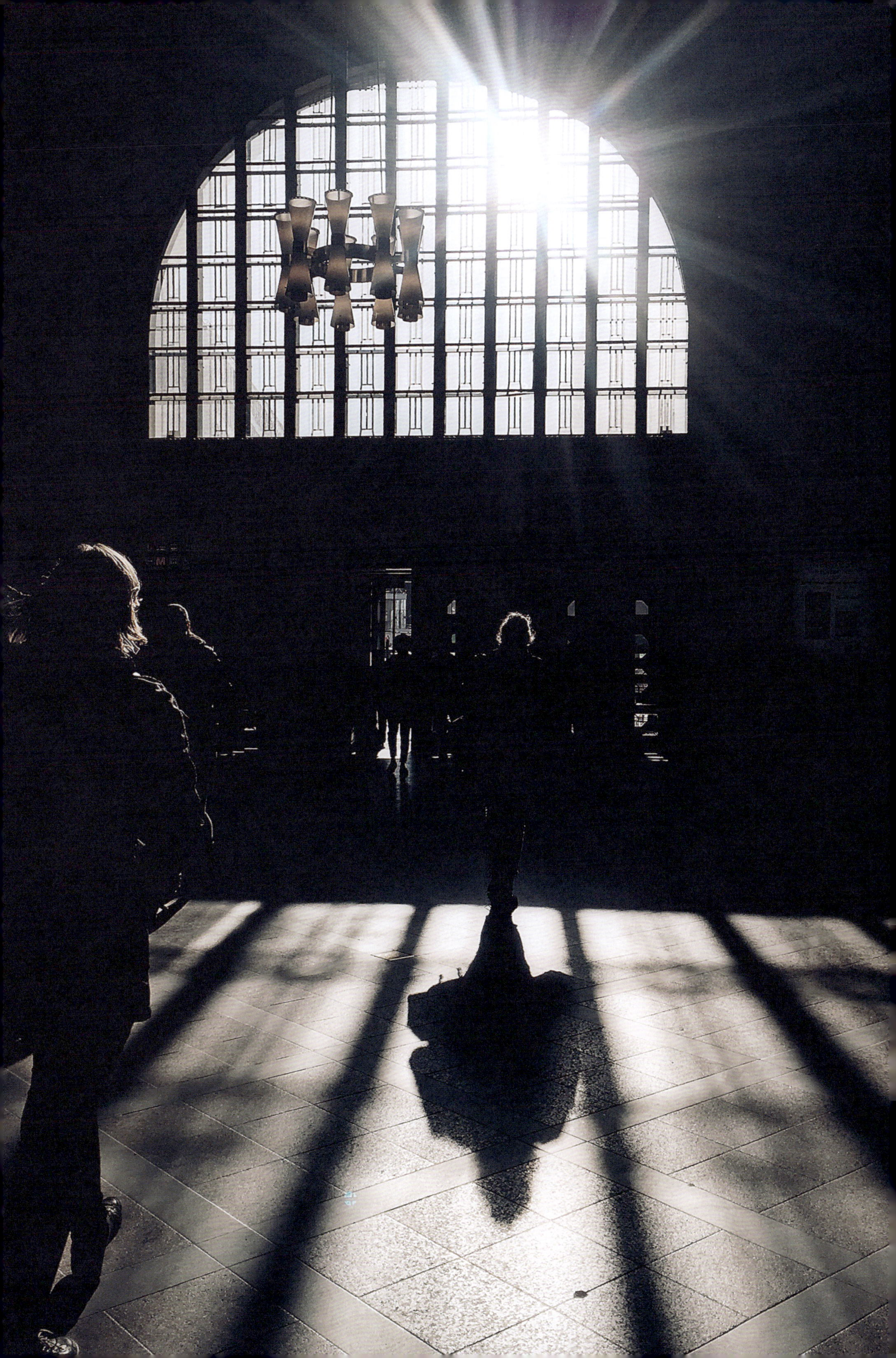

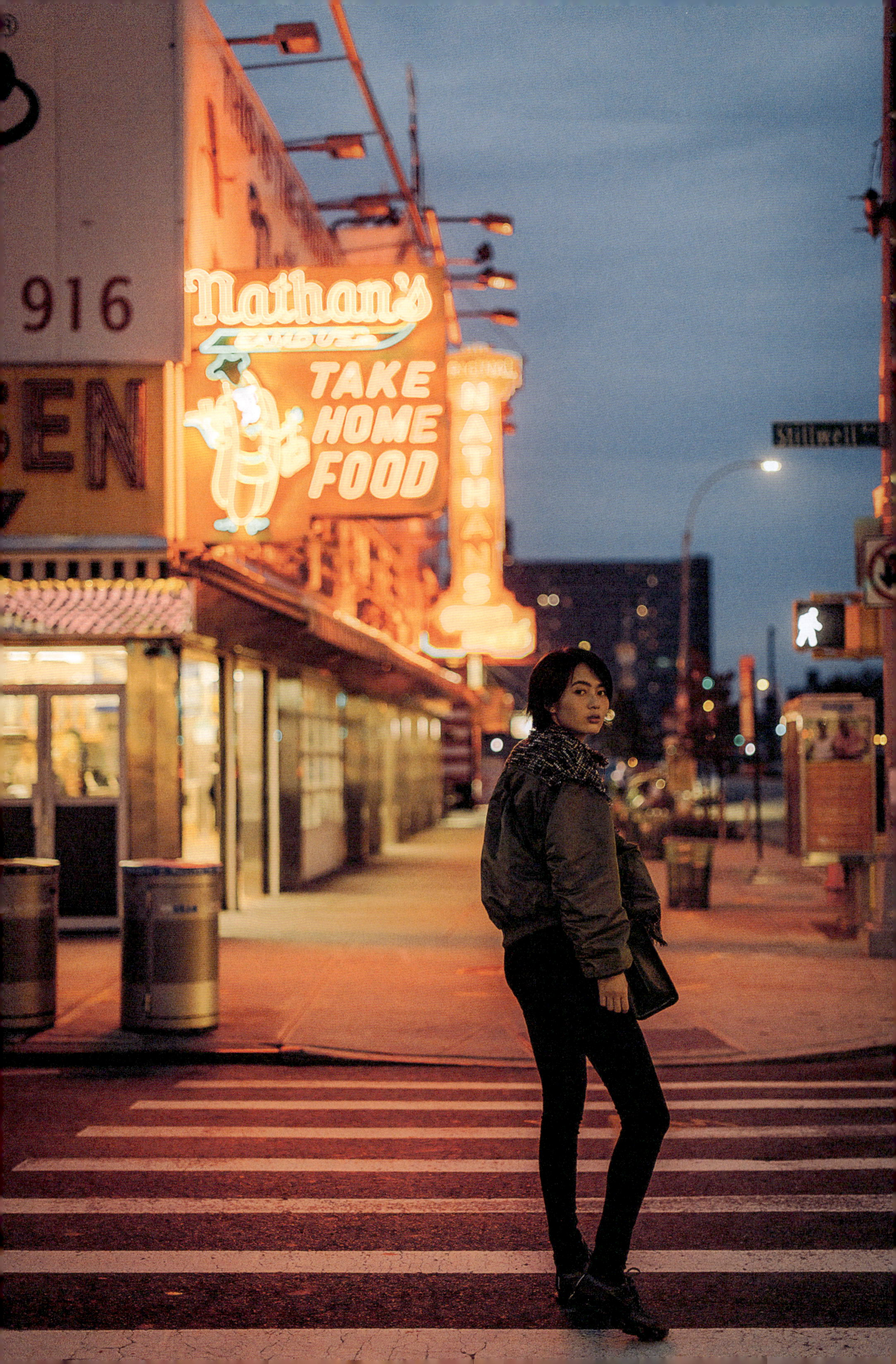
916
SEN
Nathan's
FAMOUS
TAKE
HOME
FOOD
NATHAN'S
Stillwell

THE IMAGES I CREATE TRY TO CONVEY THE ESSENCE OF THAT EXPERIENCE, WHICH MAY OR MAY NOT APPEAL WITH THE VISUAL IMPACT OF SOMETHING STAGED, BUT PERHAPS ALSO WITH THE SPONTANEITY OF LIVING AND FEELING A PARTICULAR MOMENT OF LOVE, JOY, MELANCHOLY, SADNESS, EXHILARATION OR HAPPINESS.

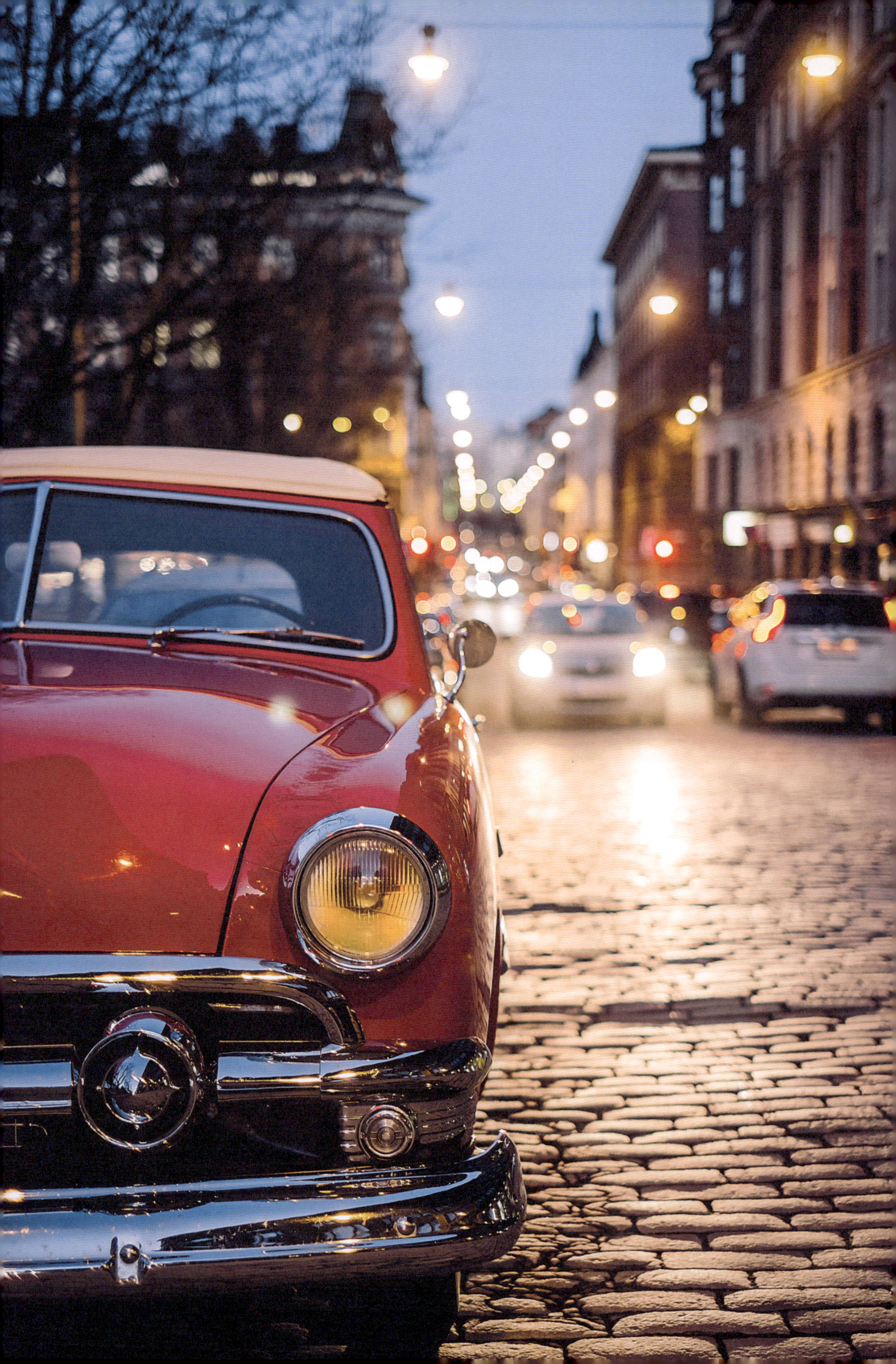

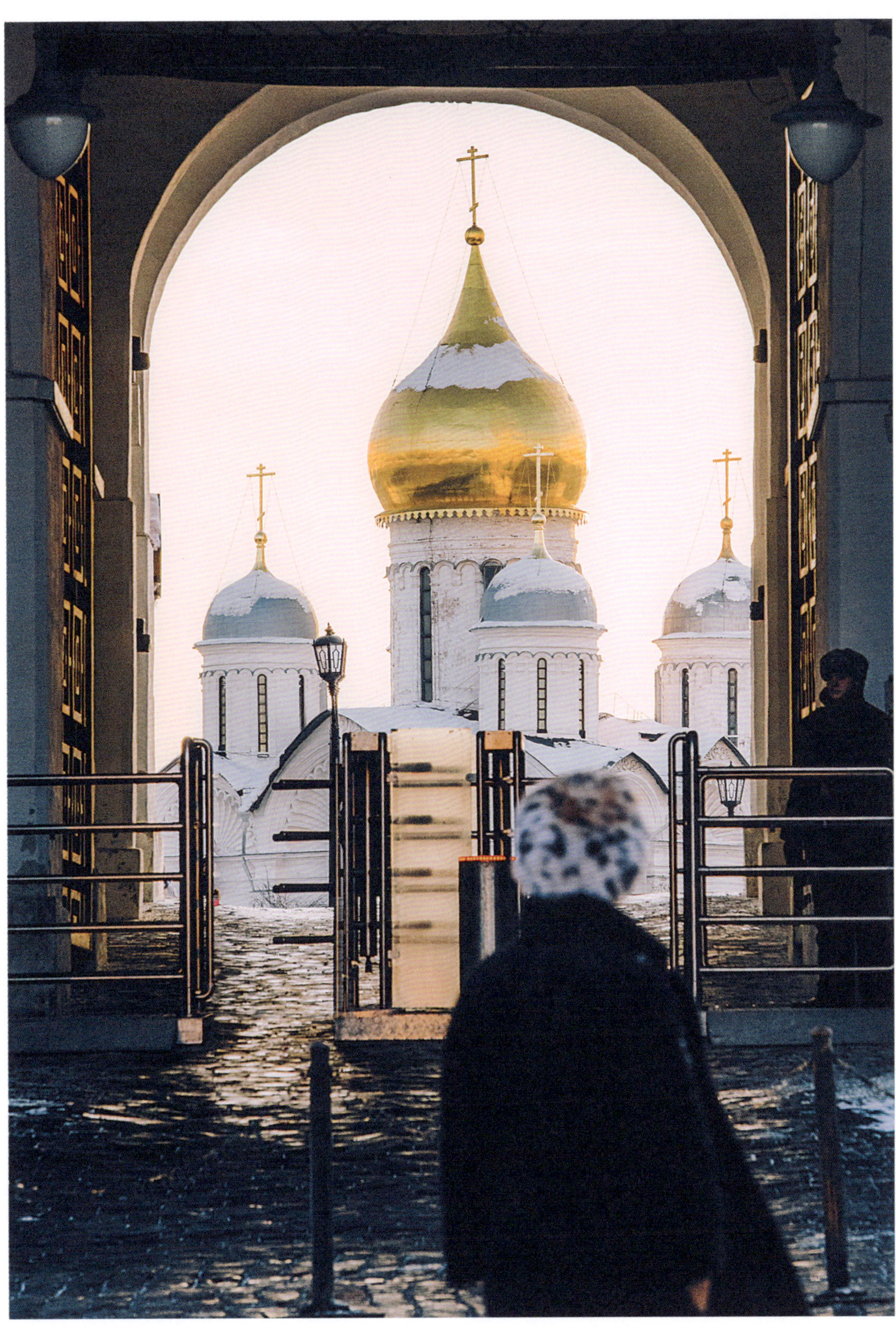

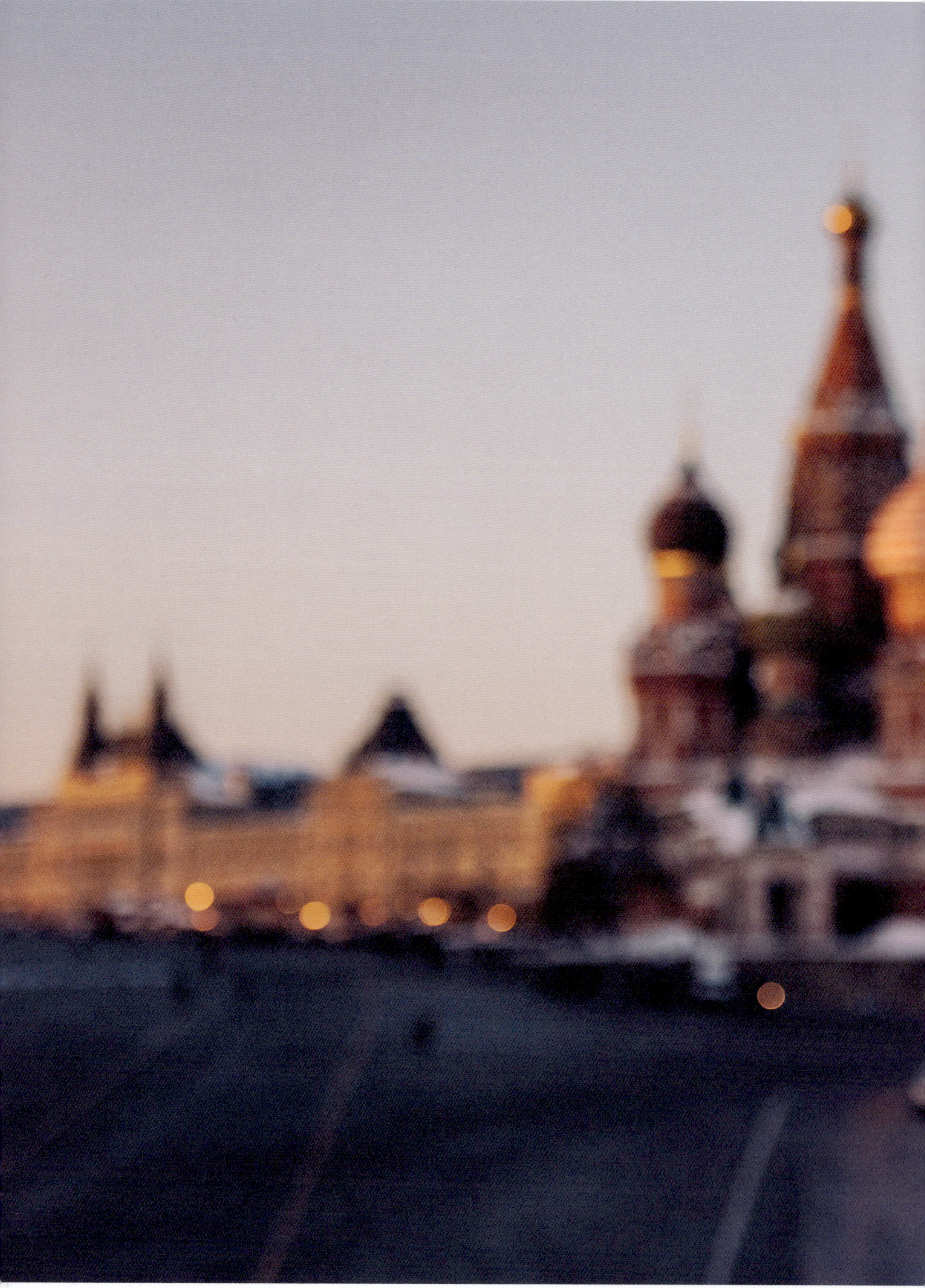

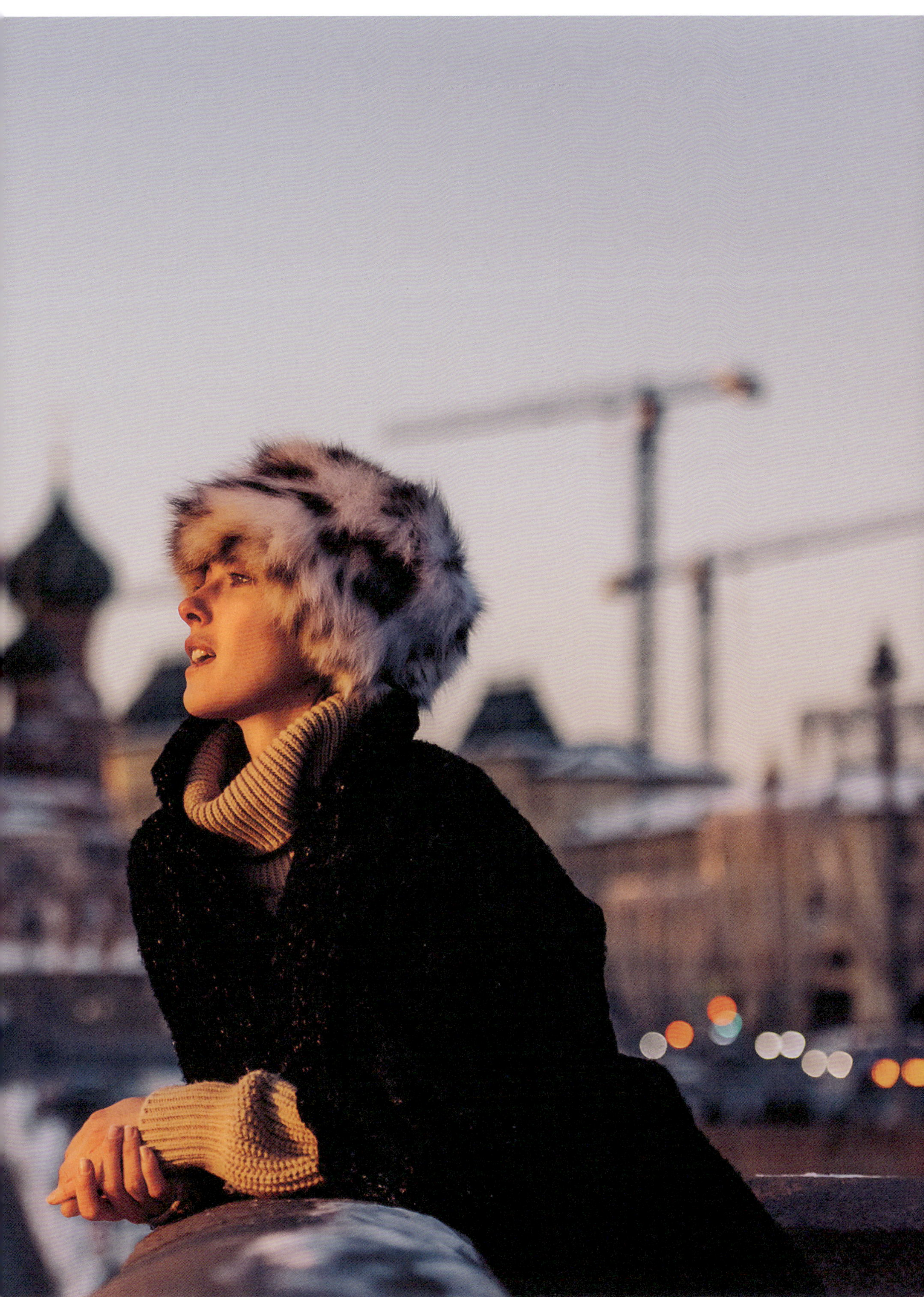

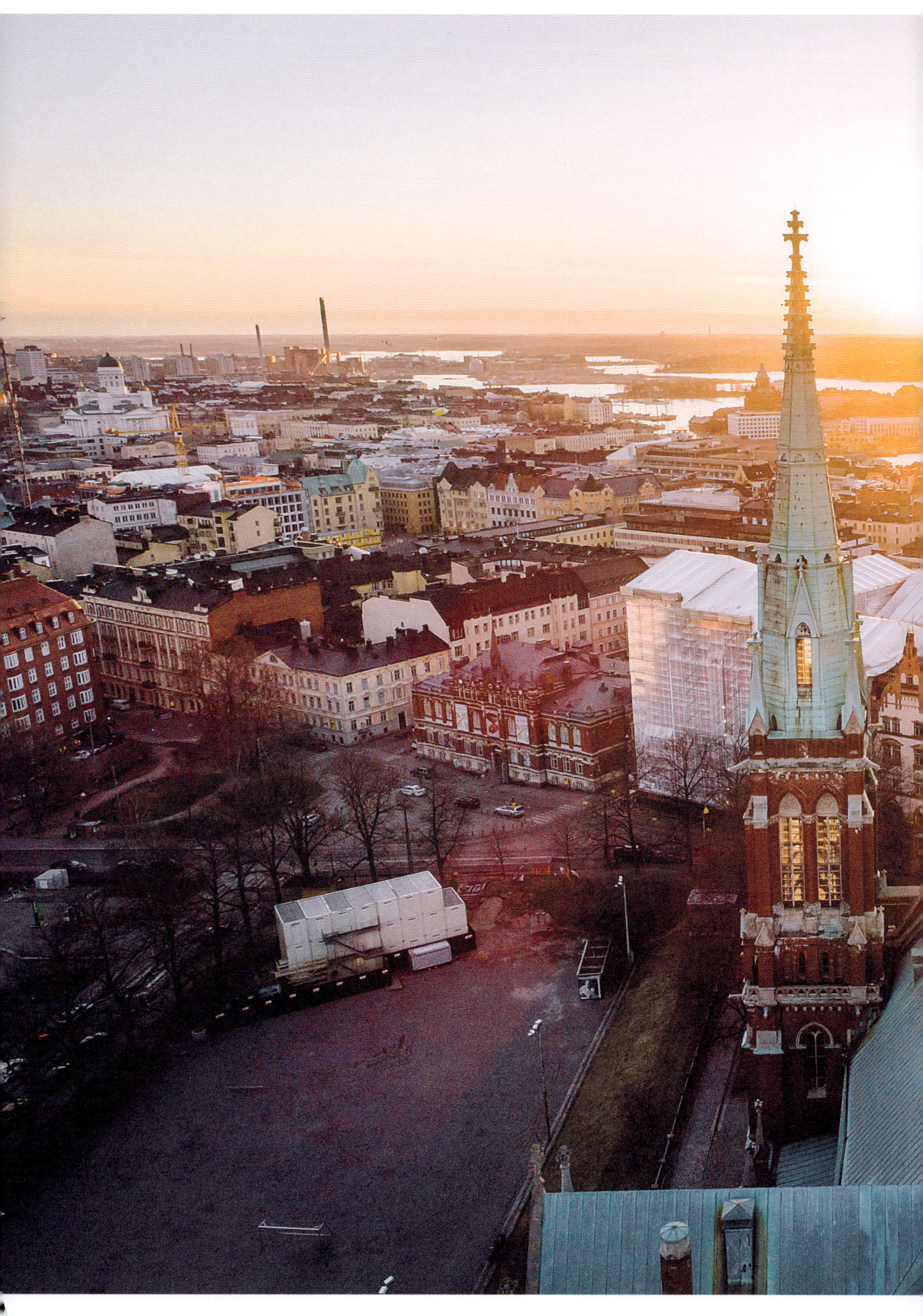

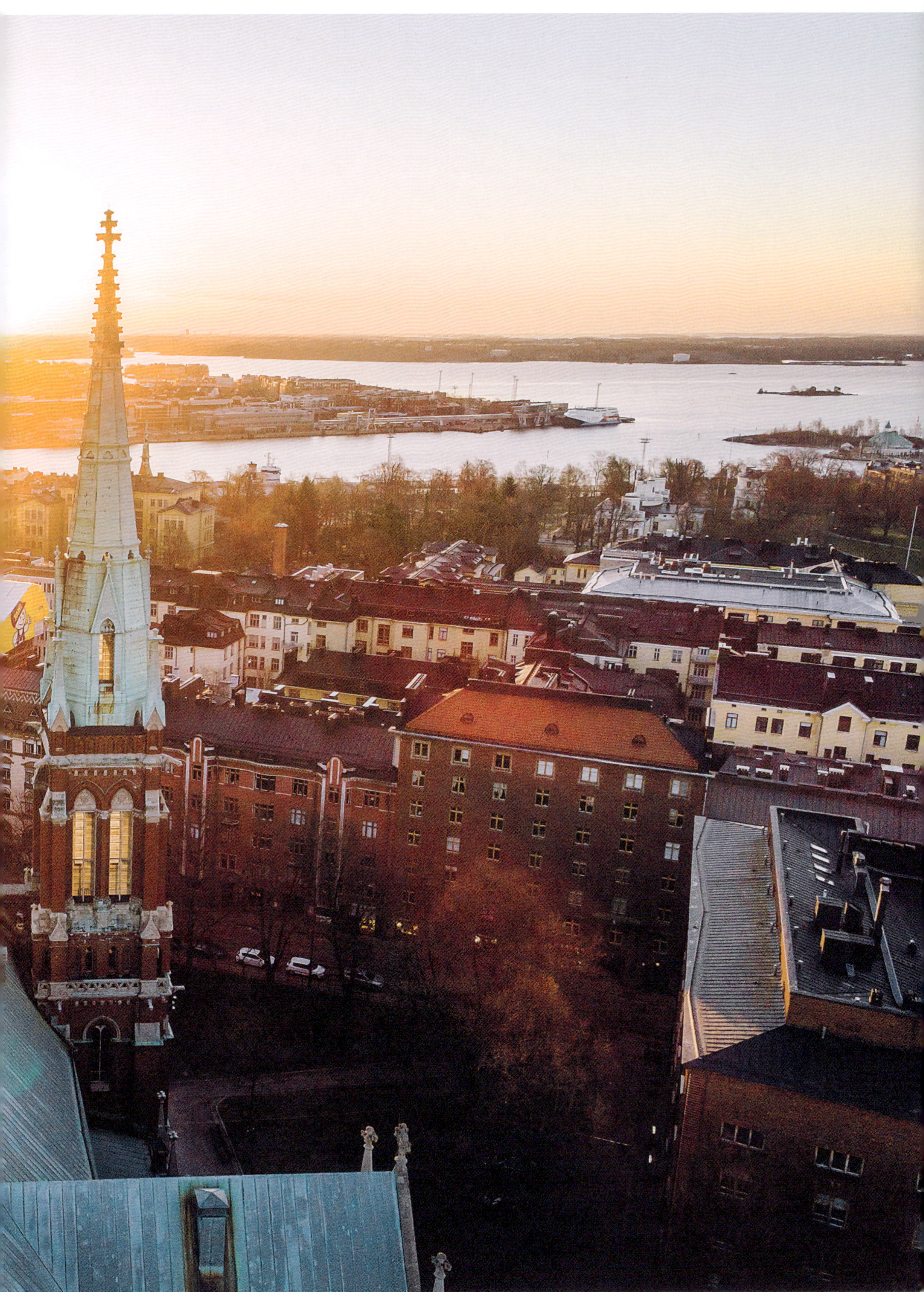

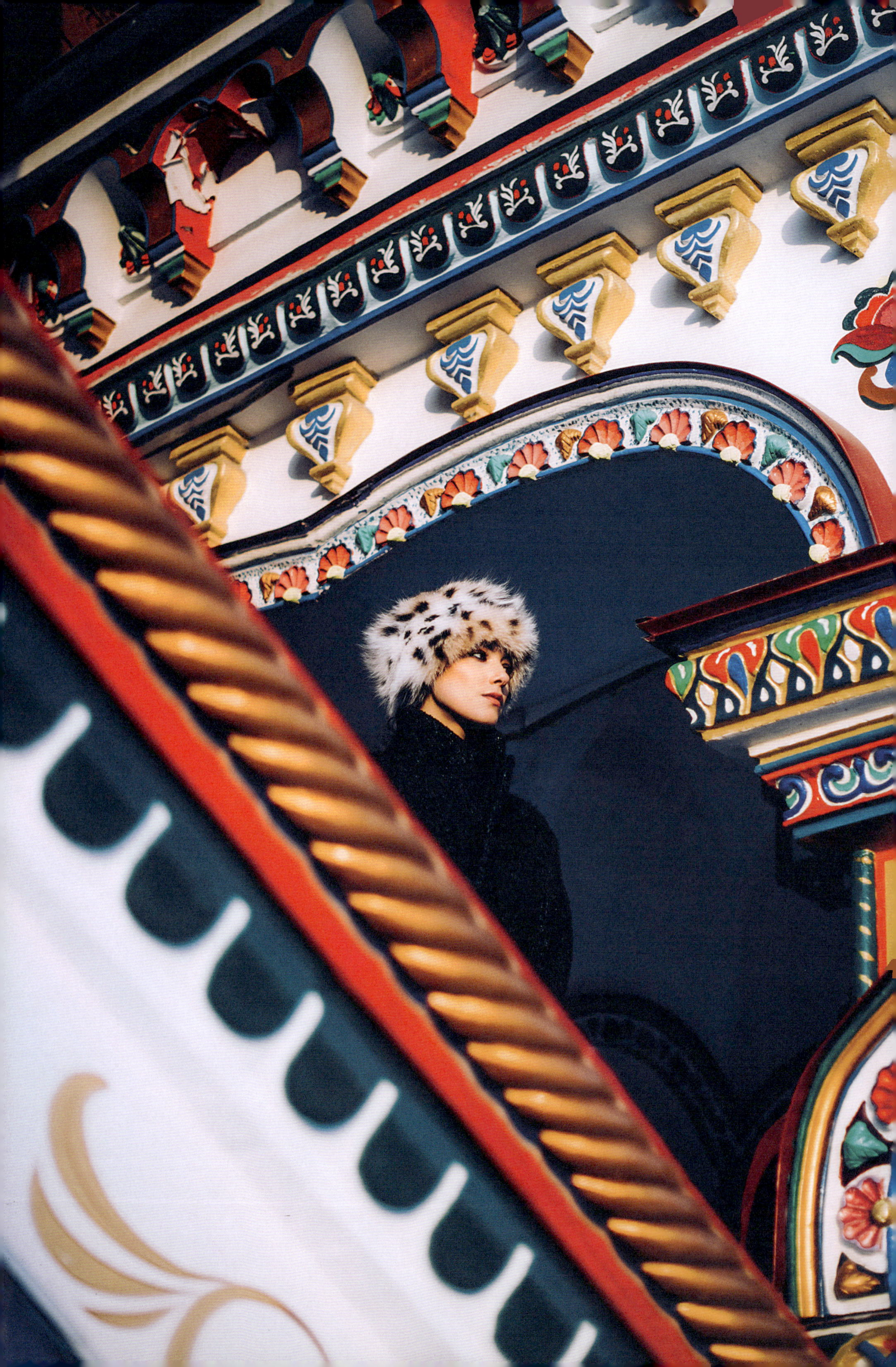

being there

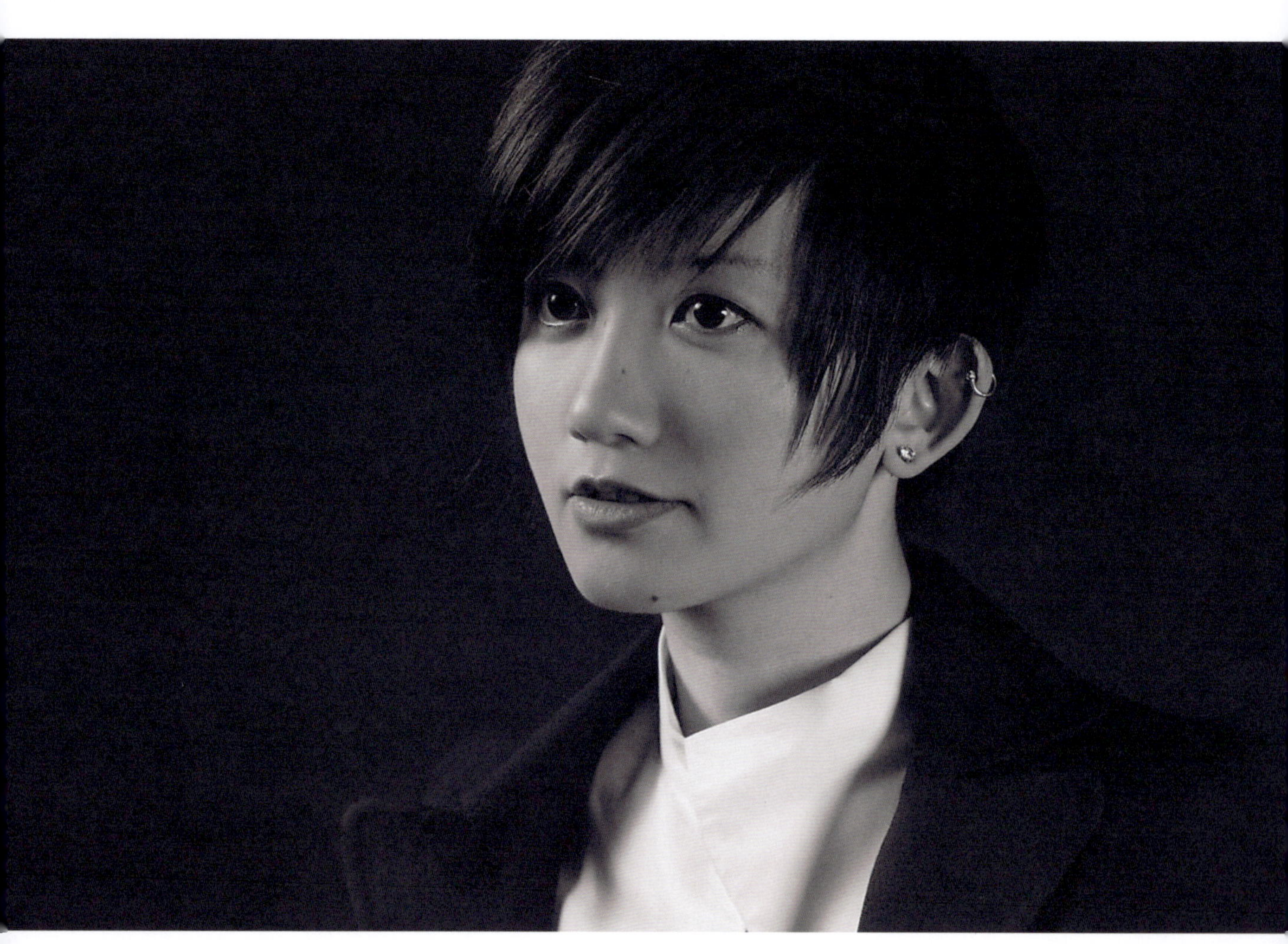

Portrait by Ruby Law

VIVIEN LIU

Vivien came to photography with a passion for capturing the urban density and architecture of Hong Kong and around the world. Her photography has attracted more than 250,000 followers on Instagram who check in to see her unique view on Hong Kong every day. Since then, her style has broadened to include portraiture, natural landscapes and product photography. She was awarded Best Female Photography Influencer by #Legend in 2017, and her work is trusted by a wide range of clients including Nikon, Jack Daniels, American Express, Huawei, Samsung, Leica, and the Hong Kong Tourism Board.

Vivien Liu has worked in architecture and planning since 2010 in the United States, Canada, the United Kingdom, Hong Kong and China. Her experience comprises a wide range of building typologies, including office, retail, hotel, residential and institutional, involving architectural design at various scales from interior to urban planning and infrastructure. Prior to founding Studio UNIT, Vivien worked as an architect at Rem Koolhaas' OMA and Kohn Pedersen Fox Associates (KPF).

Vivien attended the University of Waterloo, graduating with a Bachelor of Architectural Studies, and went on to study at Harvard University's Graduate School of Design, where she was awarded the prestigious Clifford Wong Prize in Housing Design.

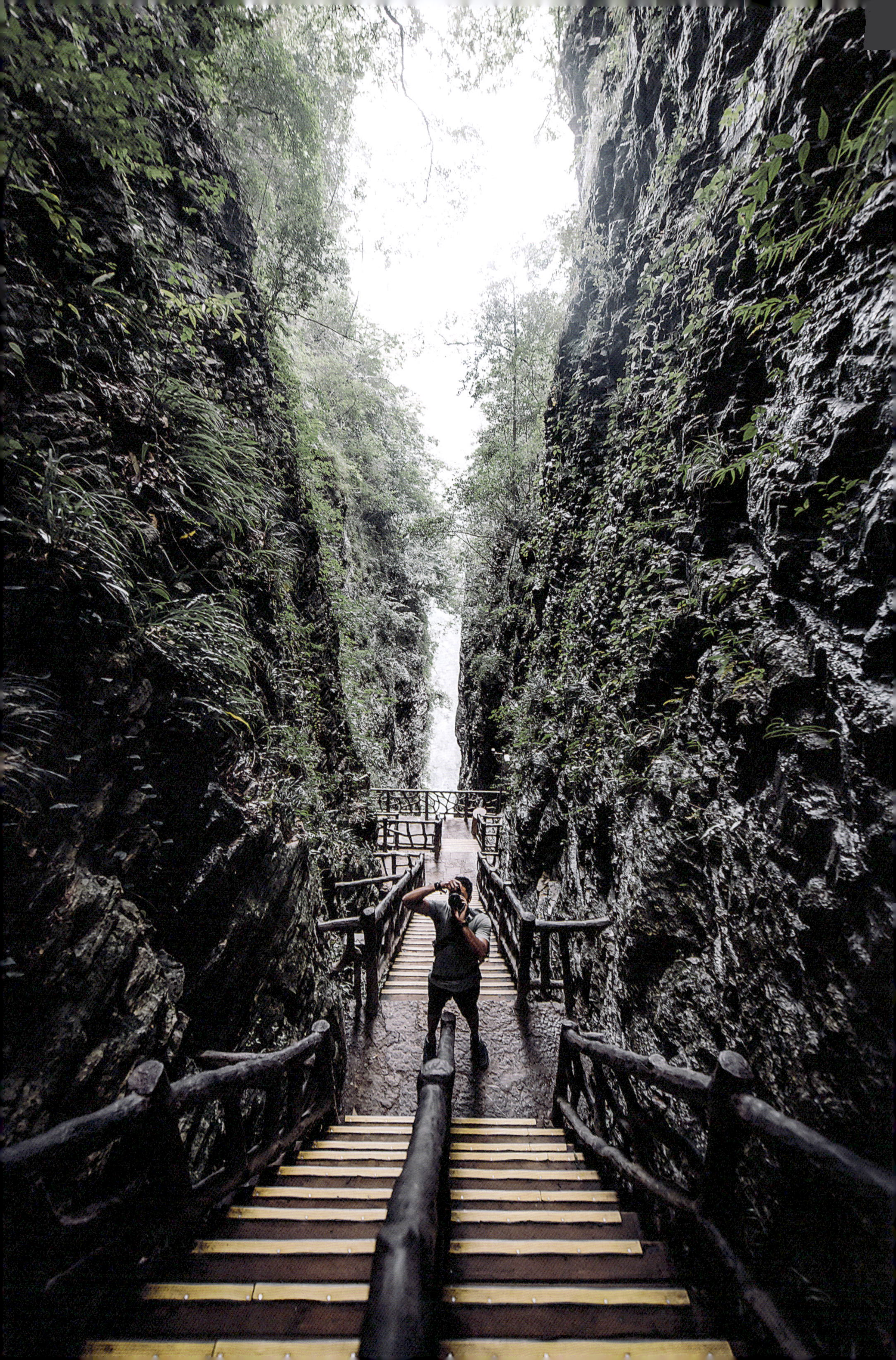

ACKNOWLEDGEMENTS

I would like to express my special thanks
to those who made this book possible:

Aida Malybaeva

Cathay Pacific Airways

Erica Tao

Julia Ponomareva

Juliana Kovalskaya

Katja Lam

Lauren Engel

Lindy Sinclair

My Helsinki

Noel Chu

Octavia Lam

Sam Landers

Selene Cheung

Varun Thota

LCCN: 2019955070
ISBN: 978-1-7326936-0-9

Printed and bound in China
First printing, 2020

Trope Publishing Co.

+ INFORMATION:
For additional information on the Trope Edition Series, visit www.trope.com

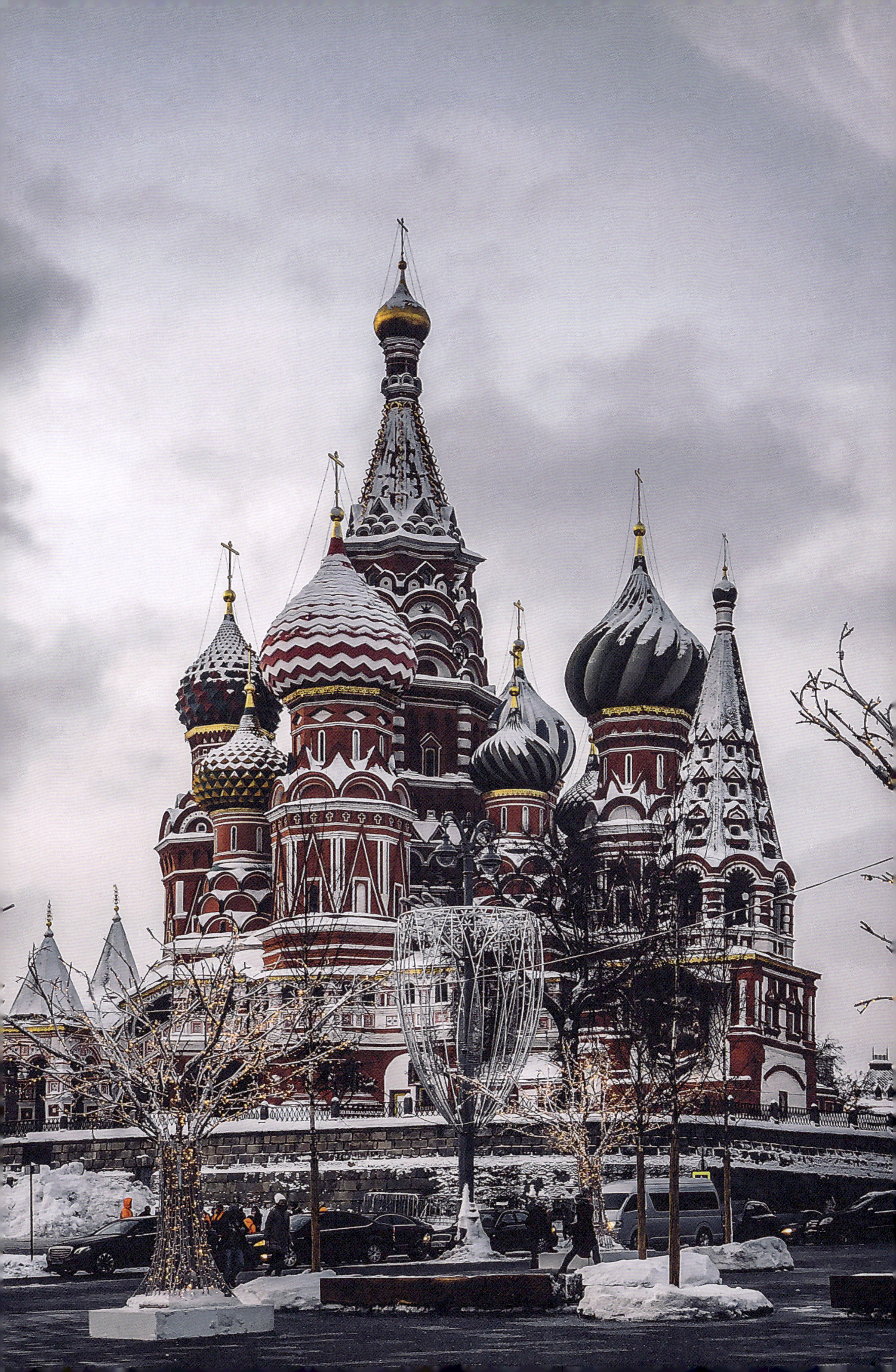

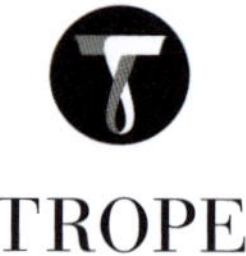

TROPE

TROPE EDITION

VOLUME IV